Women Writing

for (a) Change

A Guide for Creative Transformation

Mary Pierce Brosmer

SORIN BOOKS  Notre Dame, Indiana

"Why We Tell Stories" by Lisel Muller is used by permission of Louisiana State University Press. All rights reserved.

"Memo to the Twenty-First Century" by Phillip Appelman is used by permission of the author. All rights reserved.

www.sorinbooks.com

ISBN-10 1-933495-18-9 ISBN-13 978-1-933495-18-7

Cover image © iStockphoto.

Cover and text design by Katherine Robinson Coleman.

Printed and bound in the United States of America.

Library of Congress Cataloging-in-Publication Data

Brosmer, Mary Pierce.

Women writing for (a) change : a guide for creative transformation / Mary Pierce Brosmer.

p. cm.

ISBN-13: 978-1-933495-18-7 (pbk.)

ISBN-10: 1-933495-18-9 (pbk.)

1. Authorship. 2. Women authors. 3. Women--Authorship. 4. Self-actualization (Psychology) in women. 5. Creative writing--Psychological aspects. 6. Feminist psychology. I. Title.

PN151.B79 2009

808'.02082--dc22

2009032857

Contents

Foreword

In this compelling narrative of the creation and development of a "social purpose" school, Women Writing for (a) Change [WWf(a)C], poet and teacher Mary Pierce Brosmer offers readers a remarkable gift. The collaborative writing project whose contours she traces has grown from a few dedicated women gathered in a Cincinnati, Ohio, living room in 1991 to encompass hundreds of girls and women working weekly in communally owned or rented houses in eight states as of 2009. As the visionary force providing the "conscious feminine and linguistic leadership" that nurtured this project to fruition, Mary now shares in rich detail the philosophy, history, and methodologies that have informed her creative and entrepreneurial venture.

As editor of *The Longman Anthology of Women's Literature* (2001) I identified five central themes that characterize writing in English by women from the Middle Ages to the present—themes that appear abundantly in *Women Writing for (a) Change. Breaking silence and finding voice* lies at the heart of the work that Mary fosters in her writing circles and describes here as "foundational stories." This book's emphasis on women's poems, dreams, and journal entries reveals how fragile private reflections can be made public— sometimes tentatively, sometimes fiercely—through the listening communities that Mary and her sister-writers engender as they hear each other into speech. *Inscribing bodily experience*—the landscape deemed by poet Adrienne Rich "the geography closest in"— represents another key aspect of this project, as writers support one another in recounting their memories of bodily trauma and violation on the one hand, of bodily pleasure and integrity on the other. *Rethinking the maternal* is likewise central to this communal writing initiative, as women inscribe their lives as mothers and pay homage to the women who gave them life. In a dream that she shares in the book, Mary meets her long-dead mother in a cathedral in Italy or perhaps Spain; in poems, she remembers the living mother in whose kitchen she found both suffering and sustenance. She explores, too, her own motherhood, urging her son to "clean your room / feed the cat / check the hyacinth bulbs / and take very good care of The Parsley Garden." Other women's maternal reflections appear as well; Ginger Swope's poem, for instance, poignantly recalls her mother's "laboring breath" on her last day on earth.

Exploring women's identities as artists, workers, and spiritual beings is another central task of the writers whose testimonials Mary includes here. Fourteen-year-old Megan Miller meditates on the candle-passing ritual with which each WWf(a)C class begins: "We have the gift," she realizes, "each blazing fire in each girl's soul comes here together." Xavier University professor Trudelle Thomas revels at hearing in the writing workshop she attended "the inner musings of a minister and a car mechanic, a punk bisexual and an elderly nun." Finally, *moving from resistance to transformation* becomes crucial to the women engaged in writing for (a) change, as they challenge oppressive patriarchal systems, eschew silence and violence and war, and embrace instead a gendered empowerment and the consciousness that comes from welcoming "the planet passing through us." This book also chronicles the process by which WWf(a)C transformed itself by giving birth to new entities: a school for girls and teenage writers, a consulting business, a nonprofit to widen accessibility to programs, a public radio program, a podcast, and feminist leadership academies—one for adults and one for teens. Mary acknowledges the conflicts and failures of the communities she has launched as well as their successes, inviting the reader's trust through her openness.

Women Writing for (a) Change tells a beautifully braided story, the twenty-year saga of creating sacred spaces in which, as Mary explains, *"women's words about our lives as women* are evoked, celebrated, and woven into the larger world." Through her keen eye and generous intelligence she bears witness to the ways that women working together can "restore the social fabric" while strengthening their own voices. Her book also offers a practical guide for women's writing communities: exercises and prompts, rituals and "soul cards," and a website (www.womenwriting.org) that readers can visit. Mary Pierce Brosmer's eloquent testimony inspires readers who wish to write, and contributes meaningfully to the ongoing "herstory/heartstory" of feminist pedagogy, women's studies, and progressive activism in the first decade of a new century.

Mary K. DeShazer
Professor of English and Women's and Gender Studies
Wake Forest University

Preface

A poem should not mean
But be.
Archibald MacLeish [1]

What you hold in your hands is a book of prose written by a poet. Making poems is how I make meanings. Teaching and working for organizational change is how I weave those meanings into the world outside my study door. I am incapable of talking about things one-dimensionally; rather, I revel in making multilayered, resource-rich worlds for, and with, others.

For approval's sake, I would like to have written a straightforward book with numbered steps and defined goals, but I do not have such a book in me, nor do I believe the world needs another such book. "You can't model human behavior on math," said Frank Partnoy (interviewed by Steve Croft on *60 Minutes*), speaking on the collapse of global financial markets based with such reckless certainty on esoteric mathematical models.[2] In these pages you will find nothing to feed the insatiable appetite our culture has developed for measurement, for certainty, or for reducing complexity to bullet points and sound bites.

"I would not give a fig for the simplicity this side of complexity, but I would give my life to the simplicity on the far side of complexity," wrote Oliver Wendell Holmes.[3] Let the people say, "Amen!" I grieve that our attention-deficient culture has driven us to the brink of disaster on so many fronts, with leaders and thinkers lacking the courage and the wisdom to engage the very real and quite beautiful complexity in both nature and culture.

What you hold is a book in the conscious feminine tradition of "both/and." You will find practical and detailed ways of experimenting—as I have—with writing for change, both personal and organizational. Woven throughout the text are poems, dreams, and journal entries, the imaginal cells biologists tell us are the early and potent drivers of every new creation. By including mine, I invite yours. And I encourage you to value both interior and exterior life, background and foreground, the action-driven masculine and the reflective feminine.

While I cannot control how you will hear my voice—lacking my physical presence—I hope you will not hear my urgency for wholeness as stridency. It requires much fierceness to name what is new and protect what is still fragile and vulnerable, as noted by May Sarton in her beautiful poem, "An Observation":

> As I learn for myself we must be hard
> To move among the tender with an open hand,
> And to stay sensitive up to the end
> Pay with some toughness for a gentle world.[4]

I do not want to erase your meanings; I only want to add mine, those of a woman born three years after my country dropped atomic bombs on our enemies, those of a girl with inarticulate longings for a better world than we have created in the triumphalism of post-war modernity, with its scientific and economic fundamentalisms that distance us further and further from the wisdom of cycles, of mystery, of the feminine.

In describing my ways, I do not intend to obliterate or "make wrong" other ways, lest I become one of the "grotesques" described by Sherwood Anderson in *Winesburg, Ohio*. This passage has been a touchstone for me since I first read it as a young woman in my twenties:

> That in the beginning when the world was young there were a great many thoughts but no such thing as a truth. Man made the truths himself and each truth was a composite of a great many vague thoughts. All about in the world were the truths and they were all beautiful.
>
> The old man had listed hundreds of the truths in his book. I will not try to tell you of all of them. There was the truth of virginity and the truth of passion, the truth of wealth and of poverty, of thrift and of profligacy, of carelessness and abandon. Hundreds and hundreds were the truths and they were all beautiful.
>
> And then the people came along. Each as he appeared snatched up one of the truths and some who were strong snatched up a dozen of them. It was the truths that made the people grotesques. The old man had quite an elaborate theory

concerning the matter. It was his notion that the moment one of
the people took one of the truths to himself, called it his truth,
and tried to live his life by it, he became a grotesque and the
truth he embraced became a falsehood.

You can see for yourself how the old man, who had spent all
of his life writing and was filled with words, would write hundreds of pages concerning this matter. The subject would
become so big in his mind that he himself would be in danger
of becoming a grotesque. He didn't, I suppose, for the same reason that he never published the book. It was the young thing
inside him that saved the old man.[5]

In the name of the young thing inside us,
Mary Pierce Brosmer
October 2008

Introduction

Journal entry, undated

I have tried to imagine and solve ahead of time the problem of what kind of voice I might use for a book about Women Writing for (a) Change. The raw, vulnerable, passionate poet's voice seems unsustainable. And for whom do I speak: whom could I imagine listening in a way that would elicit, not stifle, my stories?

The answer comes in a dream:

A former student has produced a book, a slender volume of mysterious and incredibly beautiful glyphs. The subject of the book is gratitude, including gratitude to the writing school for creating what she refers to as a womb for her life's work.

Later, in a church—more a cathedral, perhaps in Italy or Spain—I meet my mother. I want to share my joy at having tapped into this deep, communal and individual creative process.

I am anxious that she understand the significance of the work and want her to see how happy my work makes me, to really have her understand my unconventional teaching, my unconventional self. In the dream my mother is youngish and soft. She looks as she looked in photos when she was thirty, holding me, her longed-for first child and only daughter.

She seems open to being included in my life, like a sister, a peer, rather than the lost, worn-out mother, whom I spent my life trying but was unable to rescue, for want of a better word.

Writing the dream, I feel a jolt of something about the phrase: for want of a better word, for want of a better World. Because words do become flesh, do create the world we live in, good women like my mother have been diminished without knowing why.

I have stumbled upon a title: For Want of a Better Wor(l)d: Women Writing for (a) Change. Wanting a better word, we write a better world, one not fueled by the diminishment or dominance of any other.

Weeks later, rereading this journal entry, I realize I have dreamed an audience, voice, and purpose to drive my book:

1. Audience: my dead mother
2. Voice: my authentic, achingly earnest, sometimes angry, always wanting love-voice
3. Purpose: to be a channel through which flows the energy of conscious love; to forge a union of feminine–masculine, yin–yang, mother–father, and daughter–son; and to participate in healing the world.

Since 1991, it has been my privilege to participate in the creation of a small school, what I later learned to call a social purpose business, Women Writing for (a) Change [WWf(a)C], in which *women's words about our lives as women* are evoked, celebrated, and woven into the larger world. The Mother School gave birth to Young Women Writing for (a) Change, the Women Writing for (a) Change Foundation, Consulting for (a) Change, the Feminist Leadership Academy of Cincinnati, and WWf(a)C schools in eight states across the country as of this writing (see appendix and chapter 1).

In the summer of 1999, I undertook the task of telling what was mine to tell about this creation. My purposes were several: to tell the story to myself as a way of reflecting on what had been made, to tell the story as a way to continue the making, and to tell the story to others engaged in expressing the conscious feminine toward the change we so urgently need.

I was writing at the end of what I think of as the Summer of the Organization/Organism, when the early patterns of WWf(a)C had emerged fully enough for me to see—and say—them. I was saying them to the writers and leaders who were entering the "better world," wanting to participate in it more fully and carrying forms of it elsewhere. It was a teacher's manual, albeit a very personal take on a teacher's manual, that addressed the two questions W. H. Auden suggested asking after reading a poem: "Who made it? How does it work?"[1]

This present telling is from the perspective of a later season, what feels like autumn to me, and I am telling it to, and toward, a wider audience as some forms of the WWf(a)C organism go to seed, and others flower. While still engaging the two Auden questions, I address others which have since emerged: "Is it possible to

keep alive the conscious feminine, the unwilling-to-be-exploited
Mother charism of the work as it attempts healthy connection with
the assumed-superior values of the unconscious masculine, Father
Knows Best?" "If so, what qualities of place and presence and what
practices will encourage life and health and discourage corruption
and lies?"

The patterns are more complicated now, but the persistent
threads of what is mine to tell in this season of my personal life, the
organizational life of WWf(a)C, and the life of the interconnected
web of which all are woven are captured in two poems I wrote in
the early eighties. Images from these poems inform the four-part
structure of this book.

Part One: Foundational Stories

Patterns

Our house was full of them:

stripe after stripe
of nosegayed wallpaper
linoleum
scrolled and
ferned

house dresses and aprons
sprigged
dotted
checked.

But in such a house
where walls and floors
were scrubbed relentlessly
clothes washed in hot water
and hung to fade

much that I needed to touch
was worn smooth,
much that I strained to hear
was bleached mute,
the faint patterns
hinting,

haunting me
still
like soft spots where bruises pale
but never heal.
I finger them.
The blood seeps back into the skin
in familiar

black and blue patterns.

Part One contains stories of the invisible patterning of family, school, church, and more, all contributing to the suppression of the feminine. Experiencing the violence done to the full expression of life in individuals and organizations, I longed for a better world, but even then intuited that I would not find it by fleeing to a new world, as do heroes in the great epics on which so much of life as we know it has been patterned. There is no escaping patriarchy; it is around us and within us, its mechanisms rapidly destroying the very ground of our physical and psychosocial being. How then to weave the new within, and with, the threads of the old?

Part Two: Groundwork

Patterns II: The Parsley Garden

For Colin

I.
The sound of the vacuum tells me you're cleaning
your room, beginning at the top of your Saturday
list of chores. I warned you strange things
would begin to grow in there
if you didn't clean it up soon.

The silence of my typewriter warns me
strange things will never begin to grow
in this poem I have been saving to revise—
if I don't clean it up soon.

Our cat noses the attic door behind me,
reminding me of the hyacinth bulbs I planted

in February. It is time to bring them out of the darkness,
to force to bloom on the page:

II.
An evening in February, just after dinner,
the candles are still lit, the violet
from Grandma's funeral blooms between us,
yellow-centered, Lenten-colored, the smell
of good rich tomato sauce (her recipe)
drifts over the table.

You are re-copying a grammar outline,
direct and indirect objects, I'm revising
a poem I call "Dinner," the cat paces around us,
and I see through the kitchen window that the rain
of late afternoon has shaded into snow.

You ask me to read a story with you,
"The Parsley Garden," by William Saroyan.
We take turns reading aloud the story
of a boy and his mother
and the cool green garden
which is the center of their lives.

III.
Suddenly, I'm both here and somewhere else,
both in the pattern and outside, looking into it,
like looking into a scene in a glass paperweight,
I see:
through a curtain of snow
past lace drapes
a cat describing circles
around an eleven-year-old boy and his mother
after dinner
sitting by their careful rows
of tomatoes, peppers, herbs,
a vegetable garden
she calls
the Parsley Garden.

I see the patterns
like fine lace
like snowflakes
intricate, fleeting, lovely beyond words.

IV.
Already, I'm wondering
how to weave it
how to hold it
how to say, to save
it.

I hear the wind roar against the windows,
the phone shrill insistently,
but for a long, suspended moment
out of time
the glass holds.

V.
"Mom, come see if you think my room is clean
enough so things won't grow in it."
I imagine you, cleaning rooms in another house,
a house where you will live a different pattern,
finding this poem in the attic.

Bring it out of the darkness and before your eyes
will bloom some part of your life planted long ago:
the boy you were, the mother I was, the pattern we made.

To that man I write this poem—
with love beyond words—
and with this list of chores attached:

Colin,
clean your room
feed the cat
check the hyacinth bulbs
and take very good care of
The Parsley Garden.
Love,
    Mom

Part Two describes the patterns we wove at WWf(a)C to make visible the weft of the emerging conscious feminine against the warp of the given masculine. Over time, and under the capable and sometimes trembling hands of many women and girls, we wove thousands of sturdy containers for holding heretofore invisible— and thus unspeakable—stories. There are many names for the emerging otherness of culture and nature, potent names from the lexicons of biology, physics, and metaphysics, all of which I embrace and luxuriate in as a poet and lover of language. For the most part, however, I use the Jungian language of "the Feminine," which I am describing for purposes of this conversation as an *energy of life and leadership available to both women and men, expressing values of transparency, hospitality, capacity to hold paradox, nurture-with-rigor, and a model of community which supports individual gifts but not at the expense of societal or planetary well-being.*[2]

Part Three: Change Writing

In Part Three you will find exercises and stories inviting you to weave the practices and patterns detailed in Part Two into your home, your family, your workplace, or other communities. You can read this section first, work and play with the practices, then flip back to Parts One and Two for detail and depth. There is a forum section at marypiercebrosmer.com where you can meet others engaged in these experiments.

Part Four: Conscious Feminine Leadership

Part Four focuses on the challenges and disciplines of leadership in service to the emerging feminine. Not for the faint of heart, or the dilettante, is this work of espousing the severed feminine in a culture so certain of her inferiority. In the leadership academy and consulting projects which emerged from Women Writing for (a) Change, we have developed a growing consciousness about how much courage is required to parent a virtually feral child back into the world.

What this book intends to do in the world is connect the powerful body of writing for personal growth to writing for transformation of culture and nature. These words made flesh in a renewed mystical body, composed of both the masculine and the feminine, make possible new stories of not only competition and domination, but of participation and cocreation.

Pete Seeger, that musician/sage/change agent, has said, "Participation. That's what's going to save the human race."[3] In my experience, what has yet to manifest widely is the holding of writing as the powerful mode of individual expression it so clearly is, alongside the holding of writing as creator of consciousness and conscious community—which it also can and must become—all the while telling the truth about what feminine power and authority can offer the world of culture and nature.

I mean to write an impassioned, but not know-it-all, account of what I have learned moment by moment—on the page in the early mornings with my own writing, watching the dream screen at night, and during a lifetime of creating writing communities.

I speak as an ordinary woman who was surprised to have conceived and given birth at midlife to a powerful and empowering movement of women and girls telling the truths of our lives. We are not exhibitionists or victims, but leaders and participants in a new and fragile possibility that truth, all manner of truths, written and heard in community, might just set us free, free to be in the web of creation, without arrogance or delusion.

I feel such urgency to rinse the world with our writing, as suggested by soul psychologist Robert Sardello: "The world is the word that passes through us and out again in the act of speaking and writing."[4] I devote myself to restoring speaking and writing to the human purpose for which they were intended. I yearn for us to connect ourselves within and without, for want of a better, a living world.

ᐧᕋᐧ

I am somewhat painfully aware that this book does not fit any particular genre. Like Women Writing for (a) Change, the life work, the community, the *communities* it describes, the book weaves not one, but several, threads:

♦   A vision emerging and becoming manifest in a particular life;

♦   The transformative power of writing in conscious community;

♦   The necessity of connection for the healing of culture and nature; and

♦   A passion for just saying what is happening, from multiple perspectives.

Learning to follow the path the words point to is the real genre. I hope you will find an invitation to follow your path, to create your patterns and to weave them into the whole, "patterns like fine lace, like snowflakes/intricate, fleeting, lovely beyond words."

Always I am trying "to weave, to hold, to say, to save it."

Part *One*

Foundational Stories

1.

Surveying the Landscape

The landscape of Women Writing for (a) Change changes so fast that it is difficult to render a stable account of it. What follows is the "now" of 1999–2008, *after* the movement had developed what remain its essential components: the Women Writing for (a) Change Foundation, Women Writing for (a) Change on the Radio, the Feminist Leadership Academy of Cincinnati, Young Women Writing for (a) Change, with its own Young Women's Feminist Leadership Academy, and Consulting for (a) Change, also known as Writing for (a) Change Consulting.

I am fascinated by the frequent references to "this place" made by writers in our communities, especially the young women who leave for college and careers and then return: "This place makes me feel sane again"; "This is the only place I tell the truth, my truth." "This place" or "here" lace their conversations about their lives past and present at WWf(a)C, despite the fact that the physical places which have housed the Cincinnati community have been several; that WWf(a)C communities exist in places as far-flung as Vermont and Oregon; and that expressions of its organizational DNA have emerged in settings as diverse as men's and women's prisons, businesses, and religious orders of women and men!

Despite the twenty-first century penchant for "virtual reality," I am devoted to the notion that everything is happening some *place*, and that real work, real change occurs only in places drenched in particularity. In WWf(a)C work, teachers and facilitators attend to "creating the space," and by this I do not mean mere, or frivolous, "decorating," though we create beauty as we can, where we can. Chairs are in a circle and there is a center marked by a cloth or rug, a candle, or a bowl of water when fire codes prohibit candles, leaves or flowers gathered from the surrounding land, perhaps symbols which community members have been asked to bring to signify their intentions or hopes. Obviously, there are times when the physical limitations of a room or the size of an audience prevent the creation of a circle, or circles, but we always work with the space to connect it to context and the larger world of meaning we hope to evoke.

I am perplexed, to say the least, when I go to workshops said to be about the creation of learning communities (in contrast to command and control systems which stifle innovation) and walk into sterile conference rooms with chairs arranged in rows facing front, rooms without centers, with little signifying purpose or meaning! Without allowing the means—the creation of space—to overshadow the end—the hope of connection—we attend to creating physical space with as much expression as possible of where we are, who we are, and what our intentions are. After all, as the engineers tell us, structure influences behavior. "This place" the writers refer to, the place of finding voice, self, and community, is equally about practices, the establishment of simple, agreed-upon rituals which signal, "you are here in this space, a landscape fertile with possibility."

I will say more about how we create space and what the practices are that say "here" and "home" later in the book (see chapters 5 and 6). For now I want to begin surveying the landscape of WWf(a)C with the story of a place that was home to our movement for ten years, 1996–2006. It would be hard to find a less likely physical place to house a community of women writers. Yet it is where most of what is core to the ecology of WWf(a)C emerged.

Ironworkers Local #44

I am likely one of the few feminists to have read—and liked—
poet Robert Bly's *Iron John*. While I can't remember quite when I
read the book, or why, I do remember that I was reading it sometime after I had initiated a sort of private and instinctive ritual, that
of lighting three candles at my altar to begin the day: the left,
Mother; the right, Father; the center, the fire of their integration.

I am more a synthesizing than a critical reader, taking what I
can use and not so much noticing the "weak argument" of a given
text. Therefore it is entirely possible that I missed the "dangers" of
Bly's book, widely regarded as part of the backlash against feminism. However, I experienced the book as an impassioned—and
understandably poetic—plea for balancing feminine and masculine energies in individual lives and in culture. Furthermore, passages about Life in the Middle, about being the "conductor of
feeling" within a family eventually illuminated my past within my
chosen vocations of teacher, community-builder, and social entrepreneur. They also supported my intuition that I must learn regular practices of *grounding*, lest the currents passing through me
"blow my circuits," to put it coarsely.

> Many of us know this sensation of conduction from early child-
> hood: the mother and father talk to each other through the
> child. The shame of the alcoholic father, for example, goes
> through your body heading east, and the anxiety of the depend-
> ent mother goes through your body heading west. Fury and
> contempt pass each other, meeting somewhere in the son's or
> daughter's chest.[1]

I write all this for a number of reasons, but for the moment I do
so as a way of saying that for ten years of its life, one might say its
young adulthood, WWf(a)C was located in a union hall:
Ironworkers Local #44. And, despite my characteristic fogginess
about dates and times, I am certain that my discovery of the vacant
space that proved so suitable to our needs for ten years was just
after I had read *Iron John*. Did I drive by the building, see the "For
Rent" sign and think: "Oh, look—a symbolic connection with *Iron
John*, so let me rent it!"? Hardly. Nor did I set out to find space in a
union hall because I am the proud daughter of a railroad engineer,
member of the Brotherhood of Locomotive Firemen and Engineers.
The move from our much smaller space on the first floor of a cozy

Victorian house to this *entirely inappropriate,* sterile, sixties-built former Masonic Lodge (!) was, needless to say, jarring. At some point I was smacked in the face with the symbolism and the irony, if you'll excuse the pun, not only of coming back "home" to my union roots, but of occupying a place which embodied what Bly wrote about in *Iron John,* and what, in the end, is my life's mission—the marriage of feminine and masculine!

The visual irony of our location, as women were quick to point out, *on top* of the Ironworkers, was lost on few visitors. The serviceable chrome and brick entrance gave way to a second floor staircase marked by an authentic road sign of yore: *Men Working.* A "WO" was boldly marked in red paint to make the sign read: *Women Working* (a gift of Lynn Goodwin Borgman).

Upper Room Spaces

There was a round table in the corner, covered by a lace tablecloth, the original tablecloth from the first Writing House, the aforementioned cozy Victorian. It was the lace tablecloth of my original WWf(a)C dream, from which I awakened to draft the first brochure announcing my intention to teach writing "in the margins," as we feminists say, outside the power centers of "regular schools" where credit is given, careers are launched, all for the price of. . . . Actually, I cannot say the price, because it differs for every woman who steps into the center to be granted a degree of authority, legitimacy, or financial security. I have made it a point to never, as my father and mother used to wisely warn, "bite the hand that feeds," for I have most surely been fed in regular schools, loving school since my very first year, and succeeding there more than in any other arena of my childhood and teen years.

I can only say that WWf(a)C is a place where women can step into the margins to learn what most of us have not learned from time spent in the centers of patriarchal power. As a peace-making social entrepreneur, I have come to believe in the power of both/and. My life and work are not about being against conventional schooling, against the way things are. Rather, I work with others to create an alternative, *the way things could be.*

Our school was housed in what we fondly called the Writing Hall: an office and four rooms (Earth, Air, Fire, Water) decorated with the paintings of artist Margaret Copfer and with handmade quilts, one of them memorializing our sister-writer Lynn Goodwin

Borgman, who died suddenly in February 1999. From the beginning we enjoyed the paradox of this huge-hearted, decidedly powerful endeavor housed in an unlikely (and unmarked) "upper room" space, in a heartland, "small town of a city," hardly known for radical activity. I am convinced that much of the power of the school has been its grassroots simplicity, its rootedness in place, and its relationships, extending through time.

Programs and Courses

The heart of WWf(a)C organism is the semester course for adult women. Offered four times per year, this course invites women to make a commitment to themselves and their writing by investing their time (2.5 hours once a week) and their money ($500) into creating a place and community that will evoke their words. We offer the course on weeknights and on Tuesday and Thursday mornings. Since there is sometimes confusion on the part of prospective students as to whether they can then come to any of these classes during a given week, I'll clarify here that each class is its own learning community and writers do not float between sections. Developing the integrity of the listening/learning community is essential to the process at WWf(a)C and these qualities develop and are nurtured throughout the semester.

The ten-week course combines experienced and novice writers in a workshop setting designed to help each woman tell what is hers to tell. Writers range in age from eighteen to ninety-six years. Writers experiment with, and teachers demonstrate, techniques of poetry, fiction, memoir, drama, and "genre-defying" writing. Class time is divided among writing, giving and receiving feedback in small groups, large group time for discussion, demonstration, or "read-around," in which each woman reads from work-in-progress to the entire community.

We offer one-day workshops on themes such as "Mothers and Daughters," "Mothers Writing About Sons," "Writing About the Body," as well as monthly tuition-free "sampler classes." Samplers offer writers an opportunity to write in community before, or instead of, taking the semester plunge.

A Community of Practice

Many women remain at WWf(a)C for consecutive semesters or consecutive years, finding that long-term participation in this stew of words and in this conscious community supports them as they grow, not only in skill, but in the courage it takes to break through to subject matter long suppressed. Marcella Allison, who was a member of the first semester class in September 1991 used to say, "I only took two semesters off: one to have a baby, one to start a business." Julia Mace likes to say that she grew up in WWf(a)C, coming to class just after her graduation from college and staying to become not only an active writer and performer of her writing, but also a volunteer and member of the Foundation's Board of Directors, and most recently a member of the Young Women's faculty. Gradually, it dawned on me that implicit in the programs, classes, and volunteer opportunities of the school was the development of women's leadership skills.

The Feminist Leadership Academy

I created the Feminist Leadership Academy (FLA) out of the stories both I and the women in the classes were living and telling about how "having our full voices" affected our work in the world. The FLA graduated its first class of fifteen women, "The Pioneers," in May 2004. Since then, women in the self-named "Builders" (2006) and "Weavers"(2008) classes have graduated and are carrying the conscious feminine into their work as community organizers, pastors, lawyers, activists, teachers, consultants, businesswomen, and more. Some women have participated in FLA as a portal to retirement from traditional careers and into work as conscious elders and mentors of coming generations in their fields and in their families. Still others enter FLA as a doorway from full-time parenting and/or volunteering into careers and paid positions. (Since gathering the class of 2006, I have expressed a willingness to accept applications from men who want to practice the conscious feminine, who want to learn to create conscious communities in work and life. Some have expressed an interest, but no one has yet begun the application process.) At this writing, the "Revolutionaries" (2009) have completed their FLA process. Some will be leaders *for* the WWf(a)c movement, and others will be leaders *from* the movement, carrying what we've learned "in this place" to other places and careers.

Young Women Writing for (a) Change

A creative writing day camp for girls and teens emerged in 1996. For me, this completed a circle. I had left high school teaching in

1992 to focus on WWf(a)C, and was/am well aware of the struggles girls face in keeping their authentic selves alive during preadolescence, adolescence, and young womanhood.

The Young Women's program began in my dining room, where a group of dedicated women gathered to read and discuss much of the available literature about the psychology of women and girls, work by Jean Baker Miller and other Stone Center writers, as well as the groundbreaking work about adolescent girls' loss of voice by Carol Gilligan, Annie Rogers, Lynn Mike Brown, Mary Pipher, and others. Young Women Writing for (a) Change is now a large—and deep—program in its own right that affects the lives of girls and teens who gather at the Writing Center, and those who gather in programs held at schools and community centers in the inner city and elsewhere. The Young Women's program, modeled on the structure and practices of the women's classes, creates communities of girls, aged eight to twelve years, and teenagers, aged thirteen to seventeen years. College-aged women, eighteen to twenty-one years, have their own community, although at age eighteen, young women are free to enroll in the adult women's courses. Young Women Writing for (a) Change programs are thriving as well in our Bloomington, Indiana and Burlington, Vermont schools.

Young Women Writing for (a) Change has a powerful intergenerational element, since many of the adult writers share their words as guest artists, volunteer their time as assistants, and raise funds for scholarships and program enhancements. The layered approach inspires all concerned, and began when teacher–mothers Shawn Dougherty and Marta Donahoe invited their daughters, members of our earliest girls' classes, to be teen assistants in the young girls' classes. The teen assistant program has become integral to our work with girls. Older girls serve as small group facilitators for younger girls; college-aged women return to teen classes as guest artists and eventually as assistant teachers. Near the end of our tenure at the Ironworkers hall, the leadership implicit in this arrangement rose to the level of an explicit leadership curriculum for young women, in the form of the Young Women's Feminist Leadership Academy, (YFLA) which by 2008 had graduated sixteen teens who have created programs for more than four hundred girls.

Writing with Men

During this same time period, Women and Men Writing in Community emerged as a quarterly weekend course, offered at the seasons' turnings: winter and summer solstice, and spring equinox. Women were curious as to what would happen in classes that included men in our feminist process. Eventually this program was discontinued due to a shortage of men interested in enrolling. Perhaps the time was not right, or perhaps my attitude was not right. I was responding to multiple requests from men—and from a few women—to "let men in." I thought, "Ok, let's find out if men really want to participate in a school established by, for, and about women." I knew there would be much to learn from such an arrangement: men developing the "bicultural skills," which women have developed after years in schools bearing the character of places created by, for, and about men. And we, students and faculty, would have much to learn about how to keep women's voices alive and full in the face of socialization brilliantly described in Terrence Real's book, *How Can I Get Through to You?: Reconnecting Men and Women*. Real makes the kind of observation only a man could articulate with impunity:

> When girls are inducted into womanhood, what is it exactly that they have to say that must be silenced? What is the truth women carry that cannot be spoken? The answer is simple and chilling. Girls, women—and also young boys—all share this in common: None may speak the truth about men.[2]

At any rate, the Women and Men Writing in Community course did not take root. After a hiatus of about five years, we began two more experiments with women and men writing together. An all-male class survived one semester with about seven writers, all of whom decided that they would rather be in classes with women. For two semesters, we were able to sustain two sections of our semester classes as co-ed. Here we noted a remarkable *transcendence* of gender, not avoidance or covert accommodation and silencing, but a real flourishing of connection through the power of words held in conscious community. At least this is how I experienced the two co-ed classes in which I served as teacher. In early 2009, men from the most recent co-ed classes are regrouping, inviting other men to join them. I see the strong possibility of writing with men having another season, one more deeply based on their understanding of how "this place" of WW(f)aC is a container for their becoming more whole.

Writing Retreats

In the summers since 1994, we have what I like to call "Big Girls' Camp," or officially Women Writing for (a) Change Summer Retreat and Reunion. For six summer days women from various class nights gather in Nerinx, Kentucky, at the motherhouse of the Sisters of Loretto for uninterrupted focus on our writing, without cooking, cleaning, professional commitments, meetings, or caretaking. Women who once attended classes at our Cincinnati school and have moved away can continue to be part of the WWf(a)C community. And women who don't live near a WWf(a)C school can attend summer or weekend retreats at several of our sister schools. We offer weekend retreats at the Moye Spiritual Center in Melbourne, Kentucky, very near the Cincinnati airport. The sisters of the Congregation of Divine Providence (CDP) share their motherhouse and the woodlands surrounding with much grace and generosity, as do the Sisters of Loretto at Nerinx.

Women Writing for (a) Change on the Radio

In the period I describe as young adulthood, the words of women writers from our school spilled over into a radio show that first aired Easter evening, April 1999 on WVXU-FM, an affiliate of National Public Radio licensed to Xavier University. The program that began as a thirty-minute segment featuring a woman reading her work and engaging in conversation with hosts about "writing and life," expanded to sixty minutes, and into diverse formats including read-arounds, readings of pieces around a certain theme, as well as interviews with established writers visiting Cincinnati. The mission of WWf(a)C on the Radio, which we phrased pithily for radio's sake, was "bringing women to words, and the words of women to the world." The program was in keeping with our vision of publishing, broadcasting, and weaving the conscious feminine into an "overmasculinized" culture. Think of it as an antidote to "talk" or "yell" radio. When Xavier University sold their broadcasting license to Classic Radio Corporation, local programming was condensed into two magazine formats in which our writers had a presence for several years. At this writing, the voice of the conscious feminine is heard on a "radio show of our own," an internet show available on www.womenwriting.org through the miracle of podcasting.

A Foundation of Our Own

During the Ironworkers years of growth and emerging complexity, I began to understand that my role involved more than teaching or direct delivery of programs. I evolved an understanding that I was responsible for stewardship of the larger entity. I left the teaching of two of my classes in the capable hands of Kathy Wade and Cassandra Towns and made some space for discernment of the kind of leadership and leadership container that would allow for "care of the system." For two years, I disciplined myself to focus time and learning effort on what Stephen Covey calls "the important," not just "the urgent." I created a large notebook in which I collected the dreams of this period, notes from interviews with women leaders and creators both local and national, and notes from my reading about entrepreneurship, social entrepreneurship, living systems, and theories of organizational development.

A challenge that was foremost in my mind at that time was how to make the benefits of this work more accessible geographically, economically, and physically since our space was on the second floor of the union hall, without an elevator for women with physical challenges. The weight of tradition and many experts encouraged me to move the work from the legal container of a sole proprietorship into the legal container of a nonprofit corporation. After all, almost all social justice work, within the margins and with the marginalized, takes this form. I was conflicted: The ownership of my own soul meant a great deal to me, nor had I felt the true work of education well-served when, as a public teacher, I worked for a board. Had I risked so much and created so much only to put myself back in a position in which I could literally be fired from my own work? I had spoken with, and read about, several women founders who experienced just this outcome when, for sake of validity and funding, they put their work in the hands of a board that took on a life of its own. Personal fears and ego aside, I had a strong intuition that the vision would be best nurtured—at least for this epoch—by the person through whom it emerged. Relying as I often do on maternal metaphors and mothering experience, I did not want the daughter I had birthed to be raised by a board of directors.

What emerged from my thinking-dreaming-reading-imagining time was a decision to have a both/and entity: the soul proprietorship would remain and, for the next phase of its life, I would be the mother. And, we would create a container, the Women Writing for (a) Change Foundation, a 501c3 corporation, with the mission of making the work of WWf(a)C more widely accessible. We would be joined ever and always by the vision of bringing the conscious feminine more fully into expression, and we would be appropriately and carefully separated by the legal and financial oversight and leadership of a board of trustees.

Let me acknowledge the chorus of "But you can't do that" I heard and sometimes still hear, but I am a mother who trusts her intuition about what is needed.

I was blessed by a grant from the Ohio Arts Council for arts leaders, which provided the services of an arts management consultant in the person of Michael McGee London who met with me throughout my years of discernment and provided the benefit of his experience to the task force which gave birth to the Women Writing for (a) Change Foundation. Michael helped me by saying that what I wanted to do could be done—in fact, it had been done. In the world of dance, for example, the school of dance is a business, joined to a dance company that is nonprofit. Just such an arrangement, Michael told me, underlay the founding of the Cincinnati Ballet that had outlived the school of dance from which it grew. "Fine by me," I said then and say now, "I only know that a board exists to conserve and widen accessibility to a vision, but I needed to be the entrepreneur/owner/mother while I am still creating, and the vision needs the both/and of growth and conservation while it's still growing."

I honor the women by naming them: Andrea Nichols, Marta Donahoe, Jenn Reid, Pauletta Hansel, Kathy Wade, Leslie Cannon, and Mary Anne Reese spent many a Friday night over wine and dinner at the union hall, giving birth to the Women Writing for (a) Change Foundation as a fertile place to grow and nurture what the LLC could not: scholarships to programs, Young Women Writing for (a) Change, the YFLA leadership program, the New Media Circle that produces our radio show, an extensive community partnership program creating after-school programs in the city and in social service settings with homeless youth.

Consulting for (a) Change

This cell of the organism seems to me to have taken shape from two sources. The first was that one day I looked at my computer folder marked "Special Programs" long enough to actually see the many organizations, and their disparate natures, with whom I had worked in efforts to increase workplace well-being, innovation, and communication. I followed my usual path to creating a business unit, by naming what had emerged. I trademarked the name Writing for Change Consulting. I began working more intentionally and recognizing that my teaching was leading me out of the original community and deeper into the world outside our doors. The second source of cultivation of the life that was growing in this area was my extensive reading of thinkers such as Margaret Wheatley, Peter Senge, Joseph Jaworski, Dee Hock, Dana Zohar, and Parker Palmer. All of these teachers-at-a-distance aided and abetted my intuitions and experiences *and* my idealism about how people can be in community, true community as derived from the origins of the word in Latin: *cum*/with, *munus*/gifts. The book *Presence*,[3] co-authored by Senge, with Jaworski, Betty Sue Flowers, and Otto Scharmer, so inspired me that I applied for membership in the corps of consultants affiliated with Senge's SoL, Society for Organizational Learning. I joined this community in November 2007, and I continue to explore what is mine to bring from the WWf(a)C universe and what is mine to take from the universes connected with SoL members.

Name Change

I do not like to change the names of things; I feel as if names are ordained in some way, even if they, like WWf(a)C itself, are unwieldy and hard to sell in marketing slogans. However, I found the fear of writing was and is so pervasive that placing writing in the foreground of the business name seemed to close doors to places it would be fun and mutually helpful to enter. So, as a result, we are translating the values and tools—one of which is writing—to help support the gifts and embrace the challenges of organizational life, in the name Consulting for (a) Change.

Home Change

And, to bring this survey of the WWf(a)C landscape to an end and to close the era of our growth in the home of the Ironworkers:

In eighteen hectic, intense months from January 2006 to June 2008, the foundation raised capital to purchase a fully wheelchair accessible home for the hearts and words of women, girls, and men at 6906 Plainfield Road in Silverton, a working class neighborhood, once a railroad community, and an incorporated village within the city limits of Cincinnati, Ohio.

A word about the "we" of WWf(a)C: During a trip to California for my niece's graduation, I responded to questions about my work. When I said, "And we also have a radio show," my niece's stepfather, Phil, asked, "We? Is that a royal we?" I replied to him with the truth about ownership of the school: I founded the school and call myself "soul proprietor," founder, and mother; but WWf(a)C is a living thing, an organism, a community affected by the words and vision of every woman, girl, or man who has ever written with us. Certainly all the writers, the professional faculty and staff, board members, generous donors, and the many women who volunteer are the "we" of WWf(a)C.

A royal we. In that sense, yes.

Exercises

1. "Survey the landscape" of an entity or system which you have participated in creating. (Examples: a family, a business, a ministry team, workplace team, social or service organization, a visionary community.) You will be invited to continue writing about and around this choice for several chapters, so choose something you really want to understand and attend to in some depth.

    Write a list of places in which important stories in the life of this organization happened.

    (Examples: Chiertlin conference room

    Picnic table at Maumee State Park

    John's garage

    Singing the blues in the Seattle Airport

    First real home: Pembroke Towers, second floor)

    Now write stories set in each place.

2. How much particularity do you observe in the stories you wrote? Were there strong images of setting? Of people? Of rituals created within the organization?

3. Who were you in this set of stories? Not what your role was, but who were you and who were you becoming because of being there? What did you contribute for health? What did you contribute for dis-ease?

4. Who was your "royal we" in this place?

5. Give the entity a birth date; draw a graph to chart its highs and lows, vitality and loss of vitality.

6. Give the entity an ending date based on either its ending, or the ending of your relationship with it.

2.

Beginnings: In the Names of My Mother and My Father

When I am asked to tell the story of Women Writing for (a) Change I begin at different points, depending on who's asking and on my energy for telling. The least vulnerable and most prosaic version of the story begins: On September 5, 1991, fifteen women gathered in a rented space in a holistic health center. Fifteen women responded to my offer to be the teacher of women who wanted to "Write for a Change," women who wanted to be open to whatever changes would occur in their lives as a result of taking themselves seriously as writers.

But this beginning, like most beginnings, was not *the* beginning. WWf(a)C began in my family's yellow kitchen, in the Roman Catholic Church of my 1950s childhood, in the schools I attended, and in the schools in which I taught. In each of these places I encountered what I now think of as the *paradox of silence and voice,* the crucible in which WWf(a)C was created.

In the Yellow Kitchen: Mother

Mama

Working in her kitchen,
making spaghetti sauce
for the men out fishing,
I find the little, wooden-handled
tool she used to cut the ravioli.

I remember her, pressing
it fiercely into the yellow dough
defining neat squares
sealing the meat and cheese inside.

The richness always inside
threatening to explode
in the boiling broth.

I search the newly-remodeled
kitchen for some trace of her,
hating the vinyl wallpaper
over the old walls,
the Formica food bar replacing
the oilcloth-covered table
where she rolled the pasta.

The only thing familiar
is this tool for crimping the edges.

I am hungry for the rich broth,
I want to be fed:
woman secrets
kitchen talk.

Instead, I am starved by silence,

the silence of her death
leaving me sole woman in family
of men: father, brothers, son
whom she fed
with the silence of her life:

crimped edges, neat squares,
hospital corners, pinched lips
holding things together.

Now it falls to me to hold things
together. She did it then so I
could be free—
or so we thought.

She hands me the tool with work-
reddened hands, her wedding band
worn thin.

Make the pasta, feed the men,
but above all, seal the edges,
hold it in.

After my mother's death, I picked up my pen, and I began to
live by writing a different story: the story of a woman unwilling to
starve in silence as a way of feeding others; the story of a woman
not holding her richness inside, not risking explosion in the boiling
broth of suppressed rage.

Writing this story, poem by poem, journal entry by journal
entry, I longed for a place where I might be heard and supported in
this disloyal work of telling the truth of my life. I did not—and still
do not—long to be published in the conventional sense; I longed to
be *heard*. I longed for the company of other truth-telling women. I
wanted to share my elation at the sweet release of not holding it all
together. My longing has been met, for I have created for and with
others a deep, loyal-to-ourselves-and-one-another company of
truth-telling, word-loving women.

At one especially low time of my life as a single mother and
"known feminist" teacher in a conservative school system, I
dreamed that I carried my heavy briefcase wearily "home," to my
mother's kitchen. I walked into a circle of my mother's friends, their
names a litany of such sweetness, I awakened to tears. Marge, Dot,
Esther, Billie, Elsie, Betty, and Mama Isabel. They were beaming and
saying, *Sit down, Mary, you look tired. Put your briefcase down.*

It was not long afterward that I did indeed put down my briefcase and the weight of teaching, grading, and schooling which I
had carried long enough.

During the months before I wrote the first brochure announcing my intention to start WWf(a)C, I had two other telling dreams. The first came in the late fall of 1990. The previous summer I had taught a course in women's literature at Cincinnati's Xavier University. I had agreed to teach the course with great excitement. Surely this would be a chance to bring women's words to the table without having to explain why I was teaching all those women. After all, the course title was Studies in Women's Literature!

It was not to be. The question simply mutated: *Why are you teaching all these feminists? Why are you teaching works by lesbians?* Despite my most skillful facilitation, despite the strenuous efforts to speak and be heard on the part of fully half the class of "non-traditional" women students, the semester became an exhausting battle of the sexes. I struggled to listen to the women, they to me, and all of us to the women writers we had assembled to hear, above the din of indignant male voices demanding explanation, justification. I later laughed, ruefully, about how we women talked in stolen moments: in the hallway during breaks, going to and from class, in the "women's room," and in journal entries and responses. Marcella Allison, who graduated from the University of Chicago with an English degree, and who later crossed over with me to the land of WWf(a)C, wrote in her journal: "Why do we always have to teach the boys?" Against this backdrop I dreamed:

> I begin to take roll in women's lit class and realize all the men—half the class—are absent! I keep wondering why they signed up for a course in women's literature they're prepared to hate! I curse this latest "tactic" on their part. I am worried about the strength of my words at the last class; did I come on too strong?
>
> The scene metamorphoses and now we are all women seated around a beautiful mahogany table with lace cloth. We are in a Victorian-era house, and we begin to talk immediately and passionately about the literature at hand. The lights blink and go out. The atmosphere grows ominous. We have to abandon our studies to focus on the threat to our environment.

A few months passed. By early 1991, I was writing in my journal, making notes, thinking on paper about a course I might offer to the women who spoke to me after my poetry readings. To my great astonishment and humble delight, women of all ages, all levels of formal education, were asking me if I would be their teacher. I was trying to imagine a way for those women to get to me and I to them, when I had a second dream:

> The dream I had Saturday evening has been heavy in me. I was teaching women only; we were sitting around a table writing plays, and they kept coming up with plays about sexual abuse. I was bewildered, and afraid of what would happen to us if we kept writing about such things, but their words were so powerful and real. I had no impulse to contain or control. But much fear. In the next part of the dream, I was hiding in an old Victorian house from someone, or several people who were trying to kill me because of the teaching I was doing.

After recording this dream, I went on to write in my journal a draft of what became the first WWf(a)C brochure, describing the values and vision of the project I was proposing.

The brochures first saw the light of day at the workshop, "Women Writing Across Difference," which I co-facilitated at Grailville, a conference center and intentional women's community in Loveland, Ohio.[1] After my reading, I casually mentioned that I had put brochures for a writing class I was teaching on the conference table. Later that evening, one of the women attending the workshop came to my room, waving in her hand a lilac registration form paper-clipped to a check. I almost didn't recognize what she was handing me, so amazed that it was, might be, actually beginning. Eight years later, at my fiftieth birthday celebration, the same woman gave me that check, laminated, and labeled, "First check ever written to Women Writing for (a) Change."

So it was that I gathered women, fourteen more by the anticipated start date of September 5, 1991, to my home school, which, though never held in my literal home, flowed out of the home, the kitchen where my mother had gathered her women friends, the kitchen where I had watched her so many times press fiercely on the handmade dough, crimping the edges. The kitchen where I had followed after, piercing the dough.

Ten years after her death, and two years into the life of WWf(a)C, I sat in the kitchen, at the oilcloth-covered table of Aunt Marie, the woman who had helped raise my mother, her husband's niece, from the time my mother was nine years old. I asked Aunt Marie to tell more about why my mother had not gone beyond the sixth grade in school. Aunt Marie told about an incident at the school in Clarksdale, Mississippi, where some Italian families had settled in the twenties as indentured farm workers on cotton plantations. Mom had come home in tears, humiliated in some way related to her darker skin, her "Dago" origins.

"After that happened, Papa [my mother's grandfather and patriarch of the family] wouldn't let her go back, even though she wanted to. She got to be very sorry she told what happened to her," sighed Aunt Marie. "And, there was nothing I could do to help her, once Papa had made up his mind."

"What did she do all day with her time, once she wasn't going to school?" I asked. My mother never told any of the stories of her life before she married my father and moved to Ohio.

"Oh, she helped out in the house and in the fields. And she sat many evenings at the kitchen table with a pencil and tablet, writing little poems. She even had some published in the Clarksdale newspaper."

Mothers: A Meditation

They visit me often now,
gather in my room
nights I cannot sleep,
nights I lie in bed sifting
house sounds for the comforting
murmur of my son's breathing,
nights I pray for sleep.

They seem to want something,
stretch white hands toward me,
want to give me, ask me,
tell me something,
and I cannot sleep,

and I hear nuns intone the sad
round notes of the Stabat Mater,
hear the click and tink of their
rosaries as they process into my room
in two swaying, candlelit lines,
their white faces rising moons
in the darkness,

Aunt Marie snaps beans into her
aproned lap, her hands are red,
knuckles swollen, nails and moons
round and white, white moons
of childhood rising, rain tapping
the old tin roof, breeze heavy
with the scent of cape jasmine
lifting the lace drapes, fanning
my hot face,

and Mother, white-gloved and smiling,
rises from the darkness of old photographs,
gardenias in her white hair, to crown
the Blessed Virgin, arms floury to the
elbows, her hair now streaked with white,
she pats fat moons of dough into dumpling
pans, lays her cool hands on
my feverish cheeks.

Suffering mothers, cool white mothers,
I love you, will tell your lives like beads,
recite your days like decades:
The Joyful, Sorrowful, Glorious mysteries
you teach. I reach for the beads, clear
and lovely in the moonlight, touch
your hands, and finally, sleep.[2]

1984

In the Yellow Kitchen: Father

If my mother was the lost poet in our family, it was nowhere apparent. You'll appreciate the extent of my shock about my mother as girl-poet when I say that her only writing was hastily scratched grocery notes in a nearly illegible hand. A game my father conducted from his place at the table was leading my brothers and me in the hilarity of trying to decipher my mother's jottings. Oats became rats, i.e., "Mom's buying rats at Cardinal Mart today!" I am embarrassed to think of my participation in this romp at my mother's expense, but much of what happened in the yellow kitchen under my father's direction was so strained, a child could be excused for the occasional release.

I did not know then of my mother's shame at her cramped handwriting and limited education. I knew my mother was ambidextrous, writing, eating, crocheting with her right hand and doing most other things with her left hand. I *didn't* know then that in school, her left hand had been tied to her body until she adapted to right-handed writing. As for reading, I never in my life remember my mother reading a book; she glanced in stolen moments at women's magazines, and that was the extent of her reading.

It was my father who gave us his love of words. Earl Keith Pierce was actually named after a character, one "Earl of the Border" whom his older sisters, my book-loving aunts, Sarah Ruth and Alberta Pauline Pierce, had discovered in a long-forgotten novel.

When I would remark how the Pierces were a book-loving family, my aunts would tartly remind me that it was the *Andrews*, their mother's family, descendents from Scottish lairds and ladies, as family history had it, who were the *literati* of the coal-mining towns in and around Hocking, Vinton, and Meigs counties in southern Ohio. All my Pierce-Andrews aunts and uncles were avid readers of everything from James Joyce and Shakespeare to Gene Stratton Porter and Zane Grey. I tried to read *Ulysses* the summer I visited my Aunt Ruth on her five-acre retirement "farm" in Vinton County. I gave up, but my aunt had read the Joyce tome for pleasure!!!

When I was born my father purchased a set of the classics for me, inscribing each volume with my name: Mary Lucille Pierce, in his beautiful looping, left-handed script. When my father wasn't working, gardening, hunting, or fishing, he was in the living room, in his recliner, reading. No matter what swirled around him in our tiny house—horseplay, television shows, phone calls and next-room conversations—Earl Keith was gone to books. He died in his sleep February of 1990, pushed back in his recliner, a novel on his chest.

I always knew, without remembering any preaching, that school, books, and a good education were the highest values. Dad had left school his junior year at Nelsonville High School to join FDR's Civilian Conservation Corps that for months into years was the only source of a paycheck for his mother, despite the fact that he was the "baby" of six living siblings. I do not know why my father did not return to school after the Depression, after testing his way into the Army Air Corps flight school, reserved then—as now—mostly for the college-educated. Perhaps he took the same dim view of the G.I. Bill as he did of V.A. loans: He felt the white-collar bureaucratic dispensers of such monies condescended to him. I do not exactly know, but I do know that he inscribed in my heart these words: "Education is something they can never take away from you." My father was one of the best-educated, most critical-thinking men I ever knew, and a rare man of his class and generation who believed that higher education was as essential for girls as it was for boys.

My father intervened directly in my education only twice; the first time to inform my first grade teacher that I was left-handed, and that he "wouldn't like to hear of any attempts to change that." The second time was when I came home crying that my eighth grade teacher, our school principal, had accused me of cheating by "letting" Johnny G. copy off my paper. When Dad heard that Sister did not believe my denial, he went back to St. Joseph's—seven years after his first visit. When I asked him, timorously, what had happened in this battle of *the* titanic forces of authority in my young life, he said, "I told her, 'my daughter doesn't lie.'" Oh, how I loved him fiercely for knowing me as a lover of truth!

If my father was—and he was—the proponent of words and books and telling the truth, he was also the reason for the crimped edges seeping rage in our yellow kitchen.

At a Veteran's Day Service at St. John's Unitarian-Universalist Church, a woman in the congregation spoke of growing up in the 1950s, and thanked the many men, her father among them, who had not, as she put it, "carried the war home." Her words cut me to the quick; for my father, who loved us deeply, also carried the suppressed rage and grief—and perhaps shame—of his thirty-seven missions at the controls of a B-24 into our yellow kitchen.

Throughout those long and long-ago years, I was plotting my escape to the relative safety of my woman's kitchen, a room spacious enough to hold the words I had swallowed in the yellow kitchen.

My father gave me the love of language, the determination and courage to resist those who attempt to silence the expression of others. My life with him, my love of him, was another face of the paradox of silence and voice that gave birth to WWf(a)C.

For My Father

I.

This morning, making breakfast,
I did more than think of you,
I was in the yellow kitchen
of my childhood with you,
Daddy, making soft-boiled eggs
the way you taught me.

Did you know then, can
you know now, if I tell you,
from the safe distance
of my woman's kitchen,
how much was at stake for me
then, cooking for you,
performing the exacting tasks
I had so little talent for:

spoon-lowering eggs
into the center of the rolling boil
at just the right moment
so they wouldn't crack,

tapping each hot egg
with a table knife, the way
you showed me,

sliding it delicately around the shell
probing for globes of yolk
and the soft—I prayed not runny—
whites.

Did you know how I dreaded, Daddy,
the telling click-tink of shell in bowl
which would betray my clumsiness?

Not that you would hit, or even scold
me for such a tiny failure,
but that you would smile

that wry, sad, but somehow satisfied
smile that said you were disappointed

disappointed but not surprised, for
already, Daddy, it was becoming clear,
as people used to say, that I was not
"the right kind of woman,"

not like the deft kitchen women we
both loved: my mother and yours.

II.
I remember, it seems silly now,
when you came home from work
with the recipe for your friend, Vick's
daughter, Susie's molasses cookies.

So delicious you said
Susie's cookies were
so sweet and so dark.

I hurried to bake a batch, my first.
And when finally the rows of cookies
lay cooling on the table
you passed through the kitchen
and smiled, "They don't look like Susie's"
was all you said, and didn't taste one.

III.
To this day, Daddy, I'm no gifted cook,
though, like my mother and yours
I have learned to feed those
who find their way to my kitchen.

I'm better, Daddy,
at poems than cookies—
or eggs.

I sent you one, poem that is,
you never said,
but if you read it,

how did you find it?

Too dark this time
but still not sweet enough?

IV.
I write to thank you, Daddy,
for all you taught me
in the yellow kitchen.

It comes in handy now.

There is an art to lowering myself
into the rolling boil at just the right
moment so I won't crack,
running a knife around my
soft insides is delicate, dangerous
work, but I have much practice,
excellent training.

Even my old knack
for shattering shells
serves me well.

V.
Won't you come to my kitchen,
Daddy?

Sit at my table and let me use
my woman's, mother's, poet's
daughter's skills

to crack you open
shatter your shell.

Won't you let me find you inside,
good Daddy, gold sun,
broken or whole,

I would love you if you'd let me,
my father, my center,
my yolk, my yoke.

Exercises

1. Write about what happened before the beginning, before what appeared to be the "official birth date" of the system you wrote about in chapter 1 and your participation in it.

2. Who was "the mother" and/or "the father"?

3. Where did she/he come from? Bringing what gifts and what challenges?

4. Who were you in the beginning? Before the beginning? How did you enter this landscape and what did you bring?

3.

In the One, Holy, Catholic
(and Apostolic) Church

As I write, I continue to imagine my mother: imagining her taking in both the light and shadow of our collective lives as women of our time, race, and class. I direct my words to listening others who will carry on the work of creating conscious containers for the words of girls, women—and men. I am thinking of the application process for our Feminist Leadership Academies. Applicants write essays, one of which addresses how their lives have brought them to the moment of this commitment. Teachers, midwives, businesswomen, attorneys, women religious, young and not-so-young, we continue to reflect on the patterns we have already woven, as a way of continuing to weave our lives. Or, as James Baldwin put it so elegantly and succinctly, "If I don't know where I came from, how can I create where I am going?"[1]

This has been a rather long but necessary way of writing myself into the possibility of reflecting on the role of the "Roman Catholic

Church of my 1950s childhood" in teaching me how to create a utopian feminist school! But I am finally ready to take that on, keenly aware of how the alternating strands of Mother and Father are in evidence here.

Mother-Father Strands

It was my mother who was devoutly Roman Catholic, and to this day, despite my chosen exile from the institutional church, I have a loving relationship to the devotions and sacraments of my childhood religion. I am grateful that my church retained a connection, however unconscious, to the goddess, through the Marian rites and traditions. The centerpiece of my home altar is a picture of the Black Madonna to whom I have a fierce devotion. The early experience of the mystical—incense and ritual, transformation in the form of "transubstantiation"—has re-emerged in my teaching to the extent that I cannot imagine a workshop, a class, or even a meeting without some ritual elements to bring people into the space and purpose of the moment.

And what of Father? Father ruled the church and the little parish school where I received a strict, no-nonsense education that has served me well in many ways. Father was as uncompromising and authoritarian at St. Joseph's, as my father was in our yellow kitchen.

The Sisters who taught us in those nailed-down-desk classrooms facing the crucifix, were, like my mother, powerful in their love and commitment, and as often powerless and seething with repressed anger as she was. I remember hearing radical feminist Sonia Johnson say she was well trained for understanding how patriarchy works by growing up in the Mormon Church. No doubt the reason some of the explicit critique I read in my early days of feminism clicked with me so powerfully and immediately was because it drew on my wordless critique of Roman Catholicism in my early years, my wearing the diminishment of the others—women, "Protestants," "pagans"—like a child-sized hair shirt. I squirmed within.

"Catholic"

I remember being surprised when I learned that "catholic" meant universal. It was not, as I had thought, a word that simply denoted my religious denomination, much as Methodist or Lutheran were names of my Protestant friends' denominations. Catholic—I believed, because I was taught—was *the* Church, inclusive of all persons fortunate enough to have heard of us. In our small parochial grade school, we gave pennies and nickels to the cause of spreading our faith to the pagans of Africa, China, and the South Sea islands. In the eighth grade, I gave a whole $5.00 to "buy a pagan baby." I cringe when I remember this process, especially naming "my" baby Priscilla, probably after some character I'd admired in one of the novels I consumed.

I cringe even more thinking about how I did not know then that my universal church, so eager to convert and include the various others of the world, did not really include women—did not really include me. If I learned much about the paradox of silence and voice in the yellow kitchen, it was certainly deepened by my years in the catholic and apostolic church.

Voice Story

Shortly after extending the scope of WWf(a)C to include classes for girls, I gave the following writing prompt to women in the adult class: Return in memory to your girlhood and write voice stories, memories of expression and suppression of your young voice. What immediately arose for me when I responded to this prompt was the memory of singing in church. From the sixth grade through my first year in college I had what I think now was a formative experience of knowing what it meant to hear my own voice in a resonant space.

> Ironically, the first place I remember feeling the power and pleasure of my voice was the Roman Catholic Church of my childhood—not the "whole catholic and apostolic church" or the antique, patriarchal, and misogynistic church, but one small parish in the midst of it: St. Joseph's in Crestline, Ohio.
>
> Our Pastor, Father Fralick, was an aquiline-nosed intellectual, Croatian, my father speculated. His nodding, wristwatch-checking parishioners greeted his erudite and lengthy homilies on scripture with thinly disguised impatience.
>
> Perhaps his insistence on not one, but two High Masses every day of the week and Saturday, was a way of protesting his

long tenure in this anti-intellectual backwater. Whatever the reason, Father's generosity—or grandiosity, depending on your point of view—strained the resources of our small, indifferent parish. We did not even have a choir in those days, and an organist only when school was in session and the sisters were in residence.

As a result of this, and the fact that I was known to have had piano lessons, I was chosen to play the organ for both High Masses, the 6:45 and the 8:15, when the "music nun" returned to the Motherhouse for the summer months.

I was paid $5.00 per week for my services, five single dollar bills in a slim, brown envelope solemnly dispensed by Father Fralick each Saturday after the 8:15 Mass, when I was to appear in the sacristy and wait discreetly in the doorway until he had finished his after-Mass rituals of chalice-wiping and host-eating.

Every summer morning for seven years, I jumped out of bed at 6:15, threw on an odd assortment of clothing, and rode my bike eight blocks from our small house on the edge of town to the imposing granite church on Thoman Street, which was almost downtown—if a town of 4,000 could be said to have a downtown.

Minutes before Father was to process into the sanctuary, I'd dash up the steps, pull open the heavy door, and slip inside the dark church. Tiptoeing through the vestibule and up the creaky steps to the choir loft slowed me down, but I had it timed so that I had minutes—maybe two—to push any number of buttons and stops on the huge organ, and then, as it hummed to life, to select my music for the day.

Maybe I'd choose Mass #XI, or maybe, in a daring mood #X. Whether the music I played had any relevance to the liturgical themes for that day I have no idea, but I am sure if I had blundered too far into the inappropriate, Father Fralick would have informed me!

I was the choir and the organist, the soloist and her accompanist. High in the handsomely carved loft, invisible to the few Mass-goers scattered below, I was fearless. I opened my mouth and my voice flew out of me like a freed bird, carrying my soul out of me into the whole, shadowy, resonant body of the church.

My girl's voice, suppressed in all other places, drifted up to the wedding cake ceiling and fell to the marble floors, bounced off the confessionals, and trespassed into the sanctuary itself, where the only women's voices I had ever heard were those of brides murmuring vows, or members of the Altar and Rosary Society whispering, as they dusted and polished.

Whether I had a "good voice" or not was somehow, incredibly, not an issue. The old people who attended these Masses told my mother, "It's like listening to an angel." But they were kind, and hard of hearing.

I look back, and remembering the modulations that came later, I marvel at the memory of the full, right feel of my voice welcomed into space. There was a bright, animal aliveness of breath, tongue, teeth, words: round here, thinning-to-a-tremble there.

It was joy, unself-conscious pleasure, perhaps my only, certainly my purest memory of it.

Fall, 1996

The full right feel of my own voice welcomed into space was an extraordinary gift, one I have tried to share with my students, trying to consciously create a resonant space where women's voices are welcomed, whether we sing in major or minor keys.

I have created Women Writing for (a) Change in part because of this positive voice experience, one I believe to have been extraordinarily rare within the institutional church, and I have also created the school because many of our churches prevented us from being heard, except in the most marginal of ways, except in support of our own exclusion.

Exercises

1. What brought you to the moment of commitment to this family, work team, dream, or business you've been writing about?

2. *Did* you commit? Write about why, why not.

3. Write a "voice story" of your own set in the context of this family, work team, etc.

4. How might this landscape have been altered if your full voice had been welcomed into space?

5. What are you doing now, in the systems you are creating by your participation, to include as many voices, in as many timbres as possible?

4.

Schooling

My life on the student side of the desk in the process called "schooling"—a term I use to refer to the traditional containers in which learning takes place in the United States in the twentieth and twenty-first centuries—was fairly unmomentous. Always a good student, though lazy enough to earn only slightly above-average grades in subjects I didn't like, e.g., algebra and chemistry, I pretty much happily skipped through: eight years in a small-town Catholic elementary school; small-town public high school; small, liberal arts, Catholic, all-girls St. Mary of the Springs; and Xavier University of Cincinnati. The incidents which affected me most share the same theme: someone in authority doubting my intelligence—and integrity. I have told of being accused of "letting someone cheat off of me," but not of two incidents of being accused of cheating while I was in undergraduate school.

I Am Nobody

I loved my dedicated college professors, mostly Dominican sisters, erudite and fiercely devoted to the intellectual formation of young women. Although I attended college in the late sixties and feminism was breaking in waves over the country, not a whisper of it came to my ears at St. Mary's. However, my classmates and I were *living* feminism in that we, not our non-existent male classmates, were the school's leaders. I was editor of the college paper in my senior year, just as the college was becoming co-educational, and the very next year the editor was a man, with a capable young woman as "his assistant"!

I especially loved my professors of English, and blossomed in an atmosphere in which it was "good" to be smart and to love words, reading, and discussion of books and ideas. Such had not been the case at Crestline High School, home of the Bulldogs.

In this vulnerable state of naïve joy, I entered my first course for English majors, Studies in Shakespeare, taught by the formidably brilliant Sister Sylvia Mahan, recently arrived from the *East Coast*! One day, in complete sincerity, I questioned an interpretation of a text which Sister offered. I was unprepared for her wrath, and for her complete shunning of me thereafter. My raised hand was ignored enough days in a row that I got the message, and sat in my private leper colony, though I still enjoyed the reading and Sister's lectures.

I think I wrote my first paper for this class about light and dark imagery in *Romeo and Juliet*. After we had turned in our papers, Sister called me into her office. Bluntly, she told me that she did not think me capable of producing an essay of such quality as the one I had turned in! She had searched various critical sources to discover how and where I had plagiarized, but had been unsuccessful. "So where had I gotten this paper?" she demanded. I assured Sister that every word, every idea was mine and mine alone. I had no way of proving this, only my words, and not a few tears of humiliation. Sister Sylvia apparently believed me; she returned the paper to me with an A+ and, without apology, granted me access to the classroom conversations from which I had been banned for questioning.

I remember at the time wondering why Sister had thought me dumb. Was I dumb? Did she know I was the first person in my family to get to college? If I had known enough of Emily Dickinson at that point, I might have walked around campus intoning, "I am nobody; who are you?" It took a while for me to recover my footing, but I don't think I ever recovered my voice fully—the questioning, naive, *assuming-we're-all-here-to-learn* voice of the first semester sophomore I had been.

The very next semester, I had a bad case of the flu on the day of a midterm essay exam in the class taught by another of my literature-teacher heroines. I made the exam up the next week, and when our papers were returned, I had a "see me after class" marked in red at the bottom of my paper. Sister (why can't I remember this one's name?) told me that my essays had been so perfect—she could not deduct one single point for either content or style—that she was convinced that I had been told the questions by another student. Again I was stunned, shamed, and hurt! Something was wrong with me that people didn't think me smart enough to do the work I was able to do! To their credit the professors did not punish me for their suspicions; both gave me the grades I had earned, but never did I pass either of them on our small green campus that I didn't feel the veil of shame come over me for something I had not done!

The crucible of silence and voice again strikes me as the applicable theme: speak or write with too much confidence? joy? clarity? trust? and you'll be in trouble. My mother had warned me often enough: "Your mouth is gonna get you in trouble." Or, as the poster (quoting Mark Twain) on a wall of the high school library where I taught for fifteen years would have it—way too cynically for my taste—*Keep your mouth shut and people might think you're stupid; open your mouth and you'll remove all doubt.*

Throughout my work in recent years has been woven memories of how speech and withholding speech serve and do disservice to communities of learners—not to mention families, work groups, and religious communities.

Slapping Robert Rose

I.

Right up front, I want to confess:
this is going to be a confessional poem.

Instead of digressing as I'm tempted
to do, temptation existing in a complicated
sequential relationship with sin itself
as I partially recall from my catechism

(You see, I'm already digressing
to avoid confessing)

Let me just admit it:

my first year of teaching
I slapped an eleven-year-old child
full across the face,
slapped an eleven-year-old child
while forty sixth-graders
in a hot classroom
at St. Philip the Apostle School
watched.

Not to worry, tongue-cluckers,
penance-prescribers,
my victim has worked
his vengeance on me
for decades now
squirming up in his maroon sweater,
baggy at the shoulders,
his blonde hair plastered
in bowl-cut bangs to his pale forehead,
his freckles the only cheerful
thing about him.

Every time I speak about
what I have come to learn about teaching,
about classroom as community,
I see Robert Rose's face
still red with my handprint
after twenty years,
and my face colors
as though he'd slapped me.

II.
Oddly enough, that's what it felt like
as though he slapped me,
day after day, watching me where I
stood under the crucifix
in that hot classroom
watching me,
and resisting, worse, scorning,
every word, every gesture,

every idea I created to teach,
to somehow reach him.

I don't even remember what it felt like—
the slapping—
it was over so fast,
it was as if my hand belonged to someone
else, as if I'd just watched a woman,
little more than a child herself,
slap a child
in a crowded classroom
in the foreign-to-me land
of inflicted cruelties.

But I remember, as if it happened
seconds ago in the most familiar
room of my life,
that Robert Rose just sat there.
He resisted by not resisting,
he didn't move, didn't speak.

Then the oily smirk
of his victory over me
spread over his face,
and I stood there,
nailed to the spot
by forty pairs of eyes,
crucified, tasting
shame like the bitterest gall.

III.
Years later, I understand enough
about power and its abuses, to wonder
what had brought Robert Rose to the place
where his only response to life
was no response.
I'll admit, however, that I still don't
understand enough about why
silence and resistance and,

above all, smirking
provoke my fury.

I don't understand why
I am, by nature or habit,
the dark storm
swirling across
cold, white surfaces.

Why I want to, and often do
fly in the faces
of pallid, wan, passive people?

Is it because I know
it is too dangerous to take them into my arms
that I take up arms against the armored,
the thick-shelled,
the shellacked,
the cynic,
the supercilious?

I cannot take them into my arms;
I know their coldness burns.
I have lost limbs,
parts I need,
through long,
sometimes even brief
exposure
to the frozen.

IV.
God save me from the sullen,
the dead-eyed, the brittle-smiled child,
who, taught to hate,
taught me to hate him,
who taught to fear,
taught me to fear him.

His freckles spread across
my dreams like disease,
I pray for him—

God save him
from teachers like me.

I think of my career on the teacher side of the desk as a long, steeply banked learning curve, leading away from that girl who, *taught to oppress* as a way of consolidating power, oppressed Robert Rose. Away from the young woman who, in her next incarnation as a high school teacher of literature, taught "like a man," was so emotionally tough and so intellectually rigorous that no one would think her stupid ever again! I think of the first eight to ten years of my public life as a Victor/Victoria experience. I was a woman vesting myself in the "drag" of male authority and sternness in order to be successful in the show biz that teaching in those days was: six shows a day, five days a week, teacher in the spotlight; students in the audience, scripts provided by the established literary canon.

Coming Out

In 1981 I was a "fellow" in the Ohio Writing Project at Miami University, an offshoot of the Bay Area Writing Project that revolutionized the teaching of writing. The tenet of the writing project that most affected me was "teacher as writer," teacher as practitioner of the craft she was teaching. What a novel idea!

In a master's program at Xavier University, I read my first overtly feminist text, *Of Woman Born* by Adrienne Rich. Rich's analysis of motherhood, combined with her transparency about her own experience of mothering three boys—I was the mother of a seven-year-old son at the time—did not explode my world so much as ground it. Finally, I connected the severed ends of my life as a female impersonator and as a ventriloquist's dummy, having men's words about women put in my mouth that I in turn mouthed to my students.

I Re-imagine the Poet as Dr. Frankenstein

(A Feminist Aesthetic)
After Hearing Adrienne Rich

When she reads
she leads me down
into the dark
cave of memory.

I close my eyes,
trust her to guide me
through the littered lair
of his/tory.

We pick our way past
the shards of a shattered
culture, stumbling over
heaped bones,
remnants of the ritual
dismemberments, sanctioned
slayings.

I hold my breath
listening, listening
down to the quick
to her words
like breath/truths
send a tremor
along my nerves.

When she flips the switch,
connects the stripped
wires: anger and tenderness
to one another
I light up—
alive and throbbing
in the exquisite thrill
of passion hot and full
body re-membered
pleasure: bowel to breast
to lung, breath expelled,
yes!

Sane Scientist, Sister, Poet, Friend—
Adrienne—
you exhume me
from the grave/art
prick/art porn/art

revivify me in the searing
light of your poetic:

words which never
sever or shame,
numb or maim.

It is a simple/radical aesthetic—
a Poetry the opposite of an/esthetic.

1988

In Xavier's graduate program I also met my first openly feminist teacher, Mary Kirk DeShazer, who inspired me, set me on the path of a whole new way of reading, and introduced a whole new literature. It was Mary who had the courage to sponsor me as a replacement for May Sarton, who had become ill and thus unable to read on Xavier's campus. Mary said, "Why not Mary?" And so I came to give the first public reading of the poems I had been writing, religiously, secretly, for the past few years, as a way of charting my course along those first treacherous and exhilarating turns in the road.

I was on fire with it, with the prospect of a whole new literature to explore, rather than a lifetime of dreary repetitions of analyzing *Moby Dick* and *The Great Gatsby* and *Beowulf* and *The Sun Also Rises*. On fire with how much liberation feminism offered to women and to men, to boys and to girls—a liberation of energies heretofore inaccessible to all of us, and now able to be put to good use in refashioning our culture for the betterment of all.

Teaching Against the Grain

I had—naively, as it turned out again—expected the justice of the feminist project to be obvious. Or if not the justice, surely, the efficacy. My high school students and I read good literature, as always, but the diversity of the voices I managed to include stimulated more discussion, more writing and engaged learning than recycling the same novels and poems year after year. The elective courses I taught in creative writing and poetry were bursting at the seams with eager students. But, teaching against the grain, as I came to call it, made me a target.

Though most of my students trusted me to value their words and ideas while urging them to further develop skills and knowledge, I began to meet a few who seemed aimed at me like heat-seeking missiles. One self-described "conservative Christian" student, for example, signed up for creative writing only to object, frequently and strenuously, to my encouragement of students to explore their own experience to find ideas for stories, poems. He found this approach dangerous, and lacking in proper structure and authority. At one point, he inserted into a class discussion his belief, based—he claimed—on scripture, that homosexuality was a sin comparable to murder. I connected the puzzling and troubling intolerance and dogmatism among a vocal minority of students with the political climate of the late 1980s. The no-holds-barred rhetoric and name-calling of the 1986 presidential race between George Bush and Michael Dukakis had filtered down to my students; some of them, abetted by radio talk "hosts," such as Rush Limbaugh, spoke of "liberal" as if it were a dirty word. Terms like *feminazi, gay agenda,* and *anti-family* began to supplant reasonable and thoughtful discussion of complex ideas.

A "Known Feminist"

My last year as a high school teacher began with an after-school visit from my principal who said he had received an anonymous phone call from a man who had asked him if he knew that he had a "known feminist" on staff. We both laughed over that one, but a few months later, things were not so funny for either of us.

For several years I had been using Natalie Goldberg's *Writing Down the Bones* as a supplemental text in the creative writing classes. The primary text was the writing itself; the journals and portfolio pieces students created were brought to class for feedback, revised, and read aloud in weekly read-arounds. As the second semester was about to begin, a colleague in the English department who was usually in the know about political intrigue in the district, warned me that it might be wise to "lay low," and not to assign anything remotely controversial in creative writing class. She had heard that the daughter of the school board president had enrolled in the course. The father/president had run for the board as a fairly middle-of-the-road candidate, only to reveal himself after election as one of God's warriors, ready—even eager—to do battle on behalf of "Western, Judeo-Christian, pro-family values." My politically savvy colleague warned me about a set-up.

I refused to plan my course around the standard of "not offending" the school board president. For all fifteen years of my tenure in the district, we had had a workable policy allowing students who might find a text objectionable for religious or other reasons to request a substitute. The policy outlined a process that was to begin with a written complaint by the parents or student, moving through a series of outlined steps toward a conclusion respecting the rights and concerns of all parties. At one other time early in my career, a parent had objected to the use of the novel *Ordinary People* by Judith Guest, and under the capable leadership of a different administration we had used the board policy to compromise without large-scale controversy.

However, eleven years later, in a different political climate and under different leadership, the school board president and his wife objected to the Goldberg text and they were not asked to follow the outlined procedure. Instead, I was summoned to a meeting with them to "justify" my use of the text. I learned that they felt it within their right and power to intervene directly in the choosing of materials: their bottom line was that no students would read this book. I was to cease using the text immediately.

For most of that semester, February through May 1992, I was pressured in a variety of ways to assign no further chapters in the Goldberg text. My principal, whose son I had taught, and who had been lavish in his praise of my teaching, now passed on to me the pressure he was getting from the superintendent. He wrote a letter of reprimand, gave me a copy, and told me he was placing it in my file. When I asked him if he believed what he had written about me he said, "No, but I have a mortgage to pay." My rejoinder was, "The price of mortgages hereabouts must be very high." I knew that the board had recently approved a renewal of his contract for three more years, and wondered why he was so unwilling to exert leadership. At the time, I was a single mother living on a substantially reduced income after an unwelcome divorce.

I continued to respectfully decline the demands that I shape my teaching to pacify one family, however influential. What I remember most from that time was a sense of confusion, that in the maddening swirl of letters and meetings and rumors I was in danger of losing my integrity. I felt confident in not losing my job: I had tenure, superior performance ratings, publications, and the strong support of my department and the community. I still have letters I received from parents expressing their outrage and sense of helplessness at the situation. One of my most treasured letters was from a local psychologist who wrote:

I have known one of your present students for over five years. Without getting into the family reasons for my lengthy contact with her, I can tell you that I have always known her to be bright, talented and with a great deal of emotional depth. Your writing class has gone a long way to giving her back confidence and enthusiasm for writing. This young woman now looks forward to going to school and is maturing wonderfully. Feeling more powerful in her ability to express herself has of course helped her self-esteem and her ability to be open and direct with others.

The mother of this young woman recently informed me that the school board was questioning your course, specifically your use of the book, *Writing Down the Bones* by Natalie Goldberg. I know this book well, and I can't think of a better writing book to use for this young woman and, for that matter, every other adolescent I have ever worked with.

I must tell you that it is rare that I ever meet a teenager in Cincinnati or Maxfield or any other public school system that has been inspired by a teacher. Routinely, it is quite the opposite; classrooms are places where joy for education is taken away and where boredom is seen as professionalism. I know there is courage, creativity, and intelligence in Maxfield; I hope there is some on the Maxfield school board.

Sincerely,
Bruce E. Levine, PhD
Clinical Psychologist

I knew that I could outlast the school board president. After all, I had taught at Maxfield for fifteen years, significantly longer than he had even lived in the community. But I also began to know that I didn't want to teach in a school where personal agenda, and more frighteningly, fascistic political agenda, could become tyranny. I was already teaching one section of Women Writing for (a) Change at night, and was beginning to see something of a fork in the steeply banked road just ahead.

All that spring and early summer, for weeks after school was out and the controversy had died down, I worked out my rage and my sense of having been shamed in multiple revisions of a poem turning on the Midas myth. The notion that kept coming to me was that some people carry into the world a repugnant fundamentalism which causes everything they touch to turn to shit, including the reputations of any of those they perceive as enemies.

Midas of the New Right

I receive a visit from a "concerned citizen"
and must listen to what he finds offensive in a book I teach

I.
You are here, Mr. Midas,
in your bright suit,
your ears high under a new
barbering job.

(Clean-shaven businessman,
elected official, churchgoer).

When you begin by citing Christ
as your personal savior
the room smells and feels as if
someone has just told a dirty
joke, but no one is laughing.

You gouge innocent-in-themselves words
from pages, leaving obscene holes
in the whole; at your touch
they begin to putrefy.
I am sickened by the sound of words
I have read or spoken so many times
with interest, delight, a chuckle,
sickened by the sound of those same words
in your mouth.

II.
On my side of the table in this
civilized room where I am summoned
to hear your complaints, we begin
to fidget, feel sticky,
dream of going home to hot showers.
I am slow to speak,

fearful of what will happen to my
words when they are touched by
yours, already hanging in the air.

III.
I am being dragged by you
and those you have gathered to help,
armed by your citizens' rights,
dragged into the seedy backrooms
of your minds:
sour-smelling, ill-lit rooms
where pimply boys drool over
women's underwear pages
in Sears Roebuck catalogs,

dangerous rooms where older men
razor out pictures of parts of
women's bodies
and tape them to walls—
before moving on to other dismemberments.

IV.
I am growing desperate now,
I have to find a way out of this room,
well-lit and respectable,
before you kick open the final door.

I will not be able to see you there,
but you will be—in the shadows
on your unmade bed.

I know what you will be doing
(as we all know, but are afraid to name
what you are doing even now under this
table where we sit to talk),

prolonging it, prolonging it,
coming finally, fiercely,

triumphantly shouting my name
my name

which turns to shit
in the memories of all the people
you've gathered here
to watch.

On perhaps the sixteenth draft of this poem, I realized that I had decided to move myself out of the reach of Mr. Midas. On July 10, 1992, the last day teachers could legally resign contracts for the following year, I drove from my home in Cincinnati to Maxfield for the last time and hand delivered a one-sentence letter to the superintendent's office: "I hereby resign my position as teacher, Department of English, Maxfield High School."

I turned my full attention to furthering the dream of WWf(a)C, to being "soul proprietor" of a school where power would be defined as transformative not coercive, a school where "teaching all those women" would be at last an accurate description of my work, a school where no student, whatever her class origins or educational credentials, would be shamed for the "quality" of her work. And no teacher would ever be sacrificed to zealots of any persuasion.

Exercises

1. Write a memory of yourself when you were in a "vulnerable state of naive joy." How old are you in this memory? (If you can't recover such a memory, invent one.)

2. Write a scene from your current family/organizational life which shows you exhibiting a similar quality of naive joy: enthusiasm for a project or idea, a new employee. (If you can't see yourself this way anymore, write about yourself *as if* you were feeling and acting this way about something or someone.)

3. Write a piece showing your participation, witting or unwitting, in "slapping down" the enthusiasm and naive joy in others, and/or yourself.

Part *Two*

Groundwork

Suddenly, I'm both here and somewhere else,
both in the pattern and outside, looking into it,
like looking into a scene in a glass paperweight,
I see:
through a curtain of snow
past lace drapes
a cat describing circles
around an eleven-year-old boy and his mother
after dinner
sitting by their careful rows
of tomatoes, peppers, herbs,
a vegetable garden
she calls
the Parsley Garden.

I see the patterns
like fine lace
like snowflakes
intricate, fleeting, lovely beyond words.

Already, I'm wondering
how to weave it
how to hold it
how to say, to save
it.

I f you are eager to begin experimenting with writing in conscious community, skip ahead and read Part Three, and refer
back to Part Two when you need or want some more detail
and more depth about the particular processes we use. I have also
included a glossary of terms in the appendix for your convenience
and in the belief that the language of a particular place is inevitable
and desirable, only degenerating into jargon when visitors are not
extended the hospitality of being taught the language.

In Part Two, I'm going to describe the basics of what happens
in the core of our WWf(a)C movement, the writing classes themselves. I want to emphasize (pretend you hear me talking really

loudly here): *None of this is carved in stone. I am describing tools which have grown (and changed) within a particular place and time, and have been transplanted to numerous other places.*

Please (my voice is going down a notch now), as you read the chapters in Part Two, understand that, as women have learned to live our lives in translation from the "given-ness" of the masculine (from pronouns to priests), you can live a while in translation and may even enjoy the experience. It will help if you trust that when I say *women* and *girls* in these chapters, it is because they are the ones who began the experiment with me and have remained faithful to it for seventeen years, at this writing. We have learned a great deal from what writer Kay Leigh Hagan calls "growing orchids in the Arctic."[1] Ours is not a *separatist forever* project, but a project analogous to that of gathering varieties of seeds and plants, whose botanical DNA and potential gifts have been nearly extinguished, in an effort to return them to the biosphere for the health of all.

Throughout this telling, but especially now that I am moving into the recent past and the near-present, I try to tell my stories as transparently as I am able, while also reminding you, and myself, that others involved in my stories tell the same stories differently. Or as poet, Lisel Muller says better:

Why We Tell Stories

Because the story of our life
becomes our life

Because each of us tells
the same story

but tells it differently

and none of us tells it
the same way twice.[2]

5.

The Circle as Conscious Container

Women, I believe, search for fellow beings who have faced similar struggles, conveyed to them in ways a reader can transform into her own life, confirming desires the reader had hardly acknowledged—desires that now seem possible. Women catch courage from the women whose lives and writings they read, and women call the bearer of that courage, friend.

Carolyn Heilbrun[1]

W hen asked to tell *how we do what we do* in Women Writing for (a) Change, I first "attempt" to describe the power of the circle. I say attempt because, as many women have attested, you have to be there—sometimes for a full semester—to experience how the circle evokes the words of women. Though I and the other teachers devise writing prompts, select readings, take responsibility for organizing and facilitating—"holding the center" as we call it— it is the primary presence of the women to one another that is the greatest stimulation to the growth of individual writers. I believe this passionately, and see it lived out over and over. This is how I learned it.

Being Heard

The first time I read my poetry in public was at Xavier University in Cincinnati where, in the mid-eighties, I was finishing a graduate degree in English. One of my professors—my first feminist professor—Dr. Mary Kirk DeShazer, writer of the foreword of this book, had arranged to have May Sarton come to campus for a reading. When she learned that Sarton was ill and would be unable to travel, Mary, who had read some of my poems asked *me* to read. As an academic whose area of expertise and publication was contemporary women's poetry, Mary had much to lose in putting forth an unknown, inexperienced poet. Fortunately, there had been ample time to let people know that Sarton would not be reading! Still, on that April night in 1986, perhaps 100 people gathered in the Terrace Room at Xavier's student center. Many of my students, colleagues, friends, my son, and even (to my great shock) my ex-husband attended. Luckily, Dr. Susan Wooley, my then-therapist, attended also; she gave me a rushed session in the women's bathroom to help me recover my composure.

I remember being terrified and awed by the privilege of being listened to and taken seriously. I remember the feeling of community in the room; I felt not as if I were performing but, in an odd sense, *serving*. Speaking my truths about my own life, I felt I was saying: "Your lives matter too, can be given words, can be given attention." I felt as if we, the listeners and I, were collaborators in a quintessentially human, humane, meaning-making process.

Their listening helped me hear things in the poems, both flaws and strengths that I had not heard when reading them aloud to myself. I felt as if what was happening in the Terrace Room was liturgical and sacred. I have a photo of myself at the podium in my high-necked white blouse, full skirt, and red ballet flats. I looked every inch the good schoolgirl or prim schoolmarm. But someone said later to me: "I couldn't believe the things I was hearing coming out of your mouth, out of any woman's mouth. I was thinking: this woman's a jail-breaker, an outlaw!"

I heard the audience members "laugh in the right places," heard a deep, attentive silence, and saw my son's cautious pride. *Ohmigod, is my Mom going to make a fool of herself*, I thought he was thinking. Years later, I learned that what he feared most when he came to readings with me was that people would want to hurt me.

I lost my fear, and once again felt my soul fly out of me, carried not only by my own voice, but on words *I* had composed: *my own voice in a much fuller sense than I had ever experienced it!*

The first person to speak to me after the reading was my creative writing professor. He—whose job it was to encourage my words—remarked, "You really care about being understood, don't you?" I immediately understood—no fool I—his condescension to my "accessible" poems. Moreover, in that vulnerable moment, his condescension felt like condemnation. When I admitted that at least *one* of my goals as a poet was to connect with people, he offered his preferred image of the poet: "As you know, I think of the poet as the hierophant above the people, inviting them to reach up toward me, upward toward some greater understanding."

Fortunately, having heard this enough in his contemporary American poetry class, where we studied only male poets, with the pleasant exception of Denise Levertov, I knew the meaning of the word hierophant: the prophet-priest. Yet I gaped at him stupidly, rendered mute by the arrogance of the image, and his invoking it at this particular moment. Not until the next day, when I moved from embarrassment to anger, did I wonder how his belief in a "hierophant above the people" reconciled with his Marxist politics.

At the reception following the reading, my professor held forth about "feminist tropes," but Dr. John Getz, the then-chair of the English department at Xavier, told me that a student had confided that, hearing me, she began to believe in the possibility of her own writing. This woman was Ellen Galbraith, who later joined a Women Writing for (a) Change writing circle in one of its earliest incarnations.

I owe Ellen Galbraith, Dr. Mary K. DeShazer, and Dr. John Getz a great deal. Alongside the opinions put forward by the "poet-hierophant," I experienced that night what would become the most important element of WWf(a)C, what Carolyn Heilbrun so elegantly calls "catching courage." Ellen was the first of many women who said they had caught courage from my words. Their words gave me courage in turn, and the inspiration to create for others what I experienced the night of my first poetry reading. Coming from parents who never had anything that they didn't also want to share with others, from a mess of fresh-caught walleye to a pan of apple dumplings, I began to gather the courage and energy to weave circles to emulate my parents' model of sharing the bounty.

In 1993, I discovered the words of Annie Rogers in her article "Voice, Play, and a Practice of Ordinary Courage in Girls' and Women's Lives." She explores the etymology of courage, and links the "ordinary courage" of eight-to-twelve-year-old girls with an old meaning of the word: "to speak one's mind by telling all one's heart." She then observes how this ordinary courage is lost as many girls reach early adolescence. Her observation is embedded in a newly emerging psychology of women based on empirical studies of girls, that have documented a striking loss of voice, of resiliency, and of self-confidence in girls as they enter early adolescence. These studies have identified this as a time of particular vulnerability and risk in young women's psychological development, as it becomes increasingly dangerous for them to speak their minds truthfully within the context of cultural conspiracies to silence women's knowledge.[2]

So it is that in a typical semester of WWf(a)C women come together to write and to hear one another's words. We catch courage from one another; often we come to call the "bearer of that courage, friend."

Women Writing

Yesterday I read
how hummingbirds
sometimes die
in their sleep.

How at night
hummingbirds can sink
into a zombie-like state
in which their breathing is shallow
and their large, wild hearts slow
to 36 beats per minute.

I began to wonder
if this might not happen
with many women
who don't have opportunities
like this women-writing-for-a-change class.

Does their breath slow
and do their hearts wind down
to a non-creative stupor . . .
and they don't even know it?

The article goes on to say
that in the daytime,
that is with the light,
the hummingbird's heart
beats 500 times per minute
soaring to 1200 beats
as they feast and fly
court and play.

I have a similar experience
when I listen
to the outpourings of the soul
of the women in our writing class—
these women have huge hearts
to fuel their flights
to places unknown
and sometimes unexplored.

Women writing for a change are
like the flock of awakened hummingbirds
coming to life
gathering, sharing,
blessing the nectar of experience.

Fran Repka, Ed.D., R.S.M.

Exercises

1. Write about listening and being listened to in your

   a) family of origin

   b) current family or friendship circle

   c) workplace.

2. Write about how would your life be different if you had the courage to create a circle for experiments in sharing

resources, for listening and being listened to, instead of waiting for "them" to do it—or to "let" you do it.

3. Why are circles less common than facing-front formations in public life?

4. Write down the names of five people in your life whom you remember, or whom you experience now, as being instrumental in helping you trust your voice and your experience. See what happens when you remember them in words and write about their role in your development of voice and self. Perhaps you could write *to* them, and even write *as* them, imaginatively exploring their stories and how their lives unfolded to have them intersect with yours in such an important way.

5. Write for five minutes about someone like my professor whom you remember or experience now as a *silencer* of your own voice, someone whose words or presence has the effect of diminishing yours, whether intended or not.

    Now write for five minutes *as* this *silencer*. (You could have her/him respond to the prompts in earlier chapters, if you really want to imagine a way into altering your reaction to this person. By creating her/him as a character doing the writing you are doing, some new alchemy will emerge.)

6.

Rituals to Create Containers

The word *ritual* can be a flashpoint, conjuring up the abuse of power some experienced in churches or families. After a talk I gave in the early nineties in which I used the word, a woman came forward to say that she was a survivor of ritual abuse, and that the word evoked horrible memories for her. In the early years of the school, a woman left the community for good when we sang a closing song, "May the circle be open and unbroken/ May the peace of the goddess be ever in your heart/Merry meet and merry part, and merry meet again." I can't recall where I learned it, but I thought it merely a pleasant melody coupled with an upbeat leave-taking sentiment. She called me the next morning to say she feared that Women Writing for (a) Change was a cult. I was shocked, horrified, and remorseful for my naive clumsiness. I was also powerless to communicate to her that the practices are about enhancing, not erasing, the divine spark of each person. In the ensuing years, several women have written of their experiences as survivors of ritual or cult abuse, and we have collaborated with them to find ways to enter the circle holding their personal experience in one hand, and the necessity of community-creating rituals, or practices, in the other.

Careful and Courageous

These stories contain lessons in how careful and courageous we have to be in claiming powerful means, and in continuing to use them in the face of our own and others' fear.

Recently our staff had a collective and rueful laugh when someone tried to access our website while working at a coffeehouse, a store in a well-known national chain. Unable to log on to our site, she discovered that we were blocked because someone, or some system, had decided we were a cult! It took requests from two writers and several months' processing time to remove us from what we like to call "the cultists' watch list."

I think it was from reading Adrienne Rich that I learned about the "principle of reversal,"[1] the notion that much of what is created to empower women, especially the language itself, mysteriously becomes its opposite in a relatively short time. Think about the honorific *madam* as but one example. It devolved into the name for a bordello manager! The words *girl* and *woman* themselves have connotations seen in "throwing like a girl," or "he cried like a woman." Actively engaging the principle of reverse, I began to see that a thriving subtext of our work was reclaiming words, symbols, and rituals that have been corrupted and used to coerce and demean. This, too, is why I am unwilling to discard the word *feminism* even though I am aware that its distortions may "scare" people. I say, if we move off that word, we lose the power to define; and, if we move to another word, it gets trashed, so we might as well stand and do our own defining.

Hospitality

Even though I prefer *not* to put words to the rituals and symbols because that can dilute the experience, we often choose to do so as a gesture of hospitality, as a way of helping newcomers be more confident that the ritual is well considered, and is a source of health and safety to the community. Each semester, faculty members use some form of the handout "Creating Space for our Words" (see the appendix). However, it is my observation that, as the years go by, such explanations have faded in importance, not only because so many of the women are returning students, but because the consciousness of the community seems to have deepened to the point at which a newcomer can *feel* the well-being and "groundedness" in the room from the very first night of a given semester.

In the end, my working-class pragmatism often saves the day for me when I am in danger of being shamed out of employing powerful means in my teaching and consulting work. That is to say, I come back to the simple efficacy of *what works to bring people together,* which must include elements pointing to the truth that hearts and souls, as well as minds, need to be acknowledged and included in learning and change efforts. I am convinced, along with writer Margaret Wheatley, that "leadership in turbulent times is spiritual."[2] Over time, simple, grounding rituals have evolved in, and become integral to, WWf(a)C work in all of its incarnations.

Creating the Space for Reverence

I have long admired the work of Parker J. Palmer and have been much influenced by his books. These words, from *To Know as We Are Known: A Spirituality of Education,* have been a powerful touchstone: "Boundaries create the space for reverence," as well as, "To teach is to create a space where obedience to truth is practiced."[3] These words, rendered in calligraphy and framed as a gift from Ellen Doyle, O.S.U., occupy a central place at the Writing Center. The boundaries of the circle, the comforting repetition of its making and unmaking at every class, communicate the reverence with which words will be held. They communicate the presence of *an acoustics of intimacy,* my image for the quality of listening which happens in an intentional and co-created space.

Opening the Circle

Opening the circle is the first item on class agendas and all agendas for WWf(a)C volunteer, board, faculty, and other meetings. Writers gather without speaking. We teach this counter-cultural sitting in silence in a number of ways. Before class, we usually have instrumental music playing softly. The music signals participants to become quiet and to listen, as does the teacher's presence in the circle, modeling silence. Stepping out of the unconscious chatter and hustle-bustle of ordinary life is something the writer must do every time she sits down to write. Even those who jot a few lines of a poem or an idea for a story while in a cafe, or in the case of one high school teacher, while monitoring study hall, are retiring to a place of silence which is the prerequisite for the flow of words. Entering the circle evokes this stepping out of the ordinary into the charged space of creation.

We have found that waiting for latecomers only causes the class to begin later and later each week, so at the exact starting time, the teacher lights a candle in a glass vase or pottery bowl. Returning to her seat, she holds the candle and silently sets her intentions for the evening. She passes the candle to the woman on her left—I came to this direction unconsciously, but realized later that clockwise movements signal the making of the circle; counterclockwise movements signal the unmaking of the circle. This woman holds the candle for her own period of silent intention-setting, then passes it to the woman on her left, and so on, until the light has been passed to every woman in the circle. The sight of women passing fire to one another is itself an inspiration.

Over the years, writers have expressed both delight and discomfort with this practice. I remember WWf(a)C leader Andrea Nichols saying, "My favorite moment of the evening is that moment when I receive the candle, can hold it and be supported in silence by the attention of the community." Discomfort with silence, with symbolic gestures in public, and with the religious associations of candle-lighting, have been some of the flashpoints around this practice. However, we have persisted because we believe that a strong, conscious container must be created to hold the power of women's words, so long suppressed in our culture. The passing of light around the circle from woman to woman physically "makes" the container, and signifies the importance of what we are gathering to accomplish both within, and against, the history of women's words pushed into darkness.

Returning the lit candle to the center of the circle, the teacher breaks the silence by reading aloud a poem, selected and practiced as part of her preparation for class. Poetry, more than any other genre, has the potential to create community and gather people into intense listening and heightened awareness. Further, as Jenn Reid, director of Young Women Writing for (a) Change, has written in "Ritual as a Post-modern Device:"

> The choice to begin the circle with a poem echoes the belief of (Helene) Cixous who claimed that feminine writing is most possible in poetry *"because poetry involves gaining strength through the*

unconscious and because the unconscious, that other limitless coun-
try, is the place where the repressed manage to survive." [4]

After reading the poem, the teacher passes a talking stone, also
from left to right. Each woman says her name and something else:
perhaps a response to the poem, perhaps a bit of her story from her
day. When each woman has thus entered the space, and we have
made our circle out of silence and words, out of light and the darkness it indicates, we look at the plan for the evening (see "Sample
Agenda" in the appendix).

Class Agenda

The teacher has created a plan for using our shared resource of
two-and-a-half hours, but has created it in response to the themes
and needs that are manifested once the semester is underway.
Agendas give women a sense of the shape of the evening to come,
and an opportunity to request, if they see the need, a restructuring
of priorities. Class agendas are e-mailed to women who have been
absent so they can stay in connection with the flow of the semester
and be prepared for the next class. Faculty members as well as affiliate site owners share agendas by e-mail weekly. This rich cross-
pollination is an example of our extended community of practice,
but does not result in boilerplate materials, because each teacher
has her own life, as does each class.[5]

Closing the Circle

The last item on every class agenda is "closing the circle."
Whatever the writers are doing at the time, whether meeting in
small groups, writing, or working in a large group, the teacher
begins to shift the attention of the group toward closing. At the end
of class, members put attention on the writing and reading suggestions for the week to come. The teacher passes 3" x 5" index cards
around the circle. Each woman is invited to write some words that
will help her leave the circle with deepened learning and with a
sense that any lingering question, concern, or suggestion has a
place to be heard.

Soul Cards

Over the years, we have posed different questions to prompt
writing on soul cards, including: *What movements, themes, or images
did you feel in your soul tonight, and/or within the soul of the community?*

What was the gift, what was the challenge of the class for you? What did you give? What did you receive? We remind participants that they write not to the teacher but to the entire community. With soul cards, participants begin to sense themselves as creators of the system developing within their class. This insight is both important and difficult to grasp. Soul cards are not complaint cards about what the system should be doing for individuals. The name, *soul cards*, is an example of how names and practices emerge in a living system. I once asked, "What is the soul of the community speaking to you as you leave?" When a faculty member transplanted the question to a class of girls, they promptly dubbed the cards "soul cards" and the name stuck!

As women finish their soul cards, the teacher rises, removes the lit candle from the center of the room, returns to her seat, and deliberately blows it out. She passes the darkened candle to the woman on her right and it goes around the silent circle from woman to woman. The ritual unmaking of the circle allows time for writers to digest feelings and ideas that were evoked by their experience of the class.

"Cleared for Take-Off"

Over the years I have also realized the importance of each woman gently closing the vulnerable space she has opened during the class in order to write and to take in the words of others. As women return to their cars, to the night, to traffic, I want them to be, and I want to be, "cleared for take-off," as it were. The circle has been deliberately constructed as a place where writers can descend into the unconscious to access words, memories, and feelings. Paradoxically, the circle and its rituals also signal the value of being conscious, not reactive, during the often intense listening and interactions of small and large group activities. The closing ritual is an attempt to return us to the conscious mind required to "go out to the world." As women leave the circle they drop their soul cards in a basket provided for that purpose. The teacher reads the cards before preparing the next class, and we ask women to read the cards before class begins. Sometimes, though not always, I make the reading of soul cards part of opening the circle at the next class. In doing this work, as in mentoring others to do it, I always seek to hold the paradox of healthy and comforting ritual alongside the value of gestures not becoming pro forma, or rote, since this can rob them of meaning and attention.

Teacher Vigilance

For the teachers, the closing ritual signals release from the hyperconsciousness we hold throughout the class. Even when we write during in-class writing time, we are learning *not* to go too deep. A significant part of our service to the writers is that of "protecting the space," which requires that teachers remain in the upper world with an awareness of the physical space and an attunement to the psychic energy in the room. I do not have the language to describe this very well, as I am not a student of energetics, but I know that it is a very real phenomenon! I have thought and spoken of it in various ways, one of which is my sense of the teacher as Demeter, staying in the world while Persephone descends to the underworld. Another way I approach this phenomenon is Jungian: that the intense light of the work of recovering the suppressed feminine attracts equally intense shadow. The work thus requires someone with the assigned role of maintaining the consciousness of the circle and the awareness of shadow, rather than denying the shadow's presence.

One of Many Examples

One of the best stories about how we learned the need for teacher vigilance occurred in the winter of 1996. We had just moved the school from the Victorian house to the Ironworkers Union hall. The physical move was less difficult than the energy it took to conduct all the feelings generated by the move. Women had felt safe, many for the first time, in the circle at the Writing House, and there was significant resistance to the move. I also suspect that my own leadership "chi" had not developed enough that I could communicate more than, "Trust me on this." I was dangerously exhausted, and "left the school" for the first time since it opened four-and-a-half years earlier—I actually left town for a week to rest. Cassandra Towns agreed to teach all four classes for the week, and we arranged for visual artist Patrice Trauth to be a guest teacher. Patrice led an activity in which each writer claimed a small area of floor space and created an "installation," an altar of precious objects and images she had brought to class. Women visited one another's altars, and then spent time writing to or about the experience.[6]

One of the writers had a lit candle on her altar, and, when Cassandra called women back to the large group, this woman forgot to blow out her candle. You can imagine the rest of the story. We had a fire, in what we later named the "fire room." Writer, teacher, and visual artist Marian Jackson saved the day by pouring the remaining contents of the thirty-six cup hot water pot on the flames! I'll never forget the feelings when I came home to a note from Marcella Allison, beginning with the words, "There is no easy way to tell you this, but . . ."

No one was hurt; the damage was minimal, and the story has been invaluable. What Cassandra said later, as we reflected on the incident, was that, confused by the presence of another teacher, she "went unconscious" and reverted to her former role in the circle: that of being there for *her* writing and of being held. Since this was not the job of the visiting teacher, no one was effectively "holding" the consciousness of the group. Thus we received a bright signal that this role must be clearly defined.

This learning is very much alive in all of our programs: classes, consulting, workshops, and in Young Women Writing for (a) Change, in which co-teaching is often used. Someone must hold the center and maintain the container for the creative and transformative work of the others. It is very satisfying to me to hear discussions such as, "Ok, now, to be clear, which one of us is holding the center during the read-around?"

The fire was a dramatic way to begin our tenancy at the Ironworkers building. Our landlord, Jack Baker, secretary-treasurer of the local, was called out on a cold night. Fire trucks surrounded the building; women stood around outside in the cold. We have returned again and again to the story as a source of both wisdom and humor. Jack still reminisces, "Remember the night you writers almost burned down the building firing up your quills?"

As I learn more about what Maria Harris calls "the educative power of ritual,"[7] I have found it very helpful to think of the rituals we use at WWf(a)C as sacraments of becoming conscious, as well as sacraments to access the unconscious. Because ritual is purposefully beautiful, reverent, even solemn, it helps us take ourselves seriously as writers, learners, and as women. I freely admit that learning to take ourselves seriously and becoming conscious makes us vulnerable. Women are safer and more culturally condoned when we choose to "lighten up," stay cynical, and trivialize ourselves and one another.

I know that it is easy to become *self-conscious* when we try to do anything expressive of depth. I often remind myself and my students that we are engaged in, among other things, a journey from self-consciousness to consciousness, as writers and as women.

On the other hand, none of the rituals is taken so seriously that someone can "make a mistake" that will bring shame down on her head, or evoke the wrath or derision of the group. I believe Donald Murray said, "Orthodoxy is the enemy." I could not agree more! To be reminded of this, I need only return to my own childhood fears around rituals: that my teeth would touch the communion host, that my new Easter hat would fall off when I tilted my head back to receive it, that I would make an unwitting mistake during Mass and be punished later for my lapse. For me, most of the power of the rituals was squeezed out by fears of violating the rubrics.

Over the years at WWf(a)C we have had some wonderfully irreverent pieces of writing about the reverential practices in which we engage. These pieces help assure us that as we learn to take ourselves seriously, we don't take ourselves too seriously. This is the kiss of death to authenticity and joy!

Below is an excerpt from a description of the closing ritual by Robin Louise Curtis. Sometimes, the silent sitting and candle passing feels as if it goes on forever in our "let's get on with it" lives!

The Candle—I

With both hands wrapped gently around the thick mottled glass, she held it to her face. This engaged her olfactory nerve and after scrunching up her nose in bewilderment, a hint of a smile crossed her lips. Ah, sandalwood with undertones of fig, she thought. She turned to the woman beside her and offered the unlit fuse. The exchange was one of her better ones, and took place without skin touching skin. The next woman wasn't so generous with the talisman and barely gave it a whiff before passing it off to her left, catching the next woman unprepared. In one fell swoop, the next student jammed the pencil with which she jotted down a last minute note to herself about that week's assignment into her purse, whispered an apology and gripped the heavy glasswork before it landed in her lap. Composing herself instantaneously, she closed her eyes and mouthed her weekly ten words. "Our Father, who art in heaven, hallowed be thy name." She never knew quite what to do with these few seconds so she opted for her mantra, the first ten words of the Lord's Prayer. With that, her eyes opened and she readied herself for the unburdening.

The next classmate read the signal and between them they deftly passed the symbol of closure.

This one looked deep into the molten lava and even reached in to poke at the warm goo. Satisfied that she would keep all confidences as she had just promised herself she would, she shyly passed the portly pillar of ornamentation onto the next departing member of the container. This woman made quite a thing of it. Waving the waxy weight beneath her nose, she marinated in the aromas of burnt wick and sandalwood. She relished this part of the evening and challenged herself each week to hold it just a little longer to see if anybody would notice. If they had, no one in seven semesters had ever said so. Her game over for the night, she relinquished the game.

Here is Sandy Lingo's description of her "trial with fire" at the Writing Hall:

September 3, 1997

This is my first class at Women Writing For (a) Change. I sense that I should have burned my bra before coming or packed a statue of Betty Friedan or begged forgiveness for wearing eyeliner.

The class began with the passing of a candle. Everyone looked very solemn. Some inhaled deeply, some waved the flame around, others bowed prayerfully over it. I think I am not quite in the writing state of mind, because all that candle made me want to do was light up and take a big ole' drag on a Tareyton. Hopefully, all the poignant writing I am about to do will purge me of my nicotine cravings.

Then we passed around a stone. As each writer pondered her writing life, she fondled the stone, rubbed it in ways that . . . oh, never mind. Maybe I am not yet deep enough.

Tonight's lesson is letter writing. Someone shared that she composed letters that her dead mother-in-law might have!?! The teacher in the group thought we might consider writing letters to a higher being (superintendent?). Those of us at the lower end of the writing evolutionary ladder will have to cut our teeth by writing to real live people.

I won't try to describe tonight to my husband.

We had some wonderful laughs when Sandy and Robin shared their journal entries. The pieces also remind me of how vulnerable we are to less well-intentioned humor and real ridicule of our frankly spiritual values and practices. This leaves us open to criticism I flinch from, trained as I was in the separation of spiritual from professional life, battered as I have felt by the take-no-prisoners strategies that fearful people employ to keep power in the hands of the "ordained."

The characterization I hate the most of "how we do what we do at WWf(a)C" is that of New Age, which I see as a sloppy, pejorative term, used the way "liberal" is used to paint someone as naive, not rigorous, and not trustworthy. I confront my own fear of this by reminding myself: I left public schools in order to follow my own instincts, trust my experience, and do radical work, in the truest sense of *radical*, which means going to the root. We are connected to, not cut off from, the roots and depths of women's spirituality and history.

The enthusiasm with which girls and young women—even the teens—embrace ritual bolsters my dedication to understanding my role as both the artistic *and* the spiritual director of the movement. Despite, or as a respite from, their fragmented, postmodern lives of channel surfing and school days divided into ever more modules, they sink happily into our rituals. I close this chapter with two descriptions of WWf(a)C rituals; the first was written by Megan Miller, when she was fourteen years old and a member of Young Women Writing for (a) Change.

The Candle—II

At the beginning of class a candle in passed around. It's a tradition. But why in the world was it started?

It is my turn. I take the worn, jean-colored bowl and stare at the candle inside. The flame seems mesmerizing. The gold and autumn orange. The blue and violet. I pass it on. I watch as slowly, slowly the candle is passed. Girl to girl, hand to hand. The calm serene glow of the candle illuminating each woman's face. The teeny, tiny speck of fire, burning wax to liquid form. It stands as a symbol, it stands as a flame in the fire each girl's soul is made of. Unique and pure. Gentle and ever-giving. Everyday it will look the same, eventually the liquid wax will reshape itself back to a solid.

Each girl here was brought here together for the same reason. Each girl so different, willing to share different depth of
their soul like a vortex never ending. We have the gift—expressing what our souls are eager to share, are thirsting to share in
writing. Each blazing fire in each girl's soul comes here together. We all give a piece of ourselves to the candle being slowly
passed around. A flame from our fire, a phrase from our piece.[8]

And here are the e-mailed words from candle-passing parodist,
Robin Louise Curtis, to the woman who would occupy her seat
when Robin left Cincinnati to return to her roots in upstate New
York:

A little message to the woman who will take my Tuesday night
chair:

When I first entered the inner sanctum of WWf(a)C, I felt
awkward with the silence, with the candle, with the saying of
my name and bringing myself into the circle. Twenty quiet
women made me nervous. I was uncomfortable reading my
writing and offering feedback to those who read theirs. I sobbed
at the women Mary chose to comprise my small group. How
could they possibly be compatible with me? I can only say to you
who may feel all of these anxieties, uncertainties and more, surrender all to what the goddess, Mary Pierce Brosmer, has created. Your writing can't find a better home of students and
teachers; your inner voice couldn't find a more loving container.

Have faith that all the ritual and quiet is there to serve your
muse, ease your mind, free your spirit and keep you and your
writing safe. WWf(a)C made me believe and made me brave. It
will you, too. And my small group? They became the most
beautiful feminine spirits to whom I am utterly devoted. Within
weeks of first coming to WWf(a)C, I came to cherish my place
in the chair you now occupy. Once a week for three years, there
wasn't a better seat in the world. So welcome to one of the most
precious experiences of my life and now, I hope, yours. I send
you love.

And when you're more comfortable, kiss my sisters for me.
(And don't miss the potlucks; they rock!)

Exercises

1. What "community-creating practices" or rituals enriched your childhood? Are part of your life now? Are part of your life now outside of church rituals?

2. Write about rituals which became either meaningless (rote), or even degenerated into means of controlling or disempowering others.

3. Experiment with a simple ritual of your own creation for entering and leaving your personal writing time and space.

4. Experiment with members of a work team or other group to create a simple ritual for gathering focus and intentions as you enter a meeting.

5. Create a simple ritual for leaving a meeting. The ritual would ideally include gratitude, a way for people to let go of what was unresolved for them and not allow it to fester or turn to gossip, a way of acknowledging what went unexpressed for whatever reason.

7.

Creating Writing Prompts

One of the ways we fulfill our mission of evoking the words of writers, and inspiring them to follow the path the words point to, is the creation of writing prompts. Whether you are writing alone or using writing in community as a tool for organizational well-being, you will find having a supply of suggestions on hand invaluable to get the writing going, or to sustain it.

What to Call Them

Calling writing prompts "assignments" is neither accurate nor helpful within the context of writing in conscious community. At best, the assigning and grading of writing is an artificial situation that helps students develop a body of work and grow in skill. At worst, the assigning and grading of writing can become a situation in which the student "writes what the teacher wants," thereby losing touch with the true source of inspiration inside herself. Many women who come to our classes are in recovery from painful experiences of being silenced by what and how they were asked to write, and by the sometimes brutal responses of teachers and classmates. One professor I know thinks it is his responsibility to separate the "real writers" from those less gifted. This approach makes me want to further explore research with dolphins that suggests they are truly intelligent because *they know enough to know what they don't know!*[1] Given the rich ambiguity that is the stock-in-trade of the arts and artists, the arrogant certainty with which some teachers approach their professions surprises me.

In the paradigm of building the new in the shell of the old, Women Writing for (a) Change teachers are attempting to create spaces that will keep the words coming. Toward this end, we offer writing suggestions, invitations, or prompts, and we not only tolerate but encourage the "or not" response, i.e., "During the week to come, write the same story in three different voices . . . *or not.*" What this actually means is:

> This exercise is an experiment with point of view and voice. It may well elicit something that grows into a short story or a novel, a series of poems or a play. However, you may be in the middle of writing and shaping something that is coming up from your own experiences and imagination. In which case, you would not follow my prompt but would follow your own prompting. The most important thing is that you are writing regularly and you are free to use my (the teacher's) suggestions, revise them to your needs, or ignore them.

Take-Homes

Teachers create take-home prompts to help writers discover subject matter, to teach specific techniques or forms, and to encourage students to experiment with particular writing routines until they find what works for them. Experienced writers find that writing to prompts can jog them out of tried and true techniques before they become mannerisms. Writers often report that their very resistance to a prompt leads them to an important piece of writing. My rough guess is that writers follow our take-home prompts about fifty percent of the time. Many bring projects-in-progress to the discipline and listening field of the circle; others discover their own prompts and projects once they set their intentions to really write.

What follows is a discussion of some of the kinds of writing prompts we have created over the years.

Topical and Seasonal Prompts

1. From one day's newspaper, choose three stories. Holding them in mind, write until you have found a thread upon which to string them. This might become a short story, a series of poems, or a journal reflection.

2. Create a character who will "have her say" about a current political issue. Here's the catch: she is not you; her beliefs are opposite yours. Listen for her voice; it will help you understand her truth.

3. Various media outlets are carrying stories about a "newsworthy" event or sequence of events in your city or nation. A friend from another city or country wants to know, "What's up?" Have your say in a poem, or tell some stories that will shed your light on the fire.

4. As Rosh Hashanah is the season of atonement, write one piece about forgiving and another about being forgiven.

5. Advent is the season of waiting for the light; reflect in writing on waiting as a theme in your life, or in the life of an invented character.

Experimenting with Form

1. Write a conversation between a mother and her young child, as the mother is helping the child dress for daycare. Look at a passage in a short story containing conversation. Now revise your piece, working with the short story to help you with mechanics, such as punctuation, as well as with the cadence and phrasing of authentic-sounding dialogue.

2. Tonight's opening poem is a sestina.[2] A sestina is a poem with six stanzas of six lines and a final stanza of three lines, all stanzas having the same six words at the line-ends in sequences that follow a fixed pattern, and with all six words appearing in the closing three-line envoi. Study the form carefully. Then write six words from one of your areas of expertise, e.g., medicine, law, education, childrearing, quilting. Use these words as the key words in your first sestina.

Writing Practice Prompts

Throughout the semester we weave in writing take-homes that will help students discover a writing practice that works for them.

1. Keep paper, pen, and a kitchen timer on your bedside table. In the morning, set the timer for ten minutes and do a "fast-write" before you get dressed. Do another ten-minute fast-write again before you go to sleep.

2. For five successive days write freely, inspired by what you see from your kitchen window. You could do another round of this practice at a window in a different room.

3. Pack your journal in your lunch bag. Take it out before you open your food, and write for at least ten minutes every day this week during your lunch break. If nothing else, you might end up with a series of vignettes or observations of the lunch crowd.

4. If you are the mother of young children who religiously reads them bedtime stories, just as religiously write yourself a bed-time story after they are asleep. No matter how tired you are, write one story a night, no matter how short. Just get started every night, and you'll be surprised at how un-tired you can get when the pen meets the page.

In-Class Writing Prompts

In addition to the creation of take-home prompts, teachers offer in-class writing prompts as well. These usually take the form of fast-writes, five- or ten-minute timed writings. Teachers ask writers to jump into these spontaneous writing activities in order to surface new material and to keep the muscle of the imagination strong and supple. Very often in-class fast-writes are the origins of longer pieces that writers work on over time.

One of the most tension-laden moments for me is that moment when I offer a fast-write, out of left field, and ask writers to *just do it*. I don't want discussion or analysis of the prompt because that puts my, or the group's, overlay on it, but it is often very difficult for me to resist the resistance of those who want me to say more about it so they can do it right. I say: "Just trust me," but I really mean, "Just trust the words."

Sample Prompts

1. What is the "big story" you are in as you sit down to write in the circle tonight?

2. Write down three "little stories" from your day. Push these through the sieve of a fast-write and see what comes out.

3. Write hard without stopping for five minutes to the phrase, "I remember. . ." Repeat the phrase every time you think you are running out of memories.

4. Choose five words from tonight's opening poem and use them to write about your current writing practice.

Visual Prompts

We have been known to use odd visual prompts, e.g., pouring a thick stream of cream into a pitcher and slowly, solemnly carrying it around the circle. One woman told me, "If you had done that on my first night, I would have been out of here. Way over my weirdness quotient!" Another time, I brought an orange for each woman. I asked them to peel the oranges slowly and intentionally, and then write.

1. The week before Thanksgiving, Kathy Wade set the table, the cloth in the center of the circle, with her mother's good china, and asked women to do a fast-write, "In My Mother's House." This surfaced a serious mother lode of material!

2. During an eight-week summer semester, Cassandra Towns relied heavily, though not exclusively, on the artwork of Frida Kahlo for writing prompts.

Where Do Writing Prompts Come From?

I find most of my ideas for topical writing prompts from my own living, paying attention, not to mention reading of all kinds: poetry, fiction, nonfiction. Reading *Animal Dreams* by Barbara Kingsolver, for example, I was caught by Cody's reflections on the awful shoes her father, Doc Homer, made her wear. This was my inspiration for a prompt to write about shoes, to which I added the layer of writing about a particular dress or other piece of clothing that carried a story. I excavated my First Communion dress from the bottom of a trunk, laundered it, pressed it, and hung it in the circle as a visual prompt to elicit more stories. Writer Linda Witt brought her first dressy dress, a beautiful black silk, and hung it next to my white organdy dress and veil. She wrote the story of shopping for the dress with her late mother. About a year later I heard a National Public Radio interview with the author of *Love, Loss and What I Wore,*[3] a delightful autobiography with stories and fashion drawings by Ilene Beckerman. Bringing this book to class inspired a whole new round of poems and stories, ranging in emotional tone from grief, to tenderness, to hilarity.

Some years later yet another spate of writing about footwear and clothing erupted in the school, prompted by Erin Queenan's comical piece about her love affair with shoes. Her piece was prompted by noticing the diversity of footwear on display around the writing circle. Sandra Grady responded to Erin's shoe piece with a series of stories based on "her life and the shoes she wore." The collection includes funny pieces about pairs of dyed-silk bridesmaid's shoes never to be worn again, and an incredibly moving series about the shoes Sandra wore in Africa while a missionary and the Birkenstocks her fiancé, Niall, was wearing when he was murdered in Kenya. The final story chronicled Sandra's searching his small Irish village for black flats to wear to Niall's funeral.

Prompted by Poetry

I find much inspiration in my regular and pleasurable reading of poetry. I often read a poem aloud in the circle, usually more than once, and ask students to listen for words and phrases that "stay in their ears." I ask them to use the phrase as a refrain, writing it down and then repeating it at intervals during a fast-write.

Many years ago I read a series of poems by William Stafford and Marvin Bell in *American Poetry Review.* The two met at a conference and decided to begin a correspondence in poems. One would write a poem and send it to the other, prompting the second poet's response with a poem of his own. I encouraged students to find a correspondent within the class and to engage in this call-and-response process. Reading about the "100 Pictures" course in Sue Bender's *Everyday Sacred,*[4] I proposed that women devise a project that required 100 takes on a given topic.

My version of this was a series of poems inspired by my only son's graduation from college, move to Iowa, and impending marriage. I got as far as number thirty-seven. An added bonus for me was that this transition and loss was the first in memory that did not trigger a bout with depression. I think I wrote myself through it one poem at a time. I called the series "One Hundred Verses on Your Leaving," and the final verse was the source for the poem Colin and his then-fiancée, now wife, Jayna, asked me to write for their wedding.

Cross-Pollination

In the end, two things prompt the most, and best, writing from women in the school: *the quality of attention* we bring to our lives because we have set our intentions to write, and *the inspiration of the other women* in the classes whose words evoke our words. Witness the conversation, described above, between the two writers Erin and Sandy about "just shoes."

For some years now we have called this phenomenon of one writer's words evoking another's words "cross-pollination," whereby a seed from one writer, e.g., the courage to take on a particular topic, a phrase, one word, a chance remark in the circle, or a writer's footwear, is dropped onto the fertile ground of another's imagination and becomes something utterly other. I like to contrast the organic and inevitable process of cross-pollination with the "anxiety of influence" which plagues most traditional (white, male) writers. So anxious are they to appear wholly without influence, heroically "original," they must symbolically "kill the father" in order to bolster the delusion.

Faculty members cross-pollinate one another's ideas for writing prompts during brainstorming sessions at monthly faculty meetings, by putting poems, news articles, and books in one another's office mailboxes, and through our weekly e-mail exchange of agendas. There is no jealous guarding of material, no hoarding, and little competition to be the "most creative teacher." It is by far and away the most fertile and generous working environment I have ever encountered. Dedicated as we are to the development and creative well-being of every woman in the school, we are equally dedicated to one another's creative and professional well-being.

In an almost magical, alchemical way, this cross-pollination serves to prompt an abundance of writing throughout all programs of the school.

Constellation

Linda Witt, who wrote about her first "little black dress," did me the honor of writing a piece from a "seed" of mine which I think beautifully describes how we are unlearning the anxiety of influence at WWf(a)C, and acknowledging, even celebrating, the star power of collaborative genius to complement the notion of star power of individual genius.

To Mary

In response to your line, "I'd like to think I am beyond the lure of a gold star."

I would give you a whole galaxy of stars.
You have created several constellations.
I was sitting in the Semester 7 Monday constellation.
We would not be shining together if not for you.
We were throbbing, pulsing, and twinkling with light.
I am learning some of your questions:
"Do stars lose their glimmer if there are more of them?"
"Who doesn't like a sky full of stars almost throbbing?"
"Who prefers a sky with one or two bright lights?"
Shine on, sister star.

Love,
Linda

Exercises

1. On index cards or slips of paper, create a set of prompts to stimulate your writing. You can have one basket with "random prompts." (Examples: "grocery store check-out line conversation," "blue things," "When I get angry . . ." "lost pets," "a cooking disaster.") You can also create a basket to hold scraps of ideas, quotes, images, all relating to one writing project.

2. In a group setting, replicate the "two basket" exercise.

    a) Invite everyone to contribute regularly to a "random" basket of prompts and then use the basket to stimulate innovation during brainstorming or problem-solving sessions.

    b) Create a basket to hold ideas, images, and quotes relating to a back-burner project. Take the basket to the first meeting to focus on this project, and begin to arrange the ideas into a prototype or rough draft.

8.

Sharing Writing in Small Groups

In 1989, Dr. Judith Jordan from the Stone Center at Wellesley presented a talk at "Re-membering Women," a two-day conference in feminist psychotherapy held in Cincinnati. I remember being riveted by her saying that in her clinical practice she saw a strong link between women's depression and their sense of not being heard, their sense that their words had little effect on their listeners. I considered my own chronic depression, my recurring dreams of trying to speak in crowded rooms, often theaters or churches, my words swallowed up in the space, absorbed ineffectually into the bodies of the listeners. I have always loved the words of New Zealand feminist Dale Spender that in our culture *women's words don't get a fair hearing.* I have come to believe that women's words, *about our lives as women,* are *least* likely to get a fair hearing. In contrast I think of how the words of women who speak what the culture wants to hear and believe about women are lapped up: in short that we are "bitches." The phenomenal success and influence of the "tough broads" like Dr. Laura and Judge Judy come readily to mind. A variation on the type is the "tough babe," such as Ann Coulter or Sarah Palin.

At Women Writing for (a) Change we create spaces where women's words get not only a fair hearing *but also a hearing that will elicit more words.* Women bring both their raw and their carefully crafted words to two spaces: their regular small group, and the whole group, the latter in the form of what we call read-arounds. I credit my friend and mentor Kathy McMahon Klosterman, professor of education at Miami University, Oxford, Ohio, for the term *read-around.*

As a high school and college instructor, I chafed at the artificiality of my being the only audience for students' words. In reality, writers direct their words to larger and more diverse audiences than one grade-wielding teacher. Within the structure of WWf(a)C classes, the teacher is a writing member of both small and large groups. She responds to writing and offers her writing for the responses of the other participants. This shift is critical, as it begins the process of redirecting the attention of the writer away from the teacher as final authority and toward her own words and the effect they have on listeners.

Although the structure and mechanics of small and large groups are very important, women frequently report that they learn the most about how to shape a story or prune a poem by hearing their own voices reading passages within a receptive space. I call this effect "the acoustics of intimacy," that quality of listening which does not require a member to distort her voice or her meanings in order to be heard. I have experienced, and other women have corroborated, the strong physical sense of being held up by the quality of listening in both small groups and during whole group read-arounds.

Creating Small Groups

By about week three of a fifteen-week semester, faculty members create "permanent" small groups after reading women's responses to a questionnaire distributed sometimes as early as the first week (see the appendix for a sample). For a week, teachers mull over the words of the women about what kind of small group experience they prefer. Faculty members agree that the week we try to create the "right" small groups is one of the most difficult of the semester. The next week women meet for the first time in their "permanent" small groups. We ask them, barring irreconcilable differences, to commit to this group for the semester, assuring them that we have taken their wishes into account when creating groups, and that we inevitably find ourselves unable to honor all requests. This is when we remind everyone that "discomfort is educational," and hope they won't throw things at us! Writer Leslie Cannon calls the randomly created small groups of the early weeks "dating around" groups, and the groups which come together after the questionnaires are completed "long-term relationship groups." Sometimes writers ask us to add in a week of "dating around" groups later in the semester just to freshen things up.

We spend class time teaching small group protocol and structure, though each semester it seems the deepening collective consciousness of the school makes it possible to spend less time on the how-to's and more time doing—and reflecting on the doing—of small group process. We have taught small group process in a variety of ways, but one of the most effective has been the creation of a fishbowl, with the large group watching as three women give feedback to a fourth member of the group who shares a piece of writing. Writers outside the fishbowl have copies of the piece under discussion, and make notes about how the interaction seemed to help the writer, or not. As the fishbowl members discuss with onlookers what happened, we try to impress on everyone that the fundamental mission of the small group is to "advocate for the piece of writing."

Small Group Composition and Roles

Each small group of four or five women is composed of a facilitator, a timekeeper, and a vibes-watcher. These small group roles rotate each week. The facilitator convenes the group quickly, then conducts a quick check to see who wants to read. Writers are not forced to read, but are very strongly encouraged to take their time. *Not bringing writing is the single most reliable predictor of small group failure.* The facilitator and the timekeeper divide the available time (usually sixty to ninety minutes) by the number of readers, leaving five minutes at the end of each session for a "vibes-watch." When a woman offers her work to the group, she is encouraged, with the support of facilitator and vibes-watcher, to take leadership of the conversation, with the facilitator as backup.

Asking for What You Want

The writer begins by asking for the kind of feedback she wants at this point in the life of the piece. If the piece is an early draft, she may want to read it aloud, then ask the group to give her "gut" responses. I have been in groups in which the writer says, "This piece is very new, extremely raw; what I need tonight is to read it to you, to have the experience of hearing my own words within the group, but I don't want any discussion of technique." In place of discussion of a piece, or in addition to further discussion, listeners can offer what we call "read-backs," words or phrases they remember or have jotted down during the reading. I usually ask for a hands-off response when I feel that the "words are still talking to the words"[1] and I am not ready for anything which might interrupt that generative stage. I read aloud to myself often as I revise, but I hear different nuances in the piece when the words bounce off the bodies of listeners, the "acoustics of intimacy" effect.

Crafting Feedback

A group member might ask the group for craft feedback. If the piece is far enough along that she wants remarks on how it works technically and artistically, she brings copies for everyone. We encourage readers to be specific, to point to specific places they found strong, as well as to places where the language was flat or vague. Rich and enjoyable discussions develop around such things as whether the voices in a short story sound "right," how a title works or doesn't, or whether the line breaks of a poem could be improved. Writers will sometimes elect to have a private session with one of the faculty members to receive in-depth craft feedback on a piece. We have also offered semester-long Craft of Poetry and Craft of Prose classes, as well as one-day workshops to which a writer will bring a piece of writing she is trying to craft.

Discussing the Subject Matter

I often find myself asking for discussion of the subject matter when I offer journal entries to the group. Hearing spirited and engaged conversation about the topic fuels me to return at my next writing session to the journal piece and begin to shape it into a poem or essay. Women's doubt about their skill and authority to offer feedback is one of the greatest hurdles to effective small group participation. While it is true that the ability to give helpful responses varies, this ability can be cultivated with practice and mentoring. The more involved in their own writing the women become, the more they are able to "read like writers," developing eyes and ears for the strengths and weaknesses of a piece. I am happiest when I hear exchanges in small group such as:

> I have been working on this short story for a couple of weeks, and you've heard most of it before, but tonight I'm bringing the last page. I just can't get the ending to end, and I don't feel very good about my working title either. So, let me know any thoughts you have about those things, or anything else which strikes you about this final section of the piece.

What follows, ideally, is an engaged conversation that will surface new possibilities for the writing. My least favorite thing to overhear in a small group is, "I'll take anything." While the writer means that she is open to conversation that includes gut and craft reactions, most of us need practice in being specific about what we want and don't want. Not taking responsibility for this makes for a rather flaccid and misguided conversation.

In collaborating on "being on the side of the piece of writing," everyone in the group has the privilege of engaging in something magical, akin to what Carl Jung called "helping the dreamer dream the dream onward."[2] The process is usually indirect, in that only the writer can write her piece, but occasionally, a group member will come up with the "perfect title," or an image that beautifully and authentically brings a story or poem together.

Proofing, Polishing, Revising, Editing

In teaching and learning about small group process, we ask writers to distinguish between proofreading comments, editing suggestions, and revision suggestions. If, for example, a piece is nearly ready for publication, a woman might ask the group to point out any spelling or grammatical errors. This is proofreading, or polishing. She might need editing suggestions, might benefit from other writers' suggestions on words, even paragraphs or stanzas that could be pruned to strengthen the piece. Poets pore over drafts, helping one another with line breaks. A revision suggestion can be large or small. For example, I have said in small groups, "If you're open to a revision suggestion, it just occurred to me that this material could also be worked into a powerful narrative poem. I am not saying the piece does not work as it is, but I could imagine another way into the material that might be a stronger piece, or even a new piece." That, to my mind, is a "large" revision suggestion.

Just What Is Vibes-Watching?

We laughingly refer to the vibes-watcher as the VW. Hers is the most misunderstood role, and perhaps the most anxiety-producing: *"Omigod, you mean I have to tell everybody what was wrong in the group?!"* Not at all! The VW stands for the necessity of reflecting on the process at the end of the time. When the timekeeper says that five minutes remain, the vibes-watcher passes the talking stone and asks each woman to speak honestly of what worked and what didn't work for her in that night's group. Having a designated person responsible for seeing that vibes-watching is not skipped is analogous to the time management axiom that "what gets scheduled gets accomplished."

No fixing or processing happens here, just statements about how each person experienced the group. Sometimes a woman will note that the boundaries she made around her piece weren't observed. She will also—hopefully—take responsibility for not stopping the encroachment. This process helps immensely to prevent misunderstandings, and to build skill in small group interaction. "What worked; what didn't work," we ask at the end of every small group, and then, hopefully, the next week we build on the insights of the vibes-watching conversation.

The Writing Belongs to the Writer

We try very hard to model "not doing the writing for the writer." We want readers to honestly report things, such as: "On the second page of the story, I thought the momentum broke down; I found myself losing interest, losing touch with the characters," without thinking—or having the writer think—that the reader will fix that page. The writer will take in the comments, not argue or defend or clarify, and return to the text during her next writing session to decide what, if anything, to change.

Underlying much of the exchange that occurs in small group is a power dynamic that is crucial to examine. I caution women to hold this paradox in offering their work to the group: *The work is yours and you don't have to change anything to please anyone;* along-side, *If your goal is to affect the minds and hearts of others you need to be open to hearing how your work does or doesn't accomplish that goal.*

To my way of thinking, the word *criticism* has lost its usefulness in the context of responding to writing. Criticism has come to mean almost exclusively "telling the writer what's wrong her work." The etymology of the word speaks of a narrowing understanding over the years: "1583, from L. *criticus,* from Gk. *kritikos* 'able to make judgments,' from *krinein* 'to separate, decide.'" The English word always had overtones of "censurer, faultfinder."[3]

Small Group Dynamics

Over the years, I have experienced two attitudes that occasion-ally manifest themselves in the small group process and are diffi-cult to manage. The first I call the "no one understands my brilliance" attitude. The second I call "unless you tell me all the stuff that's wrong with my piece and how to fix it, you're not earn-ing your keep."

Here's a story about the first attitude: During one early semes-ter of the Cincinnati school, a woman brought to a small group, week after week, sheaves of poems no one could understand. Try as we might, and we did try mightily, we were forced to admit that we just plain "didn't get it." The language was dense; it was also terribly abstract. All the poems were untitled, leaving readers noth-ing to hold onto as we thrashed around in a sea of language. There were no images or metaphors we could grab onto. This writer remained in the position of believing that "we just didn't under-stand her," and refused, despite all the modeling around her, to ground her work in any place, story, or time. This extreme of refus-ing to respond to consistent and honest reader response is rare, thankfully.

More common to my experience are writers who exhibit varia-tions on the second attitude, throwing their writing on the table with the instruction to "tear it up." I wonder at the perversity of this approach. Although as writers we must develop a detachment from our art in order to grow, why would we want something we clearly value, something that came from within us, to be savaged?

I once saw what I felt was a tragic example of this masochistic attitude. A visiting poet, a famous elder statesman of American poetry, agreed to read and to comment upon the work of a few students. A man, who taught writing in a local high school, immediately offered a sheaf of his poems to the Great Poet to be publicly "workshopped." The GP raced through the pieces; his speed made it clear he had no expectation of encountering anything of value. Here and there he would read lines aloud, dismissing them with wit and charm, offering his belief that far too many people have taken up the writing of poetry. Surely the writer—publicly pilloried for the vanity of thinking himself a poet—was humiliated, but he bore it with great bravado, summing up the experience later: "Well, at least I have been told my stuff is shit by a Great Poet!"

Women have been told "our stuff is shit" by centuries of misogyny, and we are only too ready to believe it. Therefore, I encourage writers to hold onto the belief in the value and the necessity of their words, while learning to find and then respond to readers who will tell the truth because they want the writing and the writer to grow in skill and power. As part of our reflection on small group process, how it's working, how it could work better, I often say, "Spiritual skills are as important as literary skills." For confirmation of my opinion I think back to the many stories of writers, teachers, and editors who have not reflected on the power they have and how to use it wisely.

Unconsciousness About Group Process

Unconsciousness about groups and a refusal to reflect upon and evolve purposeful and healthy ways of being together can cause a great deal of damage to fledgling, and even more established, writers. Almost everyone can tell a story about setbacks and silencings they experienced at the hands of workshop members or teachers somewhere. I would not offer the possibility of the perfect group, nor am I saying women need to be handled with kid gloves. I am insisting—it only seems to be common sense—that groups create and continue evolving ways of hearing one another that are "acoustically alive" and vibrant. This only happens when some care is given to creating such spaces.

I think of two instances from my own experience that illustrate my point. When I was a young mother, beginning to steal time to write in my journal and then daring to fashion poems from some of that writing, I saw in the newspaper an invitation to poets to attend the "Cincinnati Poets Workshop." New to the city, I called for directions and proceeded, heart and poetry in hand, to the location that turned out to be the apartment of one of the members. In the room were six writers, one woman and five men. I was the only newcomer that night. Without introducing me to the group, other than to rattle off first names, without explaining how and why they did what they did, the "workshopping" began. I remember one especially long poem by one of the men detailing his Vietnam experiences with lots of images of napalm and body bags. I read my own poem aloud, a poem about childbirth fears. I'll never forget the first comment that broke the silence after I read. The woman responded with two words, "So what?" After another long silence in which I wrestled myself into not running from the room, the Vietnam vet poet said, almost apologetically, "I don't really care for mother poems." It never would have occurred to me to offer as a valid response to his poem, "I don't really care for war poems."

Five years later I tried again, submitting a portfolio of poems to see if I would be accepted to a workshop at the University of Cincinnati taught by a poet I admired. I was excited to be invited to be a seminar member, and was able to arrange to take sick leave to cover my Wednesday afternoon absences from my high school teaching job. There were probably fifteen of us in the class. After a few introductory classes in which we read and discussed the work of established poets, we began to take turns bringing in our poems for discussion. We had no preparatory discussions or agreements about how we would respond to poems. I worried about this, but dismissed my concerns thinking: "Well, I have never been in a workshop setting before and all these people have, so they probably know how to do this; I'll just learn by following." My trust was misplaced; when the first poems were before the group, the previously serious and respectful tone of discussions degenerated into what were mostly arguments among the participants about how the poem worked or didn't work. When their work was under discussion, some writers joined in the fray, arguing the case of the poem, explaining it, or defending it. Very often the poem itself was lost while a couple of especially vocal and combative members of the seminar battled it out, wanting, perhaps, to impress our poet-teacher or the group with their "correct" readings and insights into the poem and its problems. If four writers were scheduled to bring poems to a particular three-hour class, we usually spent most of the time on the first two, and rushed through our discussions of the third, while putting the fourth off until the next week. It became clear to me that the quarter might end before we had time to attend to even one poem from each participant.

Not Walking on Eggshells

What we do in small groups at Women Writing for (a) Change, is not "walking on eggshells"; rather we're creating structures which give us freedom—and peace. I think of the various ways people dismiss becoming conscious of how groups work: *It's a waste of time; too touchy-feely; too artificial; too soft.* I put their resistance alongside our obvious need for more civil and peaceful societies. Incivility, name-calling, talk show free-for-alls are modeled daily in our media outlets, in classrooms, in families. It is frankly countercultural to participate in the work of creating communities which "hear people into speech"[4] about what matters most to them.

One of the most satisfying results of the careful way we come together to share our lives and words at WWf(a)C is that women say it begins to affect their lives outside the school. One woman used a modified small group process to bring her family together around the division of family heirlooms following her mother's death. Many women use small group techniques (and large group ritual, for that matter) in professional meetings and trainings. Many more wish they could risk introducing our practices at work or home. One of the happiest outcomes is the stories I have heard about family meetings and marital conversations being conducted by variations on small group process in which everyone gets a share of available time, everyone can speak or read without interruption, and everyone can ask for the kind of feedback they want on what they set before the family.

Audre Lorde[5] observes that most of us teach what we need to learn. I have taught others, and have given myself, what I always longed for in my own family and in the schools where I was a student: civility, equality, and—yes, I can say it—a work that is love made visible.

Exercises

1. Write for five minutes to the phrase "an acoustics of intimacy." It is arguably true that most public places have

created acoustics to suppress intimacy. Explore this idea in writing.

2. Experiment in a work group or family setting with small group protocol and practices as described in this chapter. Here are some possibilities.

a) For bringing a fresh idea to the table: *I'm thinking of taking leave to study the language and my family's genealogy in southern Italy. I'm not asking for advice, criticism, pro and con discussion. I just want you to hear me talk about it (or read this journal entry I've written about why I want to do it and how). Then I'd like you to mirror back what you've heard (or write down read-back lines and read them back to me). I want help continuing to value this idea for a while.*

b) For getting input on a project-in-process. *As you know, I've been asked to study the possibility of developing a for-profit business to help fund our soup kitchen ministry. I've had the inspiration and run some specs on starting a cooking school. After I lay out my ideas, will you give me some gut reaction, then help me develop a sense of the strengths and the weaknesses of the plan so far? I'd like to leave this hour session with a sense of whether and what to do next.*

9.

Read-Around

When I dare to be powerful,

to use my strength in the service of my vision,

then it becomes less important whether I am afraid.

Audre Lorde[1]

When I was teaching high school creative writing, with classes meeting five days per week, I designated Friday as "bring something you've been working on to share" day. Students were to bring a draft that was not the first draft, but not necessarily a finished piece, to read aloud to the entire class. They did not rise and ascend to the podium, there to deliver stilted and terrified words to drowsy classmates, the teacher in back, pen poised over grade book. Rather, we stayed in our usual circle of chairs, and read in community. Stories, poems, journal entries, and essays poured out as we went around the room. There was the feeling of festival in the room on Fridays; students began to look forward to hearing the words of others and to being heard.

We had been engaging in this Friday ritual—though I dared not use that word in a public school—for some time, when my friend and mentor Kathy McMahon Klosterman, professor of education and women's studies at Miami University in Ohio, told me about how she called out the words and learning of students in her classes in regular read-arounds. Having a name for what we were doing made the practice deeper, better integrated, and more purposeful as the years went by.

Semester classes at Women Writing for (a) Change meet weekly. During the semester, we have four or five read-arounds, roughly correlating to the flow of my high school writing classes in which students had the ongoing assignment of having one nearly finished piece to read to the class each week.

Read-Around Preparation

In the WWf(a)C incarnation of read-arounds, there is once again the conscious making of the container for the words to be received. When the community has gathered, I lift up the necessity of confidentiality. I remind writers that they have the option of passing when the talking stone comes to them and that the passing of the stone to the next woman is a graceful way of declining to read without explanation or justification. The space has been created to receive the words of every woman; but she and she alone can choose whether or not to enter that space. I ask women, if they are willing and able while listening, to jot down a phrase or image from each writer. Finally, I remind them that at the end of each woman's reading, I will sound a chime acknowledging and thanking each woman for her words. I ask women to hold onto the stone until the resonance of the chiming is complete, thereby holding onto the attention of the group, taking time to notice her feelings after reading, and then to pass the stone to the next reader.

After all these years, I am still astonished by the words filling the circle. The variety of voices, forms, and subject matter is dizzying. The emotion evoked by the pieces ranges from hilarity to sadness. The intensity of the listening and the community ethic of giving a generous hearing to everyone's words allow each woman to hear her words fully. I have heard many discussions of "how different my words sound here." Though no praise or critique is offered, actually *because* no praise or critique is offered, each reader feels her relationship to her words, and her responsibility to her words, very deeply. This returns her to her writing with greater diligence and devotion.

How It Feels to Listen

For listeners, the read-around is an incredibly dense and time-efficient lesson in, among other things, writing possibilities. Many women go home to write pieces evoked, directly or indirectly, by the read-around. The more direct evocation comes out of our standing invitation to the group to take the words, the read-back lines, home and to be open to what words are called out of them in response.

The power and efficacy of read-arounds was the seed of my idea to create a radio show. One night when I was shutting off lamps and restoring the space after a read-around, I could see and feel waves of light and energy shimmering all around me! I thought: *If only we could drop the walls and people could listen in, listen in to the wisdom and love here, what a difference it could make!* Deploring the viciousness and "gotcha" quality of call-in programs, I was intrigued by what it might be like to transfer our acoustics of intimacy to the radio. I envisioned a write-in program, where listeners really listened to the words of others, then responded in writing using a word or phrase from the original piece or writing another version of a particular story. Although the purest form of my idea for a write-in show never worked, the read-around did give rise to our seven-year presence on PBS affiliate WVXU, "bringing women to words and the words of women to the world." That program morphed into a radio show of our own, an Internet show, produced and created completely by the women and girls of the New Media Circle, and available on www.womenwriting.org.

What Matter(s)?

Women often talk about how they were inspired by read-arounds. Usually they do not say directly, "I think I'll try a chant poem like Joan did," although that sometimes happens; but instead, there is a kind of permission-giving that occurs. A story about a mother's grief at the loss of her son inspires a poem about the loss of a partner to addiction. One woman's narrative poem about her Appalachian forbears piques another woman to fictionalize an account of her mother's arrival in America as a war bride. Even more important, but less tangible, is the overall permission we give one another to take our subject matter, whatever it might be, seriously enough to attend to it in writing. This is especially important to women, for most of us have thoroughly—and unconsciously—learned that women's subject matter is minor or less important. War, for example, is a monumental subject; childbirth is not. How I would love to see a monument to the unknown mother!

More Important Subjects

I'm reminded of my tour of California fabric artist Kathleen McCabe's studio (kathleenmccabecoronado.com). I was amazed by her "Ode to Bobby Joe," a beautiful, appliquéd piece created around a pair of bell bottom jeans her brother wore during the sixties. Arching above the jeans is a fabric rendering of the bridge from which he jumped to his death when he was twenty years old. Another piece, "Caged Animal," is a collage of textiles of her son's tiny trucks, Lego pieces, scraps of his baby pajamas, boyhood caps and overalls, all under a cage of chicken wire. A fabric book which Kathleen created to accompany the picture tells the story of his refusal to live at home, his feeling like a caged animal, his numerous disappearances, until finally, on December 8, weeks short of his fifteenth birthday, he left through the back door, his mother trying to imagine the intensity of feelings that drove him, his inability to *not* travel his solitary and terrifying path. I sat on the floor of Kathleen's studio, tracing her stitches with my fingers, tears flowing, while Kathleen told me that her teacher at the University of San Diego said the pieces were *interesting*, but that she wished Kathleen would move on to *more important* subjects.

During a read-around, women hear a whole range of subjects rendered important by the hand and heart of the artist herself, not the observer with the averted eyes, closed-off heart.

The heart. How does one protect one's heart during a read-around? I remind writers, and myself, that our job is to take in the words; we don't want them bouncing off non-receptive surfaces and flying back in the face of the writer. However, it is not our job to hold on to the words, nor to do something about the feelings expressed. I remember how revelatory it was to read in Jean Baker Miller's *Toward a New Psychology of Women*[2] that women serve as the dumping ground for the emotions denied by the dominant culture. This act of letting go is new behavior to many women in the community; in effect we recycle the emotions, returning them to the circle once they have passed through our bodies.

Read-Backs

After every woman who intends to read has done so, after the resonance of the last chime has ended, we sit quietly for some minutes. Then I open the circle for read-backs. Women read back into the circle the images and phrases they jotted down during the read-around. The room becomes a kind of resonance chamber in which we can hear, in yet another way, the beauty and power of our words. Listening to read-backs, I am always reminded of polyphony, the beauty of different voices, blending, reiterating themes. Read-back time is also enormously instructive as writers hear which words hit home and notice how strong images and writing with voice stay with listeners, while more abstract, disconnected passages fall by the wayside.

Reading back was something I remember coming to instinctively, and I was not prepared for how significant a practice it has become. Many, many women have said it is the first time in their lives when they have felt *deeply heard*. Others describe what it does to them, how far it goes toward healing them of years of misappropriation, rejection, and trivialization of their words.

Finally, the teacher opens the floor for discussion. Sometimes there is none! We are worded-out, and exhalations of awe and release are all we can muster. At other times there is energy for reflecting on what we have heard. Writers might share stories of how certain pieces began, or what changes they made. Small group members often remark on the pride they feel in a woman's piece, having heard earlier drafts, and feeling themselves "on the side" of her more fully realized poem or story. Listeners sometimes have questions for writers. Writers are free to answer, or to decline further comments beyond the words themselves. Often women express a kind of "filled-up" gratitude, feelings of being nourished and encouraged in their own lives and writing by others' words.

Read-Arounds with Guests

Read-arounds afford writers a strong experience of audience, and I often talk about how the in-class read-arounds are practice for taking our words to more public places when we are ready. Once a semester we invite other women to attend a read-around. This public read-around expands our circle to include our colleagues, neighbors, friends, and family members. They offer us the gift of their listening; we offer them the gift of our words. Our guests at public read-arounds are invited into our read-around ritual practices; the teacher explains read-backs, the use of the chime, self-care, and confidentiality. I tell our guests that we are not an anonymous group in that *who* is here is not confidential; but *what* is read here *is*—until and unless the woman herself chooses to publish her work outside the circle.

In preparing writers for public read-arounds, I very often invoke the words of Brenda Ueland, who wrote *If You Want to Write*[3] in the 1930s while teaching writing at a community school in Minnesota: "Writing is not a performance, it's a generosity." I am inclined to think that public read-arounds are an invitation to hold the tension of opposites. The read-arounds *are* performances in that a woman usually stands in a central space before an audience and she has prepared her words and practiced reading them. At the same time, she is giving her words away, possibly to a woman who needs to hear just those words. She is giving herself—polished or unpolished, in-progress, perfect and imperfect, a living, breathing, close-up inspiration—to women in the audience who will be affected by the example of a woman who takes herself seriously and asks to be heard.

Lighten Up!

Someone told me about a *Saturday Night Live* skit lampooning a "serious and sensitive women's group, sort of like ours." I think of this as one of the culture's many ways of telling women to "shut up already!" As another example of "shut up already," sometime during the first year of our radio program, the co-hosts of the show which followed ours—sort of a bad, content-less imitation of *Car Talk* (which I thoroughly enjoy)—began to make cracks about us.

This culminated in a program where they requested listeners call-in to vote for the "Edgy Bad Boy Comedy" or for "Women Writing About Their Pain." You can imagine the sophomoric, woman-hating calls this elicited! This was on a public radio station, both university and NPR-affiliated, that used "intelligent public radio" as its tagline. When I asked the female producer of our show for reassurance that this would *never* happen again, I was told to have a sense of humor! I let her know that I am in charge of deciding what I think is funny, and also in charge of being fierce on behalf of women's words! Her response to my request was to assure me she would talk to "the brothers." Later in the week she re-aired the objectionable program with only a few of the most egregious slurs crudely deleted, the remainder of the humor at our writers' expense intact.

The stakes get higher and higher the more widely we read authentic words about women publicly. One of our challenges at WWf(a)C, as writers-becoming-conscious and as professional feminist teachers, is to collaborate on carving out more and safer places for women's words. We aim to be not just individual women, acting singly and heroically, but a community of women acting with wisdom and persistence.

And yes, there is always a danger of losing perspective, and always the risk that a group of people so long silent will become greedy for being heard or feel ourselves entitled to excessive attention. Overwhelmingly, however, I see women struggling to be serious enough about our writing and about our lives to give either enough space. One of the most common stoppers of women is being told to lighten up just as we are beginning to lay claim to some of our truths.

What About *Us*?

The late feminist writer and scholar Carolyn Heilbrun has cautioned, "Remember, there is never enough mother."[4] I have observed an unholy terror arising at the possibility that our enormous, unacknowledged, and undervalued energy of caring will become less readily available if we invest some of it in ourselves and one another. I call it the "What about us?" syndrome. If society is asked to give some attention to the plight of girls, there is a

sudden outcry, "But what about boys? They have problems too."
What follows is a deluge of books about how boys are really more
worse off in our culture than girls, as if it were a huge zero-sum
game of some kind. "Take Our Daughters to Work" was established to begin to address the lack of mentoring for careers in girls'
lives, and very shortly there was an outcry that it was a sexist and
exclusive initiative.

Women Writing for (a) Change read-arounds (like the school
itself) are radical in that they are simply and persistently by, for,
and about women's words. Radical in that we are going to the root
of the imbalance in our culture and, on a small scale, attempting to
heal the attention deficit women and girls have historically experienced, by keeping our attention on women's—and girls'—words.

Exercises

1. Write three stories from your experience of performing,
   presenting, or otherwise sharing something you made, or
   some expertise, with an audience. Your stories could range
   from being in a year-end, comprehensive spelling-bee in
   fourth grade, to presenting a fundraising idea to the PTA,
   to defending your doctoral dissertation, to singing in the
   school musical.

2. Consider how you might collaborate with family or colleagues to create regular experiences in which individuals
   publish, present, or perform for the whole group or team.
   Focus on practices that will allow the performer/presenter
   to also be a *learner* in the process, practices that will lessen
   "distress" and increase "eustress." (Distress is a common-
   ly referred to type of stress, having negative implications.
   Eustress is a positive form of stress, usually related to
   desirable events in a person's life.)

3. Building on a half-year's worth of in-house presentations,
   begin to widen the audience for your work, increasing
   opportunities for building social and intellectual capital in
   the wider community in which you live and work. We
   have held variations on our read-arounds with and in

museums, social service centers, in collaboration with calligraphers, choirs, and even at a film festival with alternating short films with poets reading their work.

Part *Three*

Change Writing

I imagine you, cleaning rooms in another house,

a house where you will live a different pattern

In this section, I am imagining the readers I will never meet, who live in houses far different from the ones whose patterns I have created *with and against*. I invite you into writing as a practice of personal transformation while intentionally connecting the personal to the communal and natural worlds that are also our homes.

The flow of these chapters attempts to recreate the movement of listening within, then taking the words to the world in various ways for the sake of the change in which we must participate during this liminal/millennial era. Most chapters have two kinds of exercises: personal writing practices and connecting practices based on the ones created in the houses of Women Writing for (a) Change, 1991–2008, aimed at connecting our words to place and community.

10.

Listening Within, Moving Out

April 9, 2008

1. This morning I listened
until I actually heard the birds
lifting up the day.

Won't you listen too?

Hear the bleating cheep
of fledglings keeping time
high and regular, while
a long-long-long-short
whistle joins in every fourth beat.

Now a song of three longs
wafts in from the distance.

2. I may not have bought myself a
vivid and exotic life with my
saying no to normal, but I have,
more humbly, but it turns out more

happily, acquired sixteen
(so far) years of mornings for
my soul to have her life.

3. My soul, Ms. Psyche
I presume, thanks
my worried ego,
Ms. Conventional,
and her younger cousin,
Dutiful Good Girl,

for sitting down and shutting up
long enough for Psyche to
bask among bird calls,

swim in morning silence,
come home to the world.

A vibrant thread woven into the fabric of cultures throughout history is that of "listening within." Practices as various as meditation, fasting, ecstatic dancing, many forms of prayer, ritual, and more, make evident the human compulsion to experience our connection to something larger, deeper, and wiser than our self-limited ego states.

In a conversation with host Krista Tippett on National Public Radio's *Speaking of Faith*, the late poet John O'Donohue commented, "Your identity is not equivalent to your biography. There is a place in you where you have never been wounded, where there's a seamlessness in you, where there is a confidence and tranquility in you, and I think the intention of prayer and spirituality and love is now and again to visit that inner kind of sanctuary."[1] Hindu mystics call this place of wholeness *Atman*. The multiple names—true nature, oneness, union, soul, divine essence—hint both at our longing for "it" and "its" elusiveness. A recent e-mail from a friend describes the experience as a simple, and simply profound, coming home.

Wanted to let you know that I spent Friday morning with my mom. We hiked up the mountain with the tower and sat in reflection for some time—nourishing for both of us. And Suzy and I did indeed have a beautiful weekend, weather included. A highlight was walking a labyrinth, up on a hill overlooking a big pond and the ocean. The message I sensed walking out from the center:

We are
all of us
finding our way
back.
We are
All
here.

Rick Brush
May 20, 2008

Rick's words, "finding our way back," intended as the finding our way back to the sanctuary of at-oneness O'Donohue describes so lyrically, express my abiding belief that a certain, even sacred, quality of writing practice becomes a skill of both finding Home and returning Home. Home with a capital *H* is at-home-ness with our participation in the all, a depth of belonging and peace with things as they are and ourselves as we are. Paradoxically, attempting to live at Home permanently alienates us from our small *h* home, this world, our limited bodies, beauty and gritty ugliness, as well as our wounded, changing, mysterious lives.

In the poem serving as epigraph to this chapter, I reflect on the sanctuary of quiet mornings at my desk. At first, listening and watching without writing, and then listening with the pen in my hand, I hear and see the world without: its bird-calls and shifting light. Soon there comes a moment when I know my belonging and at-oneness with my surroundings, however ordinary. This knowing puts me in alignment with my choice to live a "non-normal," unexotic life, without the riches of a secure, with-benefits job and the status I might have attained in a racing-the-clock-to-achieve-success life. The practice of daily *writing myself in* to what deeply *is* moves me *back out* into a day that will, as likely as not, be filled with events that will make me stumble into non-alignment with myself and others. But these moments will only be temporary and not as dangerous as when I lived without a regular practice of *feeling connection.*

I am convinced that I bring more good and do less harm now that I live in regular relationship with my shy soul, as opposed to immersion in my restless and irritable ego, filled with complaints, fears, and the habit of going to war with the way things are. In his remarkable book, *The Power of Now,* Eckhart Tolle calls our complaints and fears "the pain body."

Exercise 10-1: What Is Happening Now?

Preparatory Note: You will need a kitchen timer, journal, and pen at hand to do the exercises in this chapter.

Write now: Set your kitchen timer for seven minutes. Write freely, without thinking, only responding to the question, "What is happening now?"

When the timer sounds, read what you've written, underline six or seven strong-to-you words and make a small poem. Resist the compulsion to "do something" with this little poem other than read it out loud to yourself and say, "Hmmmm. Interesting."

Witness Consciousness

The writing practices and prompts in this chapter support the development of witness consciousness. Eckhart Tolle describes his initial experience with witness consciousness in his first book, *The Power of Now.* In his rooms at school where he had been living a life "deadened by mental abstraction," Tolle was near despair and felt the "deep longing for annihilation, for nonexistence . . . becoming much stronger than the instinctive desire to continue to live." He writes:

> The thought, *I cannot live with myself any longer* kept repeating itself in my mind. Then suddenly I became aware of what a peculiar thought it was. "Am I one or two? If I cannot live with myself, there must be two of me: the 'I' and the 'self' that 'I'cannot live with. Maybe," I thought, "only one of them is real."[2]

Eventually, Tolle understood that the intensity of his suffering had forced his consciousness to "withdraw from its identification with the unhappy and deeply fearful self, which is ultimately a complete fiction of the mind."[3] Based on his powerful experience of larger consciousness, Tolle developed a philosophy and practice of noting what is happening now and gradually diminishing identification with ego.

Exercise 10-2: I Am

Write now: Take up your timer and journal again; set it for seven minutes. Write freely, in longhand, an extended series of "I am's": I am . . . I am . . . . Continue using "I am" as a refrain, writing yourself deeply into the names for your selves.

Read it aloud to yourself, and let it be.

In *Presence: An Exploration of Profound Change in People, Organizations, and Society,*[4] and in his solo book, *Theory U: Leading from the Future as It Emerges,*[5] C. Otto Scharmer relates a story about his early experience of Larger Self. Leaving the 350-year-old farmhouse where his family had made its home for generations for an ordinary school day, Otto was later called from class and told to return home. When he arrived, he says, "I could not believe my eyes. The world I had lived in all my life was gone. Vanished. All up in smoke."[6]

Scharmer describes standing in the reality of losing home, and all he considered his life. "Everything I thought I was had dissolved into nothing. Everything? No, perhaps not everything, for I felt that a tiny element of my self still existed. Somebody was still there, watching all this. Who?"[7] As a consequence of this extraordinary event, the young Otto accessed a place described in terms similar to Tolle's, including a sense that as his former reality dissolved, another reality emerged. Scharmer would base much of his life's work upon his sense of a larger reality behind events that—if we are truly present—we sense and can act upon.

> My journey began with the recognition that I am not just one self but two selves. One self is connected to the past, and the second self connects to who I could become in the future. In front of the fire I experienced how these two selves started to connect to one another. Today, twenty-five years later, and several thousand miles away in Boston, Massachusetts, the question "Who is my true self?" still lingers.[8]

Exercise 10-3: Life Dissolves

Write now: Remember a moment in your life when you saw one life dissolve. Write it as if it were happening now. Use vivid details and names. Let the story well up, don't try to shape it or make it mean something.

Read it out loud to yourself and say, "Interesting." If emotions well up as you write or read aloud, this is not unusual. Keep some tissues nearby. The practice of reading and writing through tears is an excellent way to develop witness consciousness.

Dissociation

Dissociation occurs when, as a response to trauma, the Self splits off from the self. It is important to acknowledge and deal with dissociation, the shadow side of the two selves. As a response to trauma, many people note a moment when Self splits off, watching the powerless self in the grip of events which are beyond comprehension and, sometimes, indescribably violent. Self witnesses, but what has happened remains unspeakable across the chasm that has been created. Dissociation is a critical survival strategy, but one which often persists afterward as a habit of "going away." Often in later experiences of conflict, however slight, a person feels helpless to act or speak on her own behalf. Since she is not fully present, her seeing and speaking Self is unable to contact the self in the unfolding situation.

I have been privileged to participate in the lives of many traumatized women who have written themselves whole. They have built a bridge between self and Self, a bridge where healthy commerce takes place between what is happening and what the Self now has a voice to say to the former victim: "You are not the wound; you can act on your own behalf; you don't have to be a victim; you don't have to repeat the pattern. You are whole. You are loved."

Show Up

From years of witnessing how writing can heal dissociation, I have distilled the elements that seem to produce the healing. First is a regular ritual showing up at the page, without a goal other than being present to what the words will say. The intervals around "regular" differ, but to heal and move into the future, the writing practice must be more than "whenever I'm upset." "Whenever I'm upset" writing may be immediately therapeutic, but I rarely see long-term wholeness result from occasional spilling. Regular could be: an hour each morning; an hour on my Thursdays off; or Sunday evenings after the children are in bed. Ritual communicates the movement from profane to sacred space, and says to your brain,

"In this space I listen to my witnessing consciousness, and it tells me all the things I didn't know I knew."

Exercise 10-4: Make a Date

1. Write Now: Take your calendar or day planner, and commit to a series of regular writing appointments with yourself. Keep them.

2. Do a series of witnessing/paying attention practices, such as timed writings to: what I see, what I feel, what is happening now, what I'm hearing.

Make Something

The second element of transforming dissociation into healthy awareness of self is to *make something of the writing*. While holding the fact that not every word emerging from listening within is laden and lyrical alongside the fact that some of the words may be arranged for further use and appreciation, I encourage writers to practice crafting pieces to take into the world. Philosopher Gregory Bateson's "the pattern that connects is the pattern that corrects"[9] is meaningful on several levels. I suggest that when we begin to shape raw writing into forms, we discover patterns latent in the words—stories, poems, dramatic monologues, and mixed-genre pieces. The practice of connecting is highly corrective and healing of dissociation, forming a both/and between process and product that is satisfying and wholeness-making.

As an example, I offer a piece I made from six words gleaned from timed writings (sometimes called "fast-writes," writing fast and steadily enough to stay ahead of the censor within). This poem occupies a medial position in my writing, which means I would take it to an established writing circle but would not spend much time dressing it up to take it farther into the world.

And yet, the poem is significant in that crafting it during a time of illness served to strengthen the voice of my wiser self, who encouraged my surrender to the rest I sorely needed.

She Knew Her Wounded Soul

(Written to the prompt: Incorporate six words: wounded, candor, intoxication, honor, grace, slake.)

She knew her wounded soul had
begun a conversation with her lungs.

Lying in bed far longer than she ever had,
she had occasion to listen.

Lungs' candor about her intoxication with
being good pained her.

Later they became quite serious about
how she confused honor with perfection.

She lay in bed far longer than she ever had,
hearing her lungs and the wounded part of her soul

wondering whether sickness might slake her
unacknowledged thirst for solitude. Lungs

brought up a meaning of slake she didn't know,
"to undergo a slaking process, crumble or disintegrate,
from the Old English *slacian* from which
come the words slack, or loose."

"Oh my," wound in the soul said to lungs,
"do you imagine she has the grace to
loosen her grip on what she thinks of
as her self, her life
and fall into the hands of god?"

Exercise 10-5: Strong Words

Write Now: Return to the witnessing writing generated in your regular appointments. Underline the strongest words. Write a story or poem or letter using this set of words.

Acoustics of Intimacy

A third critical ingredient in converting dissociation to witness consciousness is a safe container where you can share words and be truly heard. In my own practice of creating such containers, I use the phrase "an acoustics of intimacy." This image falls into that elusive category of "You know it when you experience it; otherwise, it's hard to describe," but let me try. An acoustics of intimacy is found in the presence of nonarmored bodies, open hearts, noncompetitive and nonjudging listeners.

My experience of an acoustics of intimacy first came within the confines and boundaries of traditional psychotherapy. In containers formed for me by two different therapists to whom I owe a great deal, I heard the Self under my self as expressed in words that came back to me as an echo might, but without the hollowness of an echo. Two women—Dr. Susan Wooley, who heard me through a period of clustered losses, and Dr. Jayne Treinen-Yager, who heard me through the remaking of my life and work—provided a quality of listening that both allowed me to trust my words and prevented me from becoming obsessively attached to them.

A healthy container for writing which nurtures the soul provides a quality of listening that somehow—I wish I knew *how*—honors the emerging words while subverting the ego's tendency to hoard and make overly precious "the writer" and "my writing."

An illustration from my early years of crafting containers for the authentic words of women and girls: It was a heady and an exhausting time; I had not yet learned the level of consciousness it would take to keep the container, and my own container, healthy. I sometimes joked to myself and to my therapist that I had unwittingly made myself the lightning rod for 5,000 years or more of repressed shadow resulting from the subjugation of the feminine. During this time, people asked, "Aren't you afraid some of the women writing about trauma are going *to get stuck in victim*?" I italicize "get stuck in victim" because it was buzz-lingo of the mid-nineties. The truth-telling genie was coming out of the bottle and there was pushback in the air. "Getting stuck in victim" was, in my estimation, part of the pushback.

I was not afraid then and am not now. I felt then and still do now that our culture has barely scratched the surface of the toxic dump that is violence against the feminine, though we are beginning to see the residue surfacing in the form of environmental consequences. On the other hand, I gradually began to see a few writers becoming attached to, even identified with, the victim stories they were relating. I am still observing and learning about this, but I speculate it has to do with both inadequate generosity and an unwillingness to participate in the longer arc, a whole rather than partial process by which writing can—and I'm going to risk saying *should*—be a tool for deepening the writer's capacity to hold both her own suffering and that of her human and creature co-inhabitants.

As WWf(a)C's leaders and I engage in exercises for "seeing our system," we perceive an evolution. We continue to be an oasis for the writing of women and girls, but widened and deepened translations have emerged, connecting us to "what is needed now" in the world outside our doors. This evolution—in my opinion, both organic and inevitable—has been troubling to some whose focus remains "their writing" or "being a writer." Some writers lobbied against using community time for anything which didn't directly pertain to "their writing," even protesting time given to sharing information and needs from the organization itself, the very system which makes the writing containers possible. I began to call part of each session *acknowledging our connection to community*, clearly stating that ours was a practice of becoming conscious and connected, not a practice that would more deeply entangle us in the projects of our egos.

Re-Association

Finally then, I point to *re-association*, a word I coin for this chapter that is the opposite of dissociation. Writing can heal the divided self, but only if that writing moves the writer back into the world, increasingly generous and able to participate in healing the whole. The words of Stanley Kunitz in his final book, *The Wild Braid: A Poet Reflects on a Century in the Garden*, seem a perfect way to conclude this reflection on the vibrant possibilities inherent in writing for returning us to the world:

> The garden isn't, at its best, designed for admiration and praise; it leads to an appreciation of the natural universe, and to a meditation on the connection between the self and the rest of the natural universe. And this can come not only from the single flower in its extravagant beauty, but in consideration of the harmony established among all aspects of the garden's form.

Exercise 10-6:
And Out Again: Moving Back Into the World

1. After a week or two of keeping regular writing appoint-
    ments, spend some time observing yourself. Write one
    paragraph where you answer each of the following ques-
    tions. You may want to tell a quick story or recreate an
    event.

    Since I've been keeping the regular writing appointments:

    ♦   What is new about my awareness at work?
    ♦   What is different about my presence at home?
    ♦   What have I noticed about my physical surroundings?
    ♦   What has changed about my health?

2. Do a small experiment in creating a container for your
    words. Ask someone to listen to you read a two-minute
    excerpt from your writing. Choose someone with the abil-
    ity to "just listen." Explain that you want to hear your
    voice on the page, and that all you need is their listening
    presence and the gift of their writing down two or three
    phrases and reading them back to you.

11.

Moving Out, Family

"I understand your language."
"Of course," Kongo said, smiling.
"My blood is mixed with yours and yours with mine.
We always say that words are a kind of blood."

Pete Hamill[1]

The writer's spiral, from self back to the world, routes her first through the landscape of family. It is a landscape filled with emotional landmines. For all its intimacy—because of its intimacy—family is, more often than not, the site of an impaired acoustics of intimacy. How then, within the house of family, does a writer engage the paradox of silence and voice, where patterns that reveal are entangled with patterns that conceal?

I believe that more violence is done by not telling the stories than by telling them. At the same time, I embrace an ethic that requires me as a writer and as a family member to tell my stories in ways that will create space for others' different—even competing—stories. I believe further that the most challenging and simultaneously most life-giving stories within the context of family are stories of loss.

Origins

I am from a landscape
ill-defined and vaporous.
The streams here are squeezed thin,
leaking instead of leaping
over embankments.

In a place without landmarks—
trees or mountains
etched against the horizon—
it is easy to lose your way.

Those of us who survive here
chart our course
by the drift of faint
and nameless stars
by reading scars,
exploring erosion,
finding faults
before they open up
to swallow us.

Our mothers taught us
to walk gingerly,
to dance or stamp was to risk
falling through the thin crust.
We learned early to whisper,
tiptoe, skirt our way around
quicksand masquerading as meadow.

We live by losing
love by letting go.
Enduring the random uprootings,
careless transplanting,
we grow thin and straggly,
bear stunted fruit.

Our roots lie too near the surface,
we drown in downpours
lie parched and cracked
in periods of drought.

Because we find ourselves so often
choking and guttering,
unable to speak,
we have only a partial history,
endings without stories,
scattered notes instead of songs,
rituals without resonance.

What will it take to make
our land raise mountains
sheer and accurate in the distance?

Will the sun ever shine
bright enough to burn off
the terrible mists,
the sickly vapors?

Will my child tell whole stories?
Will his?
Will they dance,
and sing the names
of constellations?

Will they be able to push down
beyond the scars and faults?

Root themselves in the rich loam
I must believe is there
beneath the generations
or erosion?

Oh, how I pray
they will hang heavy and well-nourished,
filled with a sense of their own belonging,
their own deserving
to bear fruit
to be fruit,

plump
ripe
undamaged.

I entered the world as a daughter of the working class, from people for whom there was little talk of, and certainly no writing about, loss. The losses were too recent, too frequent; to speak of them risked opening wounds there was neither enough time nor enough energy to tend. We practiced working-class stoicism; if not grace under pressure, at least putting one foot in front of the other under pressure. While I in no way denigrate this survival mechanism, what I observe and wish to help heal with my writing and teaching is the deepening-through-generations dissociation that results from so much erosion. Unexpressed, the pain of past loss begins to take up all the space for living in the present. Writing, by contrast, has an almost magical propensity for chipping away at the gross colossus of suffering, carving out space where joy and repaired connection to loved ones can thrive.

Exercise 11-1: I Wish . . .

Preparatory Note: A box of family photos, your timer, and your favorite writing implements will come in handy as you work through this chapter.

Write now: Set a ritual space for yourself, at a time and in a place free from interruptions. Light a candle. Browse through your family photos. Now, set your timer for ten minutes and write to:

♦   I wish I knew . . .
♦   I wish I had known . . .
♦   I wish someone had told me . . .

Read what has emerged, appreciate the content, underline the strong words, and honor your feelings. Now, blow out the candle and return intentionally to the present.

Truth and Consequences

"Truth has consequences," Bill Moyers said to author and investigative reporter Phillipe Sands.[2] *Your* truth, likely to differ from the truths of your siblings or more far-flung family members, has consequences. In no way am I suggesting silence or censorship, but I am suggesting the need for an emerging consciousness about how we hold and publish the truths of our lives, when those truths touch on the lives of those in our families. Clusters of families become clans, become tribes, become nations. Who tells the stories and how we tell them does have consequences, and, if engaged with imagination and heart, far more positive consequences than high-level diplomacy and tortured official negotiations.

When we tell family stories without awareness that they are *our* stories, not *the* stories, a reduction of possibilities occurs. At a time in history when our survival depends on more diversity rather than less, we cannot afford to continue the old way that only the winners' stories become history.

Exercise 11-2: I Remember

Write now: Re-enter your ritual writing space, light your candle, set the timer for five minutes and write: I remember . . . I remember . . .

Set the timer for another five minutes and write: And I will tell . . . and I will tell . . . Finish the session with: And I will tell . . . because . . .

Notice your feelings and intentions. Begin to imagine where and with whom your telling could open out toward more diverse telling.

Long Memory

In a 2004 interview, the late folk singer Utah Phillips told *Democracy Now* host Amy Goodman, "The long memory is the most radical idea in America."[3] Phillips was also fond of telling audience members, "A revolutionary song is any song you choose to sing yourself." When we write the healing we want to see in our families, we find ways to raise our distinctive voices in order to encourage others in the clan to do the same. We begin to weave the long memory, developing a sense of individuals and families in connection to the whole.

Over the years of writing in community, I have heard many stories about family milestones as opportunities to engage truth and tell stories. Funerals or memorial services are often the richest— and the riskiest—occasions. Writers in our community attest to the difficulty of following their yearning to have a voice in the ceremonies of their loved ones, especially feelings of "usurping" or "assuming" the role of family spokesperson. At one funeral of a beloved mother of four adult children, only the sons eulogized their mother, while the daughters, who likely had complementary stories, did not speak. By contrast, Ginger Swope, a writer in our community, summoned the courage to read intimate memories of her very proper mother sitting at her dressing table and of her entertaining guests in their beautiful home, stories neither her brother nor the pastor could have told.

I Remember Her

I remember her in the kitchen
of the old house on 14th street,
apron bow-tied tight around her waist,
girdle and stockings on under
her housedress, hair coiffed,
earrings on, waiting for the
milk to be delivered, Myrlea
to come, her day to start.

I remember her at her dressing table
in their bedroom at the new house
on the Parkway. Perched on the edge
of her quilted peach satin covered
twin bed, I watched her smooth
on foundation, draw in her eyebrows,
paint her lips, use her little finger
to spread color on her cheeks.

I remember her in the E Street house,
sitting with my dad on the 4 times
recovered Duncan Phyfe sofa, wearing
her white shirtwaist, brown buttons
down the front, brown leather belt, brown
eyes looking at my dad for all the world
like he was the love of her life and
I think most times he was.

I remember her the day we took her
to live at Friends' Fellowship. We
walked through her house for the last

time talking over old memories, touching
the kitchen cabinets that Daddy embossed
with wooden fruit, taking one last ride
in the elevator in the closet. "Goodbye
for America," we always yelled on the way down.

I remember her on April 23, 2008, her
last morning on this earth, her eyes focused
inward on her laboring breath or maybe
outward beyond what I could see. "Fred,
Fred" she'd called out the day before to my
Father dead nearly thirty years. I remember
her now in the presence of her children
and their children and their children.

I remember her: Miriam Olive Fowler Swope.

Ginger Swope
May 2008

My cousin's wife invited me to speak at his funeral Mass because, she said, "You're the only one with the gift of words." At first, I demurred; I felt at too much of a distance, in both geography and years, to have a voice. At the last minute, a way to honor her request emerged on a yellow tablet I had in the car. I told the priest I would, after all, read something following communion. I include it here because, in writing and reading it, I braided layers of family stories that both positioned me in relation to my cousin, and affirmed the value of others' strands of story and connection.

Eulogy for Raymond

My name is Mary Pierce Brosmer, and I'm a Yankee—only a cousin—second at that, to Raymond.

When Mildred asked me if I could say a few words about Raymond's life, I said no. I only know Raymond as he was to me, and distance and time have put too many years between my memories and yours for them to have any hope of saying who Raymond was and how you loved him.

He was your: husband, father, grandfather, long and longer-time friend. He was only my cousin—second at that. I offer you then all I have: who Raymond was in my eyes and heart, in the humble hope that it will help you remember and hold precious who he was to you.

Only a cousin? Not exactly. Raymond was handsome, funny, magical Uncle to me and my brothers, Keith (who is with me in Clarksdale today) and Rafe (who would be here if not for a bad case of flu). He was my mother's first cousin—no, really brother!

My mother, Isabel Caliendo, lived in Clarksdale until 1947 when she married my father, Keith Pierce, by way of the WWII airmen's training at Fletcher Field, and St. Elizabeth's young women's sodality parties for pilots. John and Marie Francis, Raymond's mother and father, raised my mother from the age of nine, and loved her as their own.

Mom said she carried Raymond around on her hip when he was born (she was twelve years old, we calculate) and he was *hers*, her beloved baby brother, as Pauline, Raymond's sister, was *her* sister.

Raymond Francis was, to use Rita Marie's words, "large and in charge." He was in charge of making sure you knew you were loved and *safe by God if he could do anything about it!*

In charge of making you laugh, and straighten up to his good, high standards.

Raymond Francis made my often-homesick mother happy from the day he was born until the day she died, almost twenty years ago. For that alone we, my father, brothers, and I, loved him. And there was so much more.

Nobody was "only an anything" to Raymond. You all here know the so much more of him better than I.

That will be your consolation and your hope of healing: *your* "so much more" stories to tell.

Clarksdale, Mississippi
January 20, 2003

Exercise 11-3: Family Story

Write Now: Write a letter to a family member in which you tell what is yours to tell about a shared family event or family member.

If you encounter resistance internally, set your timer for five minutes and tell yourself, "I only have to write for five minutes." At the end of five minutes, read what you have written, decide whether you have more to say. *Don't mail it*. In the spirit of not assuming or presuming that yours is the only story, set the timer again for five minutes and write back to yourself in the another family member's voice. You could start it off, "Dear ____, I received your letter about _____. Here is what I remember . . ."

Writing Through Transition

The most challenging element of writing about and within family is that of creating spaces for holding both the light and the shadow. Greeting card verse and most Christmas letters are banal, because they incorporate only the "good stuff" and banish failure and loss as inappropriate to the season, any season! The challenge to write about the wedding of a family member offers a case in point: Why should the greeting card companies and official personages have the only words about matters so personal and meaningful to us? I suggest we return to Utah Phillips's *revolutionary* act of choosing to write and sing our own songs.

Though a festive occasion, a wedding also involves loss, as the precious child is no longer a child, and will never again be in the same relation to her or his family of origin. When my son asked me to write something for his wedding, I was unable to promise, aware of challenges in the situation: both sets of parents' divorces, and my characteristic inability to write rhetorically, ignoring paradox. The request also made me aware of the responsibility, and the desire, to weave Jayna's families into the piece with as many threads as I devoted to Colin's families.

The invitation from Jayna and Colin challenged me personally, but also challenged me to align with my mission of including the feminine voice. In this deeply personal time of transition, as my son moved out of the life we had made into "rooms in a different house," I found an opportunity to include "the mother's voice" in a traditional Roman Catholic ceremony where the language and traditions honor only "the father's voice."

The young couple became engaged on Thanksgiving, 1997, and set their wedding date for Halloween, 1998. The dates' meanings were not lost on me, nor was the significance of nearing the end of the century—and the millennium. I knew that we were in deeply liminal time. Further, I could not ignore my own and my family's patterns of "not doing transition well." I remembered how my mother had deteriorated once my brothers and I left home. From where I stood in the family line, I saw a long history of unhappily negotiated transitions, with the life-death-life spiral incomplete in most of the stories I knew.

I decided to enact re-association by writing my way through transition rather than continuing our patterns of dissociation and attendant depression, addiction, and broken relationships. In my regular "listening within" time each morning, a series of poems began to emerge. I eventually called it "100 Verses on Your Leaving."

#36

Nearing fifty, I dream and feel in archetypes, in particular:
caves, also the moon, and distant mountains.
At the same time, oh how I love my small life:
peonies' drooping elegance, my blue-veined,
but sturdy hand, reaching mango slices to my lips
on a late-spring day.

How would this translate to you, nearing 24, son?

It would have consoled me to hear someone I loved
say evenings can be as sweet, even as thrilling
as the morning you stand so joyfully in.

#37

This conundrum: when are words to
your children a gift? When are they burden?

#38

On the radio yesterday Edward Ball
and Steve Roberts of my generation pleaded
the case of remembering as vividly
as our parents' generations
executed the sentence of forgetting.

The writing I did through this liminal time had consequences. Most visibly, but not most importantly, it paved my way to a piece of long memory for the wedding.

All Hallows Eve: October 31, 1998

Dear Jayna and Colin,

You have chosen to marry on the final day
of one of the final months—not only of the year
and the century—but of what we construe
as the millennium.

On a holyday called: All Hallows Eve,
Day of the Dead, and as Samhain,
celebrated by the Celts as New Year's Eve,
a sacred day when the ancestors returned to earth
and each family lit their hearth from a common flame,
bonding all the families of the village together.

Dear son, new daughter, you are our common flame,
the light of our shared lives, the harvest of our love,
your wedding day a doorway open to your ancestors,
those:

Brosmers, Oxenders, Contis,
Pierces, Brattons, Northrups,
Bernhards, Caliendos,

generations of whom you are the flower today,
shining in your bloom of youth and hope.

You are our doorway to the millennium.
You carry forth in your bodies, more importantly,
in your hearts, the promises we made to ourselves
when we stood at the beginning of our lives, our marriages.

Dearest ones, I wish you the wisdom to accept
in your time being the root, as now you glory
in being the flower.

I cannot wish you facile happiness, an easy life—
a condo by the seashore, children with orthodontia—
I can only wish you the life you have, and what you make
of what falls into it.

Above all, I wish you the knowing that you are not alone,
not even in your loneliest hour, for you stand in an unbroken
circle of ancestors. Our wisdom, our folly,

our love, even our failures to love,
are yours to draw from, make your lives,
your marriage from.
With all my love,
Mom

Mary Caliendo Andrews Pierce Brosmer

Of far greater importance than the product of my yearlong process is that I established a new pattern: transition, which always involves loss, can be an occasion for reinvention, for spiritual growth, for joy. I am convinced, though, that the meaning-making and reinvention (called variously in this book: re-association, healing, connection) that corrects can only be perceived within the context of a conscious community. I can only "see" what I'm making against the backdrop of a container of those others, a family of writers, all of us learning to write new stories, learning to make change without making war.

Exercise 11-4: Consciously Connecting

1. Invite a group of trusted others, no more than three, to write about family. Ask each to bring a family photo. Set your timer and ask everyone to write freely for five minutes to the prompt: "What I see there . . ." Now write for five minutes to the prompt, "What I don't see there . . ."

   In a read-around (see chapter 9), invite each person to show the photo and then read as little as one sentence, or as much as the entire writing. Encourage group members to listen deeply, write down strong words from each participant and then read them into the circle. Insist upon no advice-giving, no critique, no pressure to "publish," no empty praise.

Have some gentle conversation together about how it felt to write and to be heard in community.

2. Spend your next writing appointment remembering the gathering and noticing any changes in your voice and sense of connection to others.

12.

Weaving the Social Fabric

If you don't know the kind of person I am
and I don't know the kind of person you are
a pattern that others made may prevail in the world
and following the wrong god home we may miss our star.
William Stafford[1]

It's hard to imagine someone else's life.
Robert Pack[2]

My working title for this chapter has been "Weaving the Social Fabric," but as I enter the writing and see the words atop the page, I note that they do not capture the reality I have experienced and want to explore, which is to say:

♦   I am not nostalgic for a time when a healthy fabric of community existed, and has since frayed. I read History, and experience my small "h" history as betraying scant evidence of people gathered in the fullness of their gifts.

♦   I observe that the dream of authentic community is rarely real-
    ized and even more rarely sustained. I theorize authentic com-
    munities will be realized and sustained only when we create
    conscious containers in which all truths can be told and the
    values of the feminine are integrated with those of the hyper-
    dominant masculine.

Along with economist Bernard Lietaer, I define community as a
"group of people who welcome and honor my gifts, and from
whom I can reasonably expect to receive gifts in return."[3] When I
read his interview with editor Sarah van Gelder in *Yes!* magazine,
I discovered words for much that I had intuited in my work with
Women Writing for (a) Change communities.

> *Sarah*: So fear of scarcity creates greed and hoarding, which in
> turn creates the scarcity that was feared. Whereas cultures that
> embody the Great Mother are based on abundance and generos-
> ity. Those ideas are implicit in the way you've defined commu-
> nity, are they not?
>
> *Bernard*: Actually, it's not my definition; it's etymological.
> The origin of the word "community" comes from the Latin
> *munus*, which means the gift, and *cum*, which means together,
> among each other. So community literally means to give among
> each other.
>
> Therefore I define my community as a group of people who
> welcome and honor my gifts, and from whom I can reasonably
> expect to receive gifts in return.[4]

Reading this interview was a much-needed experience of feeling not alone, and not crazy in my intuition that our survival as a
species depends on creating new cells, and nurturing the new cells
into systems where all people can be with (*cum*) one another and
all their gifts (*munus*).

Exercise 12-1: Communities: Then and Now

1. *Early Life:* Set your timer for five minutes and jot a quick
    list of places you lived and learned about community in
    your early life, e.g., your hometown, your grade school, lit-
    tle league team, brownie troop, temple, or congregation.

    Choose one place from your list and, setting the timer for
    ten minutes, remember in words the vision or mission of

this organization or place and ways it was and wasn't realized.

Read the piece aloud to yourself or to a designated listener or listeners. Ask for read-backs only. See what conversations ensue about community life, its gifts and challenges.

2. *Current Life:* Set your timer for five minutes and jot a quick list of places you currently live and learn about community, e.g., your home, work, faith community, or book group.

   Choose one and, setting the timer for ten minutes, remember in words the dream or mission of this organization or place and the ways it is and isn't realized.

   Read the piece aloud to yourself, or to a designated listener or listeners. Ask for read-backs only. See what conversations emerge about community life, its gifts and challenges.

   Explore these questions in a ten-minute fast-write:

   ♦　What is my part in this?

   ♦　How am I contributing to the community's authenticity or inauthenticity?

   ♦　What patterns from my early experience of community do I want to conserve?

   ♦　What patterns from my early experience of community to I want to surrender and not repeat?

Trying to Bridge Early and Current Life: A Story

My hometown newspaper, *The Crestline Advocate*, often features news of former residents in town to visit, with accompanying information about what they are doing with their lives since leaving Crestline. Particular attention is given to sports standouts and their playing and coaching careers. Since I have a longtime dream of growing WWf(a)C communities in small towns such as the one in which I grew up, I made an appointment with the editor of the *Advocate* some weeks before a visit home, hoping a mention of "what I was doing with my life since leaving" might plant a seed.

Journal Entry, April 12, 2004

Hard not to find this unsettling: the Editor of the Advocate blowing off our appointment. What I notice: the difficulty of being generous given a depleted supply of self-regard and self-confidence, triggered by being in a place where I had so little for so long. I was struggling to be civil to the receptionist who, it turned out, was related to a childhood friend, but I can't remember how exactly. The woman stuck with telling me her boss, the Editor, was not in, despite our long-standing appointment of Monday, 10:00 am.

I did not want to be "the bitch from the city," but I couldn't find the resources to be my usual warm, reassuring self either. Breathing into my old hurt and anger about not mattering here, being alien here for reasons I never fully understood, fighting the drowning-in-it feeling, I recovered enough to muster a "we all make mistakes" remark, though my heart wasn't in it.

I'm writing this in the McDonald's on the site of the old Garverick Funeral home, across from St. Joseph. Growing up Catholic gives you some landmarks, it occurs to me, as the old church, the school, convent, and rectory are among the least changed in an evolution in the town, which is more accurately, to my eye, a devolution. Truck traffic on Route 30, the Lincoln Highway, another constant. I feel sad, shaken, which is better than hypnotized, in a trance of impotence, which—without writing—I might have drowned in.

Writing my way out of the trance of impotence was "the third way" of coping; the only others I had known were giving up or going down fighting. Engaging the third way as a practice of rewiring my interior system enables me to create external systems. In the process, I am learning that emergent communities are both healthier and more chaotic. Dee Hock labels the new way of being in the world "chaordic" and predicates our survival as a species on our ability to dance, as it were, with chaos.

Chaord 1. Any self-organizing, self-governing, adaptive, nonlinear, complex organism, organization, community, or system, whether physical, biological, or social, the behavior of which harmoniously combines characteristics of both chaos and order. 2. An entity whose behavior exhibits observable patterns and probabilities not governed or explained by its constituent parts.[5]

What I have to add to the conversation about chaordic and self-generative systems of communities—to the point of near-stridency because it is the piece most often disregarded—is the necessity of stewarded containers and boundaried spaces or environments in which old and emerging patterns can be witnessed. Another "third way" is thus enabled. Members of a family, church, or any other organization, who are able to witness both the traditional and the revolutionary, can hold the life-giving properties of each. Oh, how I dream of a time when futile culture wars with their propaganda machines are marginalized by the profusion of culture incubators able to nurture a rich diversity of truth and meaning!

Writing as a practice of self-creation within conscious community produces what evolutionary biologists call imaginal cells, genetic communicators of new life forms. Below are some stories about how imaginal cells emerged in the nutritive soup of my life's work to fashion diverse, conscious communities.

Deep Diversity

When I began WWf(a)C, I set an intention to work with integrity and open-heartedness, envisioning an engaged and conscious hospitality that would make everyone feel welcome. This was no great stretch for me, given to extroversion and what my mother called "common sense, which isn't so common!"

While this may seem naive, how else, except by actions over time, does someone prove that she is trustworthy? I was—and am—aware that black women may well mistrust a white woman, or lesbian women mistrust a straight woman, but doing intentional and transparent work is the path I choose. Luckily, this path is also the path of learning and of collaboration. "My path" has been informed and affected by the presence and honesty of the many who share their insights as we go about creating WWf(a)C.

Years ago, I attended a read-around, a gathering in which women read their work aloud with an audience of invited guests (see chapter 9). Because my colleague was holding the circle, I was able to observe and listen differently than when I convened the group. The writing was diverse in genre, tone, and subject matter. Funny pieces gave way to tender pieces, to sad, even tragic stories and poems. I felt fed, as if I had received a "Eucharist of Truth." Young women, midlife women, grandmothers, businesswomen, lesbian mothers, stay-at-home mothers, clergy, divorced, happily married, newly-in-love women, widows, two survivors of incest, a therapist, women of means, women from impoverished back-grounds—all this and more was revealed in the writing. It was truly, not tritely, kaleidoscopic in that the words came together, and could be rearranged into an astonishing array of insights and experiences.

After the reading, I sat in the circle feeling the effects of the words while the audience stepped across the hall for social time and refreshments. Still catching my emotional breath, I overheard a woman say, "It was nice, but there's not enough diversity here for me." I wanted to scream at her, "Were you listening?" A white woman, a university professor, our guest had reduced "diversity" to skin color alone, for, to her evident disapproval, she saw mostly light-skinned women.

In my journal the next morning I used the words *deep diversity* for the first time. I offer them here, not as a replacement for more traditional projects of multiculturalism, but as an alternative, which I have found to be a powerful resource for peacemaking. In deep diversity, we look beyond the important but only partial iden-tifiers of "who we are and where we come from," and begin to explore the many traits that separate us and bind us. Deep diversi-ty opens a wider space for witnessing layered histories of ethnici-ty, race, gender, status, trauma, and religion; outsider-ship, insider-ship, and more. Deep diversity is chaordic—ordered and chaotic, and always greater than its constituent parts.

Muriel Rukeyser wrote, "What would happen if one woman told the truth about her life? The world would split open."[6] I believe that when many people tell the deeply diverse truths of their lives, worlds can come together in ways yet to be fully expe-rienced. In a conscious container, people *can* learn to "imagine one another's lives."

In their early, pre-orthodoxy-setting-in days, I was an enthusi-astic participant in liberal projects of multiculturalism, embracing strategies for widening and deepening conversation and learning across differences in race, class, gender, and sexual orientation. As a high school teacher of American (read: U.S.) literature, I grew painfully aware of the absence of diverse voices in the anthologies prescribed by the curriculum. I had long ago tired of the worship of the high modern trinity, Hemingway-Fitzgerald-Faulkner. I was bored with deadly dull essays on the "meaning of whiteness in Moby Dick." The creativity and learning required to include women, contemporary poets, people of color, working class and emerging writers energized and excited me—and my students.

As I increased my participation in multiculturalism in both civic and academic settings, I began to experience a sad and disappointing phenomenon. Almost without exception, attempts to communicate across and *about* difference resulted in deeper mistrust and further wounding! I saw people retreating into either paralysis or hyperactivity, some voices muted by fear of inadvertently offending, and other voices holding forth in self-righteous—and intimidating—rhetoric. Angry women shouted, "You just don't get it" to men, without benefit of stories to help the men get it. Angry African-Americans said, "It's a black thing, you wouldn't understand." People comfortable with the status quo sputtered, "You're trying to take something away from us that makes us uniquely American."

An (Unfortunately) Typical Story

In what became something of a typical situation for me in this phase of my learning, I was the only white woman in what was billed as a "Women Talking About Race" workshop. The session facilitator, a well-known diversity consultant, opened with a glib, "It's not my job to educate white people." One of the Buddhist tools I admire and try to practice is to substitute interest for anger, so I took my courage—and my anger—in my shaky hands, and asked the facilitator to say more about her statement and why it seemed appropriate to today's gathering, in which no one had yet betrayed an attitude of entitlement to be taught.

This was one of many times I saw spaces for learning closed by rhetoric and by experts *telling* what is acceptable or not acceptable. Oh, for the words of William Stafford in these moments: "If you don't know the kind of person I am and I don't know the kind of person you are, a pattern others made may prevail in the world." Amen. A pattern oppressors made prevails in projects in which we all seek liberation from oppression. Many people, especially those already worried about loss of their place if "we" let "others" in, flee shamed, defensive, and confirmed in their fears and prejudices. In their terror, they form the opposite of imaginal cells, or "terrorist cells," which we see constellating in talk radio ranters, defenders of the white race, Hillary-haters, and our own domestic brand of anti-modernity thuggery.

The Secret in Plain Sight: Means and Ends

As I contemplate the traditional/liberal project of multiculturalism, I recognize a taint: the misalignment between means and ends. We cannot achieve justice using unjust means, and it is patently unjust—and counterproductive—to bring people to a table where some are entitled to speak because they belong to a group historically oppressed, and others are silenced because they belong to the oppressor class (and vice versa, of course).

In theory, this may seem to even the score in a game in which, historically and systemically, men have had—and have—far more social privilege than women, whites than blacks, straights than gays. But in practice, as a practice, we must acknowledge the historical and systemic privilege *and* we must acknowledge and shift present-time, present-moment oppression, in order to build healing and healthy communities.

How painful and dispiriting it is to observe that as efforts to build multicultural understanding have increased, so have cultural divides and culture wars. I do not believe there is a simple cause-and-effect relationship here, analogous to those who claim that *women's efforts to free ourselves are the cause of violence against women*. Of course, there is backlash when the oppressed no longer want to serve the oppressors, but it is not the FAULT of the ones who want to be free. On the other hand, when liberating projects use the same means that created oppression (silencing, shaming, making someone "the other" and therefore unable to be redeemed or included) more oppression—and more violence—is the end.

My experience with building conscious communities suggests that all group members must advocate for the practice of justice within the community they are creating. Such practices shape and sustain relationships of trust and integrity. I suggest four principles:

1. Members agree to share responsibility with the facilitator ("servant-holder" of the space) for creating safe (not comfortable, or squishy) learning containers, and for naming in others, and acknowledging in themselves, unjust or silencing practices.

2. Members agree to share their stories as stories, not as "The Truth," and without censoring what they fear "might give offense."

3. Members agree to learn to recognize our shifting roles as oppressor and oppressed, as opposed to clinging to a static identity as "always oppressed, never an oppressor."

4. No shaming!

I am *not* advocating avoidance of hard truths about race, class, gender, or ethnicity. Rather, I advocate ways of helping us reveal to one another our deepest longings for community, for love, for peace—as well as our deepest regrets about its absence in our lives. This work requires us to walk through trauma stories of every kind, in order to move beyond them. There must be care, consciousness, and compassion in the formation of leaders who do this work. I have been amazed and daunted by the ways in which some diversity leaders and experts "work out their own stuff," projecting their anger and unhealed pain into the container, which it is their job to hold for others.

All of us enter communities with complex histories of both oppressing and being oppressed, and I believe that by openly bringing this to the table we can progress beyond the years of bare-knuckled litigation, well-meaning and necessary activism, research and theorizing, and begin to achieve understanding.

Exercise 12-2: Diversity Non-Workshop

Throw a potluck. Invite members of a group to draw slips of paper on which are written courses for a community supper: appetizer, entree, side dish, bread, and dessert. Ask the participants to prepare the selected course in the culinary tradition of their home or place of origin.

As people gather, encourage informal conversation around food preparation, recipes, and traditions. Once all are gathered, ask them to hold an awareness of the diverse backgrounds which are resources for this meal and provide its flavors alongside very real and sometimes awkward, if not embarrassing, differences which emerge around food: meat-eaters and vegans, fried food lovers and the fat-phobic, lovers of the spicy-hot alongside those who can't tolerate hot food. Note aloud that allergies and other health challenges can raise the stakes quite a bit.

After the meal, convene a circle in which you ask people to write to a prompt from their life with food:

- Best memory of food preparation with a loved one;
- A story about too much or not enough food;
- A major food preparation fiasco;
- A holiday meal preparation.

Hold a read-around (see chapter 9) of these pieces followed by a conversation and appreciation of one another.

High Intimacy, Low Pressure for Outcomes

I find the emotionally straitjacketed quality of much diversity work distressing. The expert advice, given from on high, does not infiltrate our communities. We are pressured to avoid offence and have witnessed a backlash against inclusion, e.g., accusations of political correctness. How little celebration there is, and how much confrontation! The goal of building connection and compassion does not align with the means: accusation and shaming.

Community, compassion, or even tolerance—that rather stingy virtue—cannot be mandated. However, we can create the conditions in which intimacy and compassion can emerge, thereby weaving a more whole cloth of social fabric. Repeatedly, I have witnessed compassion, connection, and creativity grow in the presence of these conditions: stories, the space for holding them, and a quality of attention, which I both label as feminine and insist that men can also manifest. While the feminine quality of care and attention is often overlooked, excluded, taken for granted, ridiculed as "touchy-feely," and mistrusted in public spaces, I propose that this quality of care and attention, so vital to bringing new life into the world, is essential for the health and well-being of diverse communities and the planet.

In closing, I pay tribute to that quality of attention I am privileged to witness daily in the person of my life partner, Thomas Keller.

Watching the Dead on Television While Eating Supper

October 2006
for Tom

"It is difficult to get the news from poems,
yet each day men die horribly from lack of
what is found there."
William Carlos Williams[7]

You lay down your fork and come to attention.
Someone not paying attention would miss it,
but I attend to your
no-fail attention, so frail
in the realm of what can be done.

Each evening the line of faces grows longer.

My attention falters and I mutter
"sweet Jesus, only 19 . . ."
"that one could be a grandfather . . ."
impatient for it to be over.

You lay down your fork,
food cools
time deepens
October is closing.

We are closing in on four years
of a war to bring freedom to Iraq.

Bodies stacked in Baghdad morgues
and loaded in secret onto troop planes
are free of souls, the only mission accomplished.
Each evening the line of faces grows longer.

Impatient for it to be over,
I remember other missions:
wars to end all wars
ones to stop the spread of communism
the one in Afghanistan to find Osama bin Laden,
protect women from the Taliban.

What would my father think
of his war, the one to thwart fascism
if he could see our president on television.

Our president's attention falters,
he says he never said
stay the course.
He does pay attention

to critics
to the need for a new direction
in Iraq, that his mission is now,
and always has been
freedom

Each evening the line of faces grows longer.

We eat fall foods: soups and stews,
ripe pears, an apple cake,
Soon Thanksgiving recipes will appear
in newspapers.
Each evening the line of faces grows . . .
I see your mission, my love,
how it is now and always
has been, attention.
Each day men
and women
die horribly for lack
of what is found there.

13.

Revitalizing the World of Work

Look at
what passes for the new.
You will not find it there but in
despised poems.
It is difficult
to get the news from poems
yet men die miserably every day
for lack
of what is found there.

William Carlos Williams

In fragile health and knowing he was at the end of his life,
William Carlos Williams wrote the long poem "Asphodel,
That Greeny Flower"[1] to his wife of many years who had
endured his neglect and his many adulteries. "Asphodel" is a love
poem, but the lines above are very often used, as I used them in the
poem at the end of the previous chapter, in the context of the
tragedy and futility of war.

The world of work is, more often than not, a world where women and men die horribly for lack of what is found in "despised poems" as well: patterns, purpose, meaning, beauty, and feeling. The comparison between "death by war" and "death by work" is furthered when you consider the language used in places where we gather to accomplish things. We wage sales and advertising campaigns, roll out the big guns, hammer the competition, engage in hostile takeovers, and launch initiatives.

Recently, I participated in a meditation workshop in which a very nice man asked the teacher how a "financial warrior" such as himself could "advance" in a practice without competition—without knowing whether he was winning or losing? *How is just being present valued? Measured?* he seemed to be asking, sincerely perplexed.

As I am writing this, in the fall of 2008, we are witnessing a version of the aphorism "those who live by the sword, perish by the sword," played out in the U.S. economy. Unfortunately it is not only, nor probably even very much, the financial warriors who will perish, as they bail out with golden parachutes, while those in passenger class, the modern equivalent of steerage, go down with the plane. The warriors, understandably, have resisted, with all the energy and resources at their disposal, efforts to create workplaces which are about more than winning and losing, or about the creation of true and sustainable wealth, not just machines for the making of money. (An Armenian carpet-weaver-mentor of my husband used to say, "Boys, you can't eat money!") Nor can you assuage the very real hungers I name above, hungers for meaning and purpose with the hopelessly entangled patterns and meaningless language still dominating the world of work. The fire of that world is going out, starved of the oxygen of inspiration and aspiration, dying *for want of better words.*

It's not surprising how often people in our consulting and other containers use breathing metaphors:

♦ I'm realizing I've been holding my breath for ten years . . .

♦ In this container, I can be vulnerable and breathe at the same time.

♦ I am paying attention. As I catch myself becoming the opposite of what I want to be, losing sight of the path I thought I was on, I am in this moment taking a long-overdue deep breath . . .

Wanting Better Words

People are hungry,
and one good word is bread
for a thousand.

David Whyte[2]

I dislike rolling around in generalizations and judgments about what are "good" and "bad" words. However, since I believe that better words will create the better world we so radically need, let me get to it. I think I have been clear about the better world I'm working and writing toward: hospitable to life, generous, honest, connected, inclusive of body, mind, heart, and spirit; inclusive of the knowable and the mysterious, the abstract and the concrete. The "good words" we are in want of are not necessarily eloquent; cleverness is cute, but doesn't get us far; edgy makes more war. The good words are hospitable in that they really *are* meant to be understood: bold vs. fine print. They are generous with self and story; they are transparent and earnest, honest, ample. In the lexicon of good and bad I'm developing here, the good words open us to possibility and learning because they are not "know-everything-for-certain" words. They are consolation to our own failings and imperfections; they do not put a brave face on a mess, nor do they gloss over sadness and failure. And good words embody the breath and voice of a real person, someone authentically seeking connection, not the voice of the ephemeral Oz, the man (or woman) behind the screen.

Three E-mails That Made Me Cry

1. From Karen, author of four published novels, who is currently suffering with cancer. Although I have only met her twice, she writes:

   Dear Mary,

   Forgive my delay in responding to your lovely letter. My body and I are at war, which means I only get to write when my body is feeling up to tolerating my need to change all this chaos into words.

   I am sorry to have missed your visit to class. I was just meeting the enemy at that point. This is a stealthy nemesis. The only reason I wasn't there is that I couldn't move, literally. It is so touching for you to have taken the time to write to me.

You have written a beautiful book. I can hardly wait to read the whole work.

Anyway, may whatever heaven is, send concrete blessings to you and the miracle you have helped make reality. In my own little circle, I saw women connect with their voices. More important, I saw the transformation in their entire bodies when they believe they've been heard. For good or ill.

Let me know if, and how, I can help.

Thank you again for creating a sanctuary where a jaded cynic like me could reawaken the love of turning energy into metaphor that strikes the tuning fork in the minds of others. I have remembered why I loved writing.

Love, best wishes,
Karen

2. From the CEO of an organization which supports women and girls. We have known each other for several years and have worked together on leadership and gender issues. She responded to an e-mail I sent inviting her to an afternoon experience of our Feminist Leadership Academy, as her organization "launches an initiative" to study leadership programs for women and girls that Women Writing for (a) Change has been creating since before her organization began.

Mary, yes, I know about the FLA and when the team that will work on gathering the information/details about existing programs gets started they will connect with you to gather the background, measurements, outcomes etc. as they compile an assessment of what exists in our region.

Thank you for the invitation to this weekend's program but I won't be able to attend.

3. From a representative-leader of an international organization for promoting change through the creation of learning communities and the cultivation of emotional and spiritual intelligence in the workplace. This e-mail was sent to consultants, with requests for proposals (RFPs) for work with a corporate client in the midst of a change effort. I have substituted different acronyms to protect identities.

NRPCD is in the midst of a significant effort to decentralize staff and decision-making in an effort to get closer to their clients. A major thrust of this work is to improve their approach to . . . the deployment of an FRP system that will enable tracking and sharing of information.

A recent pilot has validated the usefulness of FRP; however, there were significant challenges in getting pilot participants to quickly and fully adopt the technology.

The resistance seen on the part of some users has highlighted the critical importance of having a change management strategy as part of the deployment plan for FRP. NRPCD is looking for a partner to design and implement a structured framework and set of tools for change management as part of the project.

Why Cry?

I don't think I'm comparing apples and oranges here: all three correspondents are from my work world, and share my concern for the health of organizations and the people in them. That said, reading the first e-mail opened my heart; tears of empathy and gratitude poured onto my desk for Karen, and for the universality of fragility and vulnerability. Reading the second e-mail from a woman with whom I share feminist values, and the third e-mail from a man with whom I connect in learning-community consulting work, I wept as well.

After reading e-mail #2, I cried tears of frustration. I feel completely helpless when faced with participation in a world where "information" and "data outcomes" and blah, blah, blah trump living programs—while Rome burns. Data is to community as lungs are to fish: Data is worse than useless in community, while healthy leadership thrives in community.

After reading e-mail #3, I wept again; frustration, disappointment— even despair—filled me. How will we ever create community, which in turn creates abundance in work and the world, when we are using the tools which destroyed community: sterile, relationally distancing, almost autistic language—the jargon of the in-crowd?

Belonging

I swore, once I got me
a job where I could eat

regular, I'd never *look*
at beans and cornbread
again, long as I live,

nor scratch in the garden,
back near broke enough from
all day in the mine, then
to have to hoe them rows
of Ma's peppers and corn,

and used to think I'd die
of solemness sitting on
the porch listening to folks
swapping stories of
this strike, that cave-in
the time in 01 when
the old man run for mayor
of Buchtel on the Socialist
ticket—and got three votes.

Must be getting senile,
sitting here fat and comfortable
in Columbus, for damned
if it ain't true—

I'm longing for
a pot of beans,
pan of cornbread,
garden to work evenings,
and the soft sound of folks'
voices spilling off the porch
into the darkness.

I take the stories and the voice of "Belonging" from my father's brother, Raphael Allison "Mike" Pierce. Uncle Mike always told of the winter the old man, his father, Albert Chapman Pierce, got a deal on a fifty-pound bag of beans. He'd tell how, walking home from school, he and cousin Zella Pierce Coakley took turns posing the question, "What do you suppose we're having for supper?" before shouting in unison, "More damn beans!"

In September 1986, retired from his job as a mechanic at the Depot, an Army warehouse in Columbus, Ohio, Uncle Mike spent evenings writing stories longhand in a ledger:

> I was born in Cannelville, Muskingum County, Ohio, on Feb. 28, 1915, a legitimate son of Albert C. Pierce, a coalmine electrician, and Zella Mae Pierce (nee Andrews) housewife.

> Mining then was a brutal, man killing, maiming job & still is, despite many improvements that have been made in these later years.

> My father was a many faceted man. He was talented far above the average miner. In looking back it seems to me that very many times he was on the verge of becoming a moderately wealthy man but always his impatience caused him to draw back and try something else. I'm well aware that hindsight is much surer than foresight but it always seemed to me that he lacked that spark that drives men foreword.

> My mother was a saint among women. She must have been to have put up with dad and we kids.

> To anyone who might read this journal, much is fact, some hearsay & rumor. I guess I'm trying to depict a boy & man & his life as I remember it. I know that's boring to most—but just what is exciting about a below average person trying to write about his life?

> I don't have that biblical outlook on life, that is to raise Cain as long as I'm able (too old), nor do I have a dog's outlook on life & that is "anything you can't eat or screw, piss on it." I just don't fit either category—you take it from there.

I am the fortunate steward of Uncle Mike's memoir because his wife, Aunt Millie, called me into their kitchen on a visit and whispered, "Mike wants you to read this but he won't admit it. Take it before he destroys it, he keeps threatening to burn it because he thinks his writing is so bad. Save it for the family." I took the ledger home in a grocery sack, deeply grateful for the stories and further awed by one passage about halfway through the fifty or so handwritten pages: "Mary, I want you to know that even though your Aunt Millie was married to her first husband, Floyd, when we first met, she was a single woman, free and clear when we got together as a couple." In this sentence Uncle Mike paid me the honor of being his imagined audience, the listener who made his speech possible.

What I Want to Say About All That

Decades of at first unconscious, later deeply conscious and intentional, experiences have contributed to my certainty that the *sound of folks' voices spilling* into receptive space, their stories about life at and outside work are unalloyed gold. Largely unmined, or given only lip service in successive and largely futile projects of *re-engineering* and *quality-controlling,* stories transform workers into subjects rather than the passive, and understandably resistant, objects of workplace change efforts. I am stepping out onto a very sturdy limb here to claim that writing in consciously-held and regularly-stewarded workplace communities can significantly contribute to:

- ◆ Improved safety conditions;
- ◆ Product and process innovation;
- ◆ Improved retention of workers;
- ◆ Effective teams for project management;
- ◆ Orientation of new workers;
- ◆ Effective integration of culturally diverse team members;
- ◆ Cross-generational learning and communication;
- ◆ Capturing the intellectual capital and tacit learning of retiring workers;
- ◆ Effectiveness of policy-making groups and task forces;
- ◆ Re-educating workers for new jobs; and
- ◆ Creating a start-up business.

And this is just the short list.

Therapy for Organizations

At a convocation on social entrepreneurship at Denison University in Granville, Ohio, I heard consultant Kate Harkin say that organizational development work is something akin to being a therapist for organizations. I agree. Writing for (a) Change Consulting, a.k.a. Consulting for (a) Change, emerged from the Women Writing for (a) Change movement as a community of practitioners devoted to helping to create health and well-being in the groups with whom we are honored to work. Buckminster Fuller observed that the most powerful way to effect change is to introduce new tools.[3] We bring to the various tables we are invited to join as many skills as possible, and support organizations learning to use the tools of writing in community to revitalize their cultures.

Exercise 13-1: What's Really Happening?

Gather a group of people with whom you are working on a project. As an alternative to the usual telling of "war stories" in the break room or after work on Friday at the bar, ask each person to write a story a day for five days.

Help make this happen by brainstorming possible times and places: take five minutes at the end of the work day and write your story; write it before you go to bed; or write in the morning, remembering something that happened the day before. Or, as a group, or in partners, commit to a cup of coffee during a break or after work, and write together.

At week's end, hold a read-around of stories from the week. In this intentional reading and listening to stories, the group will begin to see patterns. This "narrative research" puts flesh on both what is working and what is not working, but do not use the read-around time to fix problems or make decisions. Sit with the stories just for their own sake and then gradually begin to gather the solutions and insights they present (see exercise 13-2).

Wasting

In *Birth of the Chaordic Age,* Dee Hock quotes Machiavelli's *The Prince*:

> As the doctors say of a wasting disease, to start with, it is easy to cure but difficult to diagnose. After a time, unless it has been diagnosed and treated at the outset, it becomes easy to diagnose but difficult to cure. So it is in politics.[4]

So it can be with organizations. With advanced age, and distanced from their conceptions in the imagination of a founder or founders, or within the exigencies and ethos of a different era, organizations waste away. Some should be allowed to die, but that is another discernment all together. Organizational therapists are typically engaged because wasting disease manifests itself in symptoms such as low morale, low profits, scandal, loss of creativity or innovation, and the inability to retain workers.

To my mind, one of the most common, wasteful, and ineffective ways to work with organizations is the default approach of most consultants: A study is commissioned. Hours are spent interviewing either individuals, focus groups, or a combination of both. Without context and conducted in isolation from colleagues, the stories are typically little more than complaints hedged in cover-your-ass org-speak and reduced to data that is then presented to managers or CEOs.

"See that top shelf over there?" a client once asked, pointing to a bookcase opposite his desk filled with spiral-bound tomes. "That's the most expensive—and I do *not* mean the most valuable—thing in this room. Every consultant who comes in here to help us with the fact that we're not getting the traffic we need to make this concept work conducts a study, then presents the findings at a much-anticipated meeting of stakeholders."

"And then what do you do?"

"Well, first we pay the bill, then we put the book on the shelf and go back to business as usual. The only time we remember the project is when someone brings up how much we paid for it, and how it didn't do us a bit of good."

When we probe into past organizational therapy gone down the budgetary drain with other poor investments, we hear variations on, "We couldn't get the fill-in-the-blank staff/workers/nurses/doctors/teachers/hourly guys behind it." Probing further about what "it" is, we learn a new formula for excellence or fiscal discipline recommended by the researchers, who have most likely taken the formula down from another expensive shelf somewhere and transplanted it, with little attention to methods for integrating and sustaining the proposed solutions. If I decipher e-mail #3 correctly, it points to an example of just such a situation. A new system of decision-making was instituted, workers "resisted," and now a "change management" effort is needed. This appears to be an example of the cart before the horse, who by now has metamorphosed into a mule, stubbornly resisting yet another in a long line of changes suggested by experts who likely never pulled a cart in their lifetimes. I speculate quite a different outcome, and quite a different system would have emerged had the horses gathered and shared their stories of cart-pulling, which were then used to inform the change effort.

The problem is always the people; the solution is another study, followed by purchase of the system *du jour*, communicated in pot-boiler jargon to the growing-more-cynical-by-the-minute workers. Several clients, especially in the nonprofit world, note that it is easier to find funding for studies where the end result is a product—a book on a shelf, or a set of recommendations—than to fund ongoing learning in community that does not fit funding cycles and is not easily measured. Everyone knows the definition of insanity: doing the same thing over and over and expecting different results.[5] Is it any wonder that most of us repeatedly ask one another and ourselves Dee Hock's questions:

♦   Why are institutions, everywhere, whether political, commercial, or social, increasingly unable to manage their affairs?
♦   Why are individuals, everywhere, increasingly in conflict with and alienated from the institutions of which they are part?
♦   Why are society and the biosphere increasingly in disarray?[6]

I offer a tentative answer: In most projects and in the leadership of these projects for change and healing we reproduce:

♦   Misalignment of means and ends;
♦   Suppression of meaning and feeling from public life;
♦   Reinforcement of that suppression by communicating in cold, empty, abstract language; and
♦   Disconnection from the vision and life stories that gave birth to the organization.

That suppression of expression in an organization goes against its very essence is apparent when you consider that the word itself is a variation on *organ*: an instrument for the expression of music and of life. An organization is a variant of an *organism*. An organism expresses its life through various organs, is organic, that is to say, growing out of its authentic self. Tragically, organizations have broken faith with their origins in this paradigm and have thrown in their lot with the false belief that they are machines, and "their people" are the replaceable parts.

Jungian Helen Luke warned that "when the means become autonomous, evil results."[7] We have ample evidence of the deadly immorality of organizations that were once the means to serving human needs, and now—in too many cases—have become ends in themselves, devouring the world's resources at a seemingly unstoppable pace. Rarely do I meet a person who believes that he or she has any power over, or within, an organization.

In "The Instruments," one of many poems using images of musical instruments, Rumi writes, "Without you the instruments would only die." In the thirteenth century, this wise poet-mystic knew something about the proper relationship between cart and horse, and about the possibility of beauty and love interwoven into work.

> Today, like every other day, we wake up empty
> and frightened. Don't open the door to the study
> and begin reading. Take down a musical instrument.
> Let the beauty we love be what we do.
> There are hundreds of ways to kneel and kiss the ground.[8]

Exercise 13-2:
What Did We Learn From What's Really Happening?

Once again, gather the group of colleagues who agreed to write stories. Do a ten-minute timed writing to the following questions:

- ◆ What surprised you most about what you heard when we read our stories at the last session?
- ◆ What seems to be working in how we work together?
- ◆ What needs work?

Invite writers to share their entire pieces, an excerpt, or allow them to pass. Discuss the themes that seem to be emerging among the stories.

Together, plan how to sustain this community. How or when might the learning point to experiments for improvements or change in your shared work life?

14.

The Planet Passing Through Us

We are living on the knife's edge of one of those rare and momentous turning points in human history. Livable lives for our grandchildren, their children, and their children's children hang in the balance.

Dee Hock[1]

. . . There is no calamity which right words will not begin to redress.

Ralph Waldo Emerson[2]

Where Are We Going?

The question grips
my grandmother's heart.

With so much—
Going

So little
We

By the time
my grandboys
are grown
will there be any

Where?

A reflection on the possibilities of *writing, women, and conscious community* as tools for healing our relationship with the planet places me on a knife's edge sharp with paradox. Nearly frozen, I must force myself to stop stewing and *just start writing*—the teacher takes her own oft-given advice!

I wrote the little poem that serves as epigraph for this chapter in response to a prompt offered by Ink Tank, an urban literary arts organization, in collaboration with the Cincinnati metro bus service. Writers were asked to compose a short poem in response to the question, "Where are we going?" Winning entries were to be posted in buses. The many ways into the question engaged me. Unexpectedly but not too surprisingly, the little grieving poem conveys the constancy of going, fixing, doing, and thinking—what my mother would call "running around like chickens with our heads cut off." I believe our incessant activity destroys and defiles the *where*, our planet.

Exercise 14-1: Being with Place

As preparation, read this excerpt about a visit to a restored medieval garden in Orsan, France:

> I sit down on a bench of braided twigs at the end of a long green walkway and observe the harmonious play of lines. The sun is shining, giving depth to the lines. I am slowly overtaken by a sense of peace.
>
> First I notice the birds and then the wind in the silver mobiles hanging from the branches of a few of the apple trees. My attention sharpens. Now I hear insects, bees and butterflies whirring around. Suddenly the sound of wind whispering in the distant trees reaches my ears.

I observe ever more intensely and my concentration grows more focused. It is as if I am hearing the sounds for the first time. Leaves rustle on the ground, then in the trees. A pigeon coos somewhere far off. *My observation is increasingly separated from my thoughts. I hear and see more and think less* (emphasis added).

Peter Van Dijk[3]

Now, without getting caught up in finding the perfect place, choose a beautiful, natural space where you will sit or stand a while. Don't take your writing tools with you.

Set your intention to be in the place as lightly as possible, feeling your way into what it is to be *with* rather than *in*. I picture *in* as making a dent upon a place by your presence; *with* intrudes less.

Without trying to achieve a goal, see if you can be with this quality of presence long enough to experience the lessening of thinking. Allow the place to make a dent upon you. Avoid thinking about what you might write about this experience. Be *with* the space for at least fifteen minutes.

Now, go to your writing place, set a timer for ten minutes, and write to the prompts:

- In my standing still in the world, I received . . .
- In my standing still in the world, I gave . . .

Read your piece out loud. Plan at least two more pilgrimages to this place, which you have made literary by writing about it, not in the old way of bending it to your artist's will but in the way of allowing it to be with you and you with it.

Writing Biophilia?

Here, as best as I can articulate it, is my challenge: For reasons made clear in the bedrock stories of this book, I have a fierce devotion to language, truth telling, and stories as instruments of healing. I recognize the slippery slope of this belief within the context of culture, given how words often delude, mislead, and inflict outright violence. The slope turns to black ice when I try to explore how language might heal our alienation from nature. Philosophers and neuroscientists tell us that it was language itself that first set us out on the long journey away from nature. Assigning words to things gives us sometimes helpful, and sometimes disastrous, distance from our experiences.

The most persuasive, and to me, disturbing, account of the disruptive quality of language creation is put forth by Leonard Shlain in *The Alphabet Versus the Goddess*. After a trip to Mediterranean archeological sites in 1991, Shlain began to investigate the disappearance of the goddesses from the ancient western world.

> At nearly every Greek site we visited, [the guide] patiently explained that the shrines we stood before had originally been consecrated to a female deity. And, later, for unknown reasons, unknown persons reconsecrated them to a male one.[4]

Through extensive research and his experience as a vascular surgeon operating on carotid arteries supplying blood to the brain, Dr. Shlain proposes a neuro-anatomical hypothesis. He posits that alphabetic literacy, with its high level of abstraction and linear patterning, wires the human brain in ways that reinforce ascendancy of the linear, abstract, and predominantly masculine left hemisphere. Shlain's theory explains much about the intractability of masculine over feminine, men over women, thinking over feeling, and combat over cooperation.

Shlain's theory seems of particular importance as we negotiate environmental and economic crises balancing fewer and fewer viable options on a thinner and thinner knife's edge. The reliance on left-brain thinking generates a panicked and futile insistence on doing over being, on theory over practice, on research over re-creation, and on short-term tactics over sustainable vision. In the midst of what feels increasingly like madness, or impaired brain function, I am asking if we can create a practice of naming, i.e., writing, that can restore balance to the web of creation and to the "neural net" that is our brain.

We are told that Adam's naming of things in the Garden of Eden gave him dominion over the earth. I propose we develop practices of naming which give us *feeling with* our co-creatures, and help us cultivate biophilia—a love of life or living systems.[5] This would include but not be limited to:

♦ Understanding that concrete, patterned, experiential language, e.g., stories and poems, is more valuable than the impersonal, abstract, almost autistic language expected of "authorities" on our present crisis.

+   Supporting and funding conscious communities of on-the-ground creators-in-the-ruins, rather than putting most of our resources into traditional combat-oriented activism.

+   Cultivating leadership from the feminine, with girls and women as teachers and stewards, rather than the more common appropriation of "feminine paradigm" by men who become its experts and theorists.

Exercise 14-2: Looking for Clues

1. Return to an early memory of yourself in the out-of-doors. Who else is there? What do you see, hear, taste, touch, or smell? What do you feel in the scene?

    Set your timer for ten minutes. Write freely to and about this memory of place. Read the piece aloud to yourself or to a designated listener, asking for read-backs only.

    Then, write a reflection on the story that leads you to some insight into how you, given your experiences, can participate in a healthy connection to the planet.

2. Using the organizational practices described in chapters 8 and 9 of this book, invite several others into a circle to write and share stories of their lives in relationship to the natural world.

My Clues

In 2005 I wrote a poem from an early memory of being outdoors with my father and brothers. Now this poem points like a slightly bent twig toward a new paradigm, down a trail I might walk.

On His Birthday

For Earl Keith Pierce: coal-miner, bomber pilot,
railroad engineer, avid reader, Father.

The sons take to the woods,
wait for the sun to rise
on the pact they hatched
in darkness:

to honor their dead father—
eighty-five today had he lived—
by bagging turkeys, one for
each brother,

both remembering the
father who taught them
not the sport
but the sacredness
of the hunt.

The daughter takes to her desk,
waits for the sun
to rise on memories of her
father, their father
who, had he lived, would
be eighty-five this April day.

She remembers
his religion: honesty above all,
his prayer, the naming of things:
trillium
mayapple
dutchmen's breeches
black walnut,
sycamore, sugar maple
paw-paw, puffball.

She remembers the day
a walk in the woods
opened onto a carpet
of magic morels
along a creekbank
behind Clearfork Reservoir.

She remembers watching
their father watching them:
sons, daughter whooping
into the windfall
picking the golden

mushrooms, precious
even in those
greener days,
a full peck basket
to bear to their mother's kitchen.
She understands she lives
harvesting his teaching,

treasuring what is given.

A member of the baby boom generation, growing up working class in a small Ohio town, before air conditioning, I experienced the outside world of creeks, farm ponds, and large wooded tracts as "always there" open space, safe space. I was also the only daughter in a family of hunting men. Because I was the oldest of my siblings, the honorary son until my brothers came of age, I went to the woods with my father and he taught me to hunt for berries and mushrooms, wildflowers and greens to gather for my mother. These early alone-with-dad hunting and gathering days formed a foundation of respect and love between us. I also believe them to be the DNA of my life as a practicing poet, a lifelong teacher, and now, perhaps a guide along the knife's edge suggested by Dee Hock. Dad taught me the names of things and I loved those names, and when he was out-of-doors, I loved my father's ability to teach. In the woods and in the large gardens he made to help feed us, he was in his element—a patient teacher, eager to share his knowledge and skills. Outdoors we were fellow creatures, not the irritable father and anxious-to-please daughter confined to the smaller spaces of our indoor life together.

At the age of seven or eight, I went on my first—and last—gun hunt. My memory of a trampled cornfield rimmed with trees is vivid, as is the sense of moving out of my body when our beagle, Susie, flushed a rabbit. Dad took aim and made a clean shot to the unfortunate creature's head. I cannot remember what happened beyond Dad putting the rabbit into the pouch of his hunting coat. Nothing was said, which was not unusual, but what was unusual was that our silence around my tear-streaked face was one in which we both felt the inevitability—and I think, even the acceptability— of our difference.

In the 1950s, my generation and I were moving into an era in which relatively few of us hunted and gathered our food. Forever and always, my father was a man for whom a childhood scarcity of food coupled with his skill in bringing rabbit or squirrel meat to the table shaped his relationship to nature, heightening his awareness of the food chain and his place in it. In my body and in my writing, I hold the paradox of that tectonic shift away from subsistence hunting and gathering and resist simplistic categories of pro- and anti-gun, pro-woman/anti-male, pro-environment, anti-hunting and grazing. I resist "going to war" to save the planet, rushing to stereotyped judgments of hunters or the poor in emerging nations. I bring these paradoxes to the creation of communities that learn to treasure what is given and attempt to learn sufficiency in an era of appalling extremes of excess and of scarcity.

Enough

(from *Poems to a Coming Grandchild*)

1. Crows caw me awake from a dream of you
which slips into darkness, does not return to light.

Peering into morning from between parted blinds,
I am startled by the wind-torn oak
bending so near my face,
and the odd solemnity of four crows
pacing, stern-legged, in the sodden grass.

This is my second rising.

Shall I tell you, grandbaby-dreamed,
how I came earlier into morning,
(3:49 by the cold-eyed clock,)
into the awe-full sound
of wind deep in old trees,
the sound, to my ears, of mourning?

Believing that you,
baby-before-breathing,
understand darkness,
may I tell you of my despair?
Tell you, while the rain streams
over my safe house,

that I, your coming-to-be-grandmother,
am part of a way of life that is death.

Everything I need to live this life
is far away from itself and me,
a life without that much life
lived for too much comfort.

2. Yesterday in a waking nightmare,
I watched a raccoon in the glare of midday
pick its way across tumbled concrete,
obscene shards of parking lot
from a last-generation strip mall.

And last summer a herd of deer,
does and fawns, streamed across
Erie Avenue at sunset,
pushed into my astonished headlights,
their hooves unimaginable clicks on concrete.

3. I would not sentimentalize.

I still carry the body memory
of my father's hunger, his pushing
in ever-widening circles from home, trying
to flush a rabbit, a squirrel, a groundhog: any
taste of meat in a beans-and-bread boyhood.

My mother's father foraged even farther:
pushed from Southern Italy
to a sharecropper's shack in Northern Mississippi
into the glare of Klan-hate for dark skin, foreign ways—
all for the meaty taste of enough
on his immigrant tongue.

My people, your people
lived close to the land,
raised crops, mined coal
for those distant,
well-fed
owners of too-much.

4. I am awake in the morning,
praying to mend my own distance,
the too-muchness of my life,

praying that you, unimaginable grandbaby,
pushing out of darkness toward your own hungers
might learn, as we have not,
what it means to live on the earth
as if it, and you, were Enough.[6]

Recognizing the Old; Encountering the Emergent

In *Last Child in the Woods: Saving Our Children from Nature Deficit Disorder*, I found tantalizing clues pointing to the old, the emergence of the new, and the association with writing and with girls. Richard Louv interviewed children about their connection to and disconnection from the natural environment. A young man described his relationships with nature as "shaky, at best":

> "Like most, I exploit what it gives me and I do with it what I please," he said. He thought of nature as a means to an end or a tool. Something made to be used and admired, not something to live. "Nature to me is like my house or even like my cluttered room. It has things in it that can be played with. I say play away, do what you want with it, it's your house." He made no mention of the senses, saw or understood no complexity. [7]

I think back to the heroic model of nature writing I remember from my youth—"man vs. nature," the lit teachers used to say—and the memories resonate with this young man's sense of nature as about and for him. He, his needs and whims, are the locus of meaning in relationship to nature. Hemingway's and London's heroes and the writer-adventurers in my father's hunting and fishing magazines took their trophies, tested and shaped themselves against the elements. In American literature and life, nature, like the war in Hemingway's *In Another Country*, was "always there" for the hunter, writer, and artist to wrestle and shape.

A second story from Richard Louv embodies a different quality of presence to nature. A fifth-grade girl, "wearing a plain print dress and an intensely serious expression, [told the author] she wanted to be a poet when she grew up."[8] The girl-poet describes how peaceful and happy she felt in her special place in the woods, with a "big waterfall and a creek." She lay on a blanket and looked up to the trees and the sky, sometimes even falling asleep. *"When I'm in the woods, I feel like I'm in my mother's shoes"* (emphasis mine). I recognize the archetypal pattern here, as the girl in the story is naming her—our—mother, nature, Gaia, our source of food and nurture that we are destroying. Louv describes the end of the interview:

> The young poet's face flushed. Her voice thickened. "And then they just cut the woods down. It was like they cut down part of me."9

De-Centering the Self

I encountered the notion of the "de-centered" vs. the "localized" self from reading *Presence: An Exploration of Profound Change in People, Organizations and Society.* This language helped me turn the learning crystal yet another way, casting new light on the ways Western culture since the Enlightenment has shaped us into creatures who inhabit space as if where we are standing is the only locus of meaning.

I will add a slight digression here which is not meant to offend, but which feels important and true. Men have for a long time been standers in the center, and many women, myself included, resist being invited to de-center ourselves when we have so long lived on the fringes. To manage this as a writer and as a member of the almost always de-centered class I move to the larger container of what is needed now, and how women can teach men about de-centering the self in service of the whole, not as a variation on "knowing one's place."

Human creativity in the arts and science, our inventions and cures, have both happily and unhappily put us outside the limits of many natural processes. Happily, we have witnessed the creation of beauty in art, poetry, music, architecture, the eradication of some diseases, and the lengthening of life expectancy. We are given more years in which we might grow in wisdom and consciousness. Unhappily, we have seen the unintended but obvious consequences of overpopulation straining the planet's resources, the rise of the "super-heroic" notion of genius and artistry that has sadly declined into the culture of celebrity, and the dangerous delusion that we can exercise power over all earth's forces to win our way, eradicating even death itself.

It is my hypothesis that writers can practice and teach others to de-center the human by using the very tools we used to inscribe ourselves onto nature in an alternate way. Rather than perceiving nature as a *tabula rasa* awaiting our definition, or the "virgin" wilderness awaiting our artistic penetration, writers can highlight our experience of nature as a living system in which we participate humbly and "learn our place."

At the beginning of the end of the first decade of the twenty-first century, as I write this, nature is no longer "always there," and I posit that those of us in love with words, those of us who want better words for a better world, can—in community and with intentionality—find clues for writing as a tool for creating a relationship with nature more appropriate to the present planetary reality.

Consecrating the Desecrated

Many of us, like Louv's young poet, have lived to see places which felt "a part of us" cut down, desacralized by concrete, strip malls, perhaps even by the homes—or second homes—we ourselves have built in an ironic attempt to "get back to nature." The knee-jerk, archetypal way—so finely articulated in that most American of novels, *The Adventures of Huckleberry Finn*—is to "light out for the injun territories," to colonize or appropriate more land, farther out, to escape the blight behind us, only to make more when "there" becomes another "here." Philip Appleman captures the futility of this on-the-move, on-the-muscle paradigm in a beautiful, poignant poem.

Memo to the Twenty-First Century

Towns fingered out to country once,
where brown-eyed daisies waved a fringe on orchards
and cattle munched at clover, and
fishermen sat in rowboats and were silent,
and on gravel roads, boys and girls
stopped their cars and felt the moon and touched,
and the quiet moments ringed and focused
lakes, moon, flowers.
That is how it was in Indiana.

But we are moving out now,
scraping the world smooth where apples blossomed,
paving it over for cars.
In the spring before the clover goes purple,
we mean to scrape the hayfield, and
next year the hickory woods:
we are pushing on, our giant diesels snarling,
and I think of you, the billions of you, wrapped
in your twenty-first century concrete,
and I want to call to you, to let you know
that if you dig down,
down past wires and pipes
and sewers and subways, you will find
a crumbly stuff called earth. Listen:
in Indiana once, things grew in it.[10]

Exercise 14-3: Sitting Shiva

Invite some friends to sit with you in a desecrated, de-natured, or otherwise soul-damaged outdoor space, such as a strip of green space between or around a development. Try not to be showy or melodramatic about this, but sit together, collaborating on ways to appreciate, through language, this marginal space.

1. What practices will you use to ensure healthy qualities of human relationships while you're there (see chapter 16, "Care of the Container")? Who will commit to leading and ensuring these practices?

2. How frequently will you meet and for what length of time?

3. Learn the names of things in this place, names of weeds, grasses, or trees, if any. Use the names in pieces you commit to write between meetings, pieces not necessarily about this place but using the names of things in it. Name the names of the broken things you see in the space as well: Coors cans, used condoms, broken glass. You are not here to pretty up, or sentimentalize. Hold read-arounds (see chapter 9) in the space, sharing pieces written about and because of your commitment to this place.

4. Don't plan to publish or otherwise use what you write
    here, except among yourselves, because of the healing
    energy and restoration you are evoking. If your practice
    garners publicity, and others want to join you, or establish
    their own group practice, see what quality of conscious-
    ness your group can cultivate to keep the essence of the
    practice, that of engaging language and community to
    grieve, to praise, to appreciate, and to be present to a pil-
    laged place.

How, Save in Poetry?

I will end this reflection as I began it: with Dee Hock, with concern and love for the grandchildren, and with poetry. Listen first to
the poetry of Hock's questions from his chapter, "In Search of a
More Liveable World":

♦   Did the silence of a billion nights shape the owl's gentle voice?

♦   What happens within owl when it hears owl?

♦   How can we know so much *about* owl, and nothing of what it
    is to *be* owl?

♦   Do our intentions toward owl shape owl becoming?

♦   Do owl intentions shape our becoming?

♦   How did evolution organize owl, man, earth, and all therein as
    a vast, harmonic—infinite cohesion of infinite complexity—
    infinite coherence of infinite diversity?[11]

Such questions capture my hope that language can shape
humanity's intentions to be with owl and all our siblings with neither sentimentality nor brutality. And I believe we can create, for
want of a better world, the communities in which to practice—
populated by women, men, girls, boys—reinitiated by women into
a belief in the great both/and of things.

Returning for a Picnic

After Seeing a Great Blue Heron at Pine Hill Park
June 2007

1.

With our picnic parcels, bats and balls,
card decks for after-lunch downshifting
we create our world:

Two Grandmothers and the Mother
of radiant, still-in-their bodies
boys on a cool June day.

Max and Joey, Joey and Max,
the preciousness of them
opens—and breaks—my heart,
or perhaps it is: breaks my heart
open, as if it were not open to the point
of anguish for the world already.

2.
In my enthusiasm to see—and have
Max and Joey see—the heron
I surprised here last week,
I hail a wheeling-low hawk.

Though both are birds of prey,
the Great Blue's delicate wading
and dipping, perhaps the fact

that it swallows fish, which I cannot see
save the sunlit flicks of their bodies,
vs. the Hawk's terrifying swoop and

talon-grasp of rodents and fowl,
which I can witness more fully,
accounts for my sentimentalized

yearning for the heron, vs.
my shiver-tinged awe for the
looming hawk.

3.
How, save in poetry, shall I
gather the golden happiness of
children and parents, sprinkling
of still-able grandparents,
such plenty:

containers of melon and cherries,
bags of sliced-thin cheese, ham,

good bread, even a smuggled bottle
of summer wine, ice cream, of course,
above all: glorious-bodied boys,
blowing bubbles, racing and climbing,
tossing field-corn to ducks and
a few geese guests, with the
hunting hawk, the disappearing planet?

Part*Four*

Conscious Feminine Leadership

To that man I write this poem—
with love beyond words—
and with this list of chores attached:

Colin,
    clean your room
    feed the cat
    check the hyacinth bulbs
    and take very good care of
The Parsley Garden.
        Love,
        Mom

The stories in this section describe the very daunting challenges I faced when I attempted, as intentionally as possible, but without the admired skills or recognized credentials of traditional models, to foster the growth of the new within the universe of the old.

I was unprepared for the myriad and mysterious ways in which systems and people variously ignore, dilute, or purposefully destroy the new. I was also unprepared for the physical and emotional costs of both expressing a new paradigm and being a responsible steward of that expression. In my leadership life, I have had to relearn the most difficult lesson of my life as a mother (now grandmother): the new will either be strengthened by its exposure to the desperation of the old paradigm and its frightened leaders, or it will die.

I will describe leadership qualities and practices I learned for nurturing the new during the death throes of the old. I have included stories of my efforts to integrate conscious feminine leadership into the wider culture.

What qualities of presence and self-care does it take to bring the unwelcome news that the emperor is naked and has been for quite some time? I believe that the work of new paradigm/conscious feminine leadership is hands-on and humble. At its heart is caring for (not neglecting or exploiting) what I call the containers: the organizations, businesses and nonprofits—and homes—of which we are the vaunted leaders.

I chose the stories in this section from a treasure trove of encounters in which the conscious feminine met the unconscious feminine and unquestioned masculine. I chose sparingly because I wanted to tell the stories in enough detail that I writing, and you reading, might see the patterns, and might learn from them.

15.

Care of the Container

When reading the lace, the Reader must look
for one of two things: something that enhances
the pattern or something that breaks it.

Brunonia Barry[1]

The most important set of practices I have learned for both growing the new in the shell of the old and for providing compassionate care for dying organizations, falls into a category I call "care of the container." The leader of a conscious writing community, or any other kind of community, must regularly create places where participants can "see the patterns," patterns that either enhance or distort life.

At Women Writing for (a) Change we aspire to an engaged and conscious stewardship of relationships and resources; in our parlance, caring for the container. By *container*, I mean the organizational universe, encompassing all aspects of how a group lives: time, physical space, money, relational agreements, food, and ritual. The word container has many analogues: eco-system, home, womb.

Anything that maintains the delicate balance between open space and boundaries and allows life to emerge is the container.

The medieval alchemists attempted to transform lead into gold in a crucible they called "the container." I imagine the alchemists had servants or apprentices to clean their containers, to dump ashes, and to burnish the metal. I do not imagine, but know to be true, that in organizational life at the nadir of patriarchy, we have flown high into abstraction and distanced ourselves from life by the use of technology. Not only do we neglect our containers, we don't even see them.

For example, a healthcare worker might say to the CEO: "How can we deliver health care, when we don't have health among ourselves?" This is similar to a shaman standing at the seashore and telling the villagers, "There's a large boat with cannons sailing into the harbor." The villagers do not recognize the danger because they have no frame of reference for *large boat*, no language for *cannon*. Actually, caring for the container is more daunting than being the shaman in the fable because the shaman had authority and status in his culture and his meanings got a fair hearing. Today, we quickly label the woman as crazy who asks, "If we say we're experts on community, why aren't we a community? Why is this place a mess? When did the container fill up with unresolved anger, unexamined ideas, and unconscious, even stultifying, behaviors? When did this become 'the way things are'?"

Within our WWf(a)C communities writers sometimes resist practices that keep them from "just getting the writing done," forgetting that writing "gets done" because of, and within, community. The conscious feminine leadership we practice at WWf(a)C includes stewardship of the great both/ands of creating and caring, individual and community, self-awareness and awareness of other, product and process.

Conscious feminine leadership sees and names *all* the work of an organization as valuable: emotional as well as intellectual, practice as well as theory.

In our collaborations with other organizations and with consulting clients, we have struggled to incorporate care of containers. While the word *stewardship* has much currency in organizational development and leadership conversations, the conversations rarely descend to the level of practice.

As I revise this chapter, first drafted in 1999, I am challenged to manage my outrage as I witness a cascade of environmental and economic crises. We are supposed to trust, again, the same experts who rush in with the same tools: contradictory and arcane theories, quick fixes, fear, and urgency. The only thing that keeps me writing is the possibility that we might make the world anew by finally considering new/old tools, dismissed and devalued in the headlong flight from the embodied feminine.

Tools for Organizational Care

I will describe practices that evolved in WWf(a)C and trust your ability to translate them into your world.

Caring for the Container happens in a variety of ways in our work. One example: At approximately the halfway point of any program, we devote a large portion of one session to care-of-the-container activities. During the preceding week, we ask writers to reflect upon their writing lives, what they have accomplished during the semester, and specific ways membership in the class either has supported or has not supported their writing. We ask them to consider the elements of class: large group discussions and demonstrations, the functioning of small groups, writing prompts, teacher facilitation, ritual, the use of time, the physical space itself—anything and everything affecting the learning experience.

Care of Container Prompts

Please write freely to the following questions with regard to (a) your individual writing practice; (b) class practices; and (c) small group practices this semester:

♦ What hopes, dreams, fears, or doubts did you have at the start of the semester? What did you bring to this class?

♦ What have you realized so far? What has changed? What still needs to happen? What is working? What is not working?

♦ At the middle of our time together, what questions are you holding about your writing? Your life in this community? Any aspect of this community, from rituals to practicalities?

♦ What are the gifts and challenges of your participation in this semester? Write one story to illustrate each.

♦ How is your life different because you commit to writing and writing in community?

♦ What aspects of the container serve your writing life? What aspects of the container do not serve it?

♦ What has been the quality of your presence this semester to your writing, your small group, and your participation in large group activities?

♦ Choose two lines from tonight's opening poem and allow them to lead you into reflection on what themes are emerging for you so far this semester.

Care of Container Read-Around

When we convene the care-of-the-container class, women read what they have written in response to teacher prompts (or to prompts they devised for themselves) in their small groups. Later in the evening we have a large group read-around in which women read their reflections on the container.

In my care-of-the-container writing and sharing, I try to model the importance of naming both the light and the shadow, the gifts and the challenges of my own writing, and my own observations of the community's gifts and challenges.

One colleague asks writers to name only what hasn't worked for them this semester, as a way of eliciting shadow. I have mixed feelings about "calling in the shadow," given its propensity for showing up and taking over, but I take the point, and feel the possible usefulness of the practice with any group addicted to happy talk.

Another care-of-the-container practice is to have fast-writes written on identical sheets of colored paper. The women put all the writings in a basket, pass it around the circle and choose one piece, other than their own, to read aloud. This can be a wonderful way of getting diverse themes out into the community for contemplation, without people having strong attachments to them.

The variety of ways we care for the container allow the ritual to remain safe and prevent the practices from becoming pro forma. Anything this crucial to the work, and, for some, this challenging, requires different styles so as to avoid privileging one person's comfort zone over another's.

The halfway point care-of-the-container session is a complement to shorter practices used in every session. (1) In small groups, the closing five minutes are devoted to passing around the stone for each woman's reflection on what she saw, heard, and felt during the sharing of writing. (2) In the large group, the last five minutes of the session are used to capture in writing, on 3" x 5" index cards called "soul cards," each person's thoughts and feelings about any element of her experience.

Care of the School

In 1999 we instituted semi-annual Care of the School meetings. At the end of the fall-winter and winter-spring semesters, participating writers join with faculty members to put our attention on all aspects of the largest container at that time: the school itself. Kathy Wade designed and facilitated a prototype for all-community "wisdom circles," including time for women to write our hopes and concerns for the school, the gifts and challenges of our work there, and any other school related issues. Writing time is followed by time to read and discuss themes and concerns raised by the writing.

Care of the Faculty

Monthly faculty meetings begin with care-of-the-container writing. After the circle is opened, we fast-write for ten minutes to a prompt such as, "What is the light and what is the shadow of your life as a faculty member at WWf(a)C since last we met?"

One holiday season, I gave each teacher a copy of Parker Palmer's *The Courage to Teach* and we read a chapter per month as preparation for the faculty meeting. The writing prompt was often a quote or insight from this brilliant book. One of the teachers said, "Reading this book is sort of like painting the Golden Gate Bridge; when you reach the end of it, it's time to start over." The text is rich and supportive of teaching and living authentically. I believe the book is relevant to working with integrity in any vocation.

We have a read-around of these fast-writes, do read-backs as a way of lifting up the themes that struck us most deeply, and then weave a conversation around those themes before moving on to our discussion of curriculum and our "ecology of work" (my term for the pieces of teaching and administrative work members are doing, or want to do, or want to move away from doing). The facilitator will have solicited the remaining agenda items from the staff before the meeting.

At the final semester staff meeting in December and May, we attend in some depth to the gifts and challenges of our working together, our web of relationships as colleagues. In 1998, I asked Carolyn McCabe, PhD, a skilled and profoundly spiritual therapist, to create a space for us to speak our truths to one another. Christiane Northrup, who said she had hired a therapist to work with her staff in Maine, served as my inspiration. Northrup sought someone who could facilitate truth telling among the partners. Another inspiration was my sense that we, as a faculty, were beginning to project mother-daughter stuff onto one another. I felt we were "doing good badly," by getting stuck in the messiness of unconscious material. I suspected we needed a major house-airing.

Speaking Our Truths

Carolyn McCabe designed a process far beyond anything I could have imagined! Each semester she had either a face-to-face or phone conversation with each faculty and staff member for about thirty minutes. Based on that listening, Carolyn designed a ritual in which we said our words to one another. Significantly, Carolyn divorced us from our comfort level with the written word, and moved us into spoken word and gesture. Each session was a work of art, combining Carolyn's deep listening and gift for ritual with her ability to act in the moment. One of the most memorable things Carolyn asked us to do was to take a position in the circle with respect to the distance from anger each of us liked to have, with a lit candle representing the anger. I will always remember us moving around the space, sizing up the distance from the fire, and from one another as it turned out, and then finally choosing a position.

Celebration

As a fan of food and celebration, I insist that this final semester meeting include both, for I feel incredibly happy that we do this work together. "This," I have often said, "is our real job security": our certainty that spaces will be created to tell our truths about our work, to reflect and learn together, and to celebrate.

Care of the Movement: Wisdom Circle

In the same way that the world and economies are being forced to grapple with the effects of untrammeled growth, organizations can also experience sprawl. While WWf(a)C has not pursued a strategy of growth for growth's sake, an energetic community of creative people can give birth to more projects than there are containers to hold. In October 2008 when the stock market dropped hundreds of points per day, media pundits reminded viewers that in October 2007, the U.S. stock market reached its highest point. In what seems to me now an odd coincidence, I had the intuition in October 2007 that the growth of the WWf(a)C movement as a whole warranted a container of its own, a community to discern what was living and what was dying back in our shared universe. This is the invitation that I crafted to invite members to that community.

An Invitation from Mary Pierce Brosmer
Founding Director, Women Writing for (a) Change

Dear Community,

After the ravages of Katrina, I heard an interview with jazzman Dr. John, who was talking about the special culture of New Orleans in an NPR interview with John Burnett. About rebuilding the city, Dr. John said, "Transmission of culture has to have a place to happen."[2]

While we are not rebuilding a city, our WWf(a)C communities have experienced an enormous amount of change within the last eighteen months. Our place to transmit and continue creating our culture is in the container, where we practice rituals, writing, listening within and to one another.

Will you join us in an especially critical wisdom circle to name all that has been called into being and the kind of systems emerging? Your presence will help all become more coherent and integral.

With thanks,
Mary Pierce Brosmer

Please join faculty and staff of Women Writing for (a) Change and Women Writing for (a) Change Foundation as we gather together in a Wisdom Circle at 6906 Plainfield Road, Silverton, on Monday, November 19, 2007, from 7 to 9:30 pm.

We will gather as a community to reflect on the gifts and challenges of supporting the existence and healthy life of our movement. All the containers in our movement will be represented:

Foundation Board of Trustees   Ellen Doyle

Foundation   Andrea Nichols

Community Partnerships   Marissa Williams

Young Women Writing for (a) Change   Jenn Reid

Young Women's Feminist Leadership Academy   Jenn Reid

Radio Circle   Annette Wick

Author's Fundraising Event   Beth Fritsch

Finance Committee   Susan Branscome

Cincinnati WWf(a)C   Kathy Wade

Men Writing for Change   Forrest Brandt

Feminist Leadership Academy Stephanie Dunlap and Bron Park

Affiliate schools:

Bloomington IN site-owner   Beth Lodge-Rigal

Indianapolis site-owner   Mindy Flask

Traverse City site-owner   Anni Gibson

Consulting for (a) Change   Mary Pierce Brosmer

The Wisdom Circle will revisit the mission and vision of WWf(a)C, to share our stories and celebrate our journey. Mary Pierce Brosmer, Founding Director, will hold the circle.

A potluck dinner will begin at 6 pm. Please RSVP by November 15.

If memory serves, a circle of forty women and men gathered on that evening. Here is the container I crafted for evoking the wisdom of the community:

Wisdom Circle Agenda

7:00   Gathering the Community

7:00   What is the Vision, the Spiritual/Organizational DNA of the WWf(a)C movement and how has it emerged? (Mary Pierce Brosmer)

7:50   Writing Time

From your vantage point, what has emerged?

What is emerging?

What is needed to hold emerging life?

And/Or:

What has emerged in you in the WWf(a)C circle of life? .

What is emerging?

What are you creating to hold what is emerging?

8:05   Read-Around, with read-backs

8:45   New information from and for the system: What is emerging?

9:15   Returning within, checking in and around

9:30   Closing

Here is what I wrote that night in the fifteen-minute fast-writing time, and read aloud when it was my turn to have a voice in the read-around:

What is emerging for me in what I guess is the third season of WWf(a)C life: the season after my direct involvement in the day-to-day.

I am imagining new "buck-stops here" Mothers, owners for the school, a younger generation of women writers, FLA-trained, apprenticed in all the containers of the organism, who will own the school and be its stewards and upstanding social entrepreneurs.

If this happens gradually, with Kathy and I still available for consulting as they create the new phase, they will be free enough and at risk enough to boldly go forward, and Tom and I will be freed up to visit our grandsons in Toronto or wherever they might be in three–five years.

Also emerging: a desire to see if spending more time on the consulting container emerges as a joyful experience of companioning people to more conscious and efficient and healthy workplaces *or* is it beating my head against a wall I'm not wise or strong enough to move?

If I do this, I will have to create a community of practice around that work, another container, and I haven't had the freedom or energy to create that.

I can imagine transitioning the FLA in five years to new leadership, that will create the FLA containers and invite me to tell the stories of founding and emergence.

I will be sixty; I love my work; I love new challenges; I want to be part of earth community. I will not, however, fight and resist and go to war with the hellish way things are in the Empire. What we resist, we discovered in the 60s, not only persists but buys more weapons for the wars. I will give all my energy to creating alternatives, third ways, new worlds where people choose to be.

Process Does Not Take Over Product!

I am convinced that our commitment to reflecting on what we do in community is essential to the ongoing vitality and health of the school. There are always those who object—often strenuously, although less so over the years—to "wasting our time" on process. Once again, my working-class pragmatism serves me well in being faithful to care of the container activities in the face of objections: *it works*, and, as the community has become accustomed to it, works efficiently, even elegantly. The precious commodity of time is wasted much more egregiously when attention is *not* paid regularly to the container, resulting in paralysis and crisis.

Because the Stakes Are High

Moreover, I would be remiss in not repeating: "the stakes are very high" in this work of making space for the feminine. We come to the circle, whether we are conscious of it or not, to break taboos around female speech; we come to the circle carrying our own fears of feminine power. And, to put it mildly—and redundantly—this work is not supported by the world at large.

Under such internal and external stresses, largely invisible because so normal, women's work often implodes, leaving damaged and disillusioned participants wondering *why*. I believe the why is simple: attention was not paid, or too little attention was paid, and often too late, until finally the unsaid had reached a volume too great to be heard.

Three-Year Lifespan

Marion Woodman has said that women's groups have a three-year lifespan.[3] She believes that women come together hungry for the feminine, and then begin to project what Jungians call the "inferior feminine" onto one another. I offer evidence that supports Woodman's theory from our own work at WWf(a)C and in the story of a writing group in another city.

A member of WWf(a)C who had moved to another state asked me to help her start a writing group there. Significantly, this woman did not want to be the leader or facilitator; she wanted to "be held, not to hold," or at least not to hold all the time. I give her much credit for her clarity about the difference between the two roles.

At their request I worked with a group of writers to develop a shared leadership model for their group. I emphasized the necessity of care of the container, and taught them the ways that we did this in WWf(a)C. Very quickly, however, the group began to neglect care-of-the-container practices. The pre- and post-writing group lunches, that included wine, began to assume more and more importance as time went on. Women "just wanted to write." Unacknowledged competition for leadership set in.

Nearing the end of three years, the group struggled around a number of issues. They contacted me to discuss another visit to revitalize their group. After listening to some of the concerns and stories of the members, I returned and facilitated a workshop in which the writing was almost completely focused on the *community*—in effect, a weekend's worth of care-of-the-container activities. My interpretation of what happened as a result of this workshop was that the group split along the lines of what had not been evident before: those who were completely resistant to care of the container and insisted "We just want to write, not do all this new age mumbo-jumbo," and those who believed that the safety and vitality of the group had been seriously compromised by the ongoing failure of the group to do so.

I learned volumes from this experience. For one thing, if I were asked to foster a shared leadership version of WWf(a)C again, I would decline. Without even more caring (caring for the leadership team itself, for example), a shared leadership model becomes one *without* leadership: "If everyone is in charge; no one is in charge." I have discovered in the ensuing years what I knew even then but was too lacking in confidence to admit: the "leader" serves the group by holding its conscious center. Her centeredness and her capacity for grounded holding must be cultivated. An exchange of energy must occur between the holder and the held. Those for whom the space is held pay their leader to both acknowledge the importance of her service and to make it possible for her full dedication to the work. Moreover, all of this must be named and acknowledged because a group lacking someone whose vocation it is to lead will most likely founder.

Founder makes me want to mention in this chapter how very carefully I have worked in recent years to learn how to allow space for a living system to come to life, a system *that will make possible even more life*.[4] I believe that a shadow side of the feminist and postmodern project of flattening hierarchy is that we have, predictably, "thrown the baby out with the bath water." I have heard women criticized for being "hierarchical," when they were honestly trying to serve by leading or teaching. These women leaders were trying to create a space for themselves and others to act. I made the grave mistake, in my early attempts to mentor other women to do this work, of thinking, "If I can do it, anyone can; I certainly don't want to put myself 'above' this woman, so talented in her own right." This was another face of not knowing how to teach others, not knowing how to deliver the bad news, as it were, that leadership for life involves lots of messy, slow work, as well as discipline and *staying put*.

It is important to this discussion of care of the container to note the critical role of the leaders who will take the heat on behalf of regular housekeeping, lest the nest be fouled. Given the prevalence of shoot-from-the-hip leadership that scorns reflection and cannot imagine just saying what is happening, I have come to believe that leaders in the tradition of the conscious feminine work must be cultivated and supported. Conscious feminine leaders need more training than simple turn-key techniques that inevitably become rote and shallow. Training for conscious feminine leadership is entrainment, opening to and committing to ongoing practice within a conscious community in order to transform the container of Self.

Conflict

Regular attention to care of the container does not forestall conflict; it *includes* conflict, making numerous spaces for it to be named, but not "fixed." It is challenging to make care-of-the-container processes more than "course evaluation." Within this challenge is the deeper challenge of inviting participants in the community to "see their participation" in the system, thereby encouraging their responsible participation in changing what does not seem to be working. Likewise, it is challenging for leaders to avoid reacting defensively or rushing to fix things. The work of sustaining community, the work of inscribing the feminine more fully into the world, will never be comfortable—we know that not much worth doing *is* comfortable. However, when we pay attention, we can work together over time in ways that are empowering and healing. Paying attention is hard work; it is difficult to "take the time," but I am unwilling to replicate the stagnant, bureaucratic, unresponsive systems now imploding for lack of stewardship and cultivation of wisdom.

Exercise 15-1:
Care of the Container for Your Organization

Carefully craft an invitation to members of a work team, community, or other group to participate in care of the container. As you craft your invitation, spend some time developing your process of engaged hospitality and transparency about your motives and hopes.

Here is a prompt you can use or adapt: Set the timer and write for ten minutes about what you consider a failure on your part. What did you learn from it? What would you do differently next time? Is there something you could have used from the group if you had known to ask?

After a read-around, ask participants to return for a session on a success and its lessons.

With leaders in our success-obsessed culture, there is nothing like meditating on "the fortunate fall" to open space for connection and moving into a new era of creating around what really is happening in the system.

Blessing

I approach this work in the belief that most of us want to be better stewards of our shared world, but we easily lose our way without conscious containers where we practice countercultural values of truth-telling, vulnerability, and noticing the messes we've made, while trying to prevent worse messes. Scarcity of consciousness plus scarcity of community eventually equals the scarcity of moral conscience about which most of us wring our hands, without examining our complicity-comfort in the faltering status quo.

Though I take a stand for ongoing stewardship of organizational life, and have found it natural and obvious to care for containers, I do not believe I have been a good teacher of these skills to others.

As many of my poems attest, I learned from my mother and her humble, daily, beautiful, not-valued work that made our home safe, clean, and love-filled. However, like my mother before me, I have found it easier to "do it myself" because I often don't have the stamina to care for the container while simultaneously:

♦ Teaching others to do it;

♦ Holding them accountable for helping to clean up messes and hew to values they do not see, or see as priorities (punctuality, for example, and promptly returned calls, and meeting people as they walk in the door and introducing themselves, standing up and speaking up when in a large crowd so everyone can hear, etc.); and

♦ Facing their anger when I pull back the curtain on the disciplines necessary for sustaining habitable spaces, from homes to organizations to the planet.

In my career—and life—I have experienced broken relationships when I pointed out the injustice of having some people doing "invisible mother work," freeing others to create, to perform, to do only the things they love to do. The sweaty, hands-on, concrete work of the scorned feminine prepares the space, and the calm, cool, and collected, expert masculine enters and takes charge. Not in my world, if I can help it.

In an early journal snippet crafted into a poem right after my mother died, I took up the work of carrying the content of her love into new forms, such as poems, learning and change communities. I see myself holding the gifts of the traditional feminine alongside

the gifts of the emerging conscious feminine, holding the value of
both in the name of The Mother, the archetypal container, no empty
vessel She.

Eucharist

for Isabel Rose Caliendo Pierce

In the loaves of your good bread
cooling in the open window
solid slap of your bare feet
crossing and re-crossing the kitchen floor

bedsheets hung white and hot
in the sun

memory of your worn hands
smoothing and folding,

I recognize your choices,
the life you made

    which seemed to me then,
    your unmaking.

With you now, I kneel proudly down
to my own choices:

Words, solid as your scrubbed floors,

Words, hung white and hot on the tongue,
    Your Bread, My Poetry
    Our Blood,
    Mother,

    making us One.

16.

Writing the World of Work:
A Story from the Field

I have never been able to clearly distinguish between success and failure, so they shall appear as they were, irrevocably interconnected.

Dee Hock[1]

Perhaps the greatest mistake was to completely underestimate the degree of individual cultural change such an organization required, both in self and others. Nor did I anticipate how pervasively and persistently old concepts would reassert themselves, or the covert, tenacious resistance new methods would evoke.

Dee Hock[2]

Weave real connections, create real nodes, build real houses. Live a life you can endure: Make love that is loving.

Marge Piercy[3]

In this chapter I tell a story about how conscious feminine patterns of creating and caring for containers are easily overwhelmed by established patterns of urgency, constant doing, and fear. I chose only one story from many encounters between the conscious feminine we are trying to birth, and the unconscious masculine patterns so ingrained, even in women's organizations, as to be invisible. I also hope to show how container creation and caring can be translated into established organizations.

I chose this story because the project was dear to my heart. I sensed great promise as two women's organizations engaged in cross-pollination and mutual respect. Additionally, it illustrates the fairly common failure to enact a fair and sustained hearing of the conscious feminine. Dee Hock, who wrote about his efforts to create VISA as a living system which would be part of a new planet-saving paradigm, advised, "It is painful to think and write about failure and weakness but it is an essential part of the story."[4]

Exercise 16-1: Bright Beginnings

Give yourself the gift of a longer portion of time, at least thirty minutes, to choose and then write about an experience of entering a project with high hopes, idealism, and good intentions all around, only to find the outcome was not what you'd hoped, and without clear understanding of why. If you are able to find colleagues who were involved in this project with you, invite them to write their stories of this experiment.

Diagnosing and Healing Like a Poet

I describe our form of organizational consulting as "like poets" because we intend not only to foster the expression of the organism, but also to help make something, as opposed to merely measuring. A poetic response to organizational and personal life is that of crafting or creating, as the etymology of the word indicates: "Poetry: from Gk. *poema*, 'thing made or created'; from *poein*, 'to make or compose.'"[5]

We work with groups to clear a space in which they can see or create patterns that will support the organism as it changes and grows, or changes and dies to its former self. We attempt to connect the system, as a poet connects words, bringing new insights and ideas into being, building real houses, making work lives people can endure. "Connections are made slowly, sometimes they grow underground," writes Marge Piercy in "The Seven of Pentacles." If you did the exercises in the earlier chapters, you engaged in this kind of process. In the underground richness of story, reflection, and conversation, coworkers and leaders can observe connections that already exist once there is a place for the connections to be seen. With regular practices of "making real," i.e., saying what is happening from where each person stands in the organization, participants can also make connections that do not yet exist but will help the system flourish. This non-interventionist, impossible-to-measure healing of systems is what we attempt to practice within our own organization and with client-organizations.

And what of diagnosing like a poet? My own first inclination is to go straight to the stories and symbols of the organization as rapidly as a physician would go to the vital signs of a presenting patient.

♦   What are the founding stories of the organization?

♦   To what extent are present members of the community familiar with the history of the organization?

♦   Where in the stories, the symbols, and the tools of the organization are there clues to what is needed now?

Diagnosis is, or should be, an art—and a collaborative art at that. Thus the stories are brought to community for discernment. Sometimes we discover that the organism is wasting away because it has lost its connection to the potent stories and symbols that brought it to life. At other times, the defining stories are no longer in alignment with the stated values and mission of the organization. Either way, diagnosis is sometimes as simple as saying, "There is a need to remake the organization in light of its organizational DNA, the information that created its unique life."

A Challenge of "Just Saying What Happened"

As the writer of a story that is interwoven with threads of others' stories, I am humbled, sometimes to the point of muteness. Humbled to be the only teller here, I am aware of my responsibility to remind you that I am not writing "the story"; I write *my* story, what I saw, felt, and experienced from where I was standing. Others, who stood in different places with relationship to the events I narrate, have different—and doubtless competing—versions. As a facilitator/consultant/teacher, I have committed my life to opening the space for heresies—that is, unofficial, non-dominant, "private" accounts of things. This whole book, it occurs to me, is a "her-essay." As a writer, I am not an anthologist, nor a researcher, nor a collector of others' stories, and I do not attempt those forms here. I place my writing alongside an intense lifetime of personal and professional hearing others into speech. Anything different would extinguish the fragile self that emerges for me when I write—the self of the poet, "her-essayist." The kind of writer I am and must be is the congenital twin of the creator of communities which allow others to emerge as the kinds of writers they are and must be. To separate one from the other is to put both at risk.

I am committed to being ethical in how I tell communal stories, so I am telling true stories as I experienced the events and themes, while inventing names and other details so as not to hurt anyone unwittingly by my telling.

Finally, The Story

A few years ago, I began conversations with the CEO of an organization whose mission was working with girls. Admiring theories of organizations as living systems, "Joan" expressed frustration at the challenge of putting theory into practice. Her organization was in the midst of a major reorganizational effort, and she was eager to make the reorganization an "opportunity for cultural transformation."

"Opportunity for cultural transformation" immediately piqued my interest. Joan and I began a series of conversations to explore how she could provide leadership which would effect transformation while she managed the challenges of a reorganization which mandated combining several formerly separate business units into a new entity.

As preparation for our work together, I encouraged Joan to read *A Hidden Wholeness*, a powerful book in which Parker J. Palmer describes circles of trust.[6] I was very impressed by Joan's "first things first" work of attending to her own "leadership container." Every two weeks in a series of coaching/mentoring conversations, she brought the stories of her work to the place I created for and with her. Joan already had practice in journal writing; I gave her prompts to elicit stories from her work life, especially as she was in a critical moment for any leader, a moment when a major change effort was in progress.

Weeks and months went by, and the complexity of the transition naturally increased. I urged Joan to invite members from the business units, managers, and first-line staff, at least, to begin to work in circles, but she felt that the logistical details needed to be attended to first. *I* believed that the stress on the workers could be turned to energy if we first attended to making community: gathering the people, building the relationships, establishing agreements and practices for truth-telling, understanding one another's cultures and structures, and inspiring one another's creativity and hope. I knew that investing resources in bringing the system together in community would enhance, not hinder, the flow of "external work." I worried that the tyranny of the latter would so dominate that, by the time we *finally* got to the work of creating the new in the shell of the old, fatigue and cynicism would have set in. But I could not influence Joan to do both at the same time to balance the effort.

Researching Like a Poet

In the meantime, I was conducting research, reading the history of the organization, a biography of its founder, the manuals, and websites. At the same time I learned from conversations with managers and with Joan about the strengths and challenges of current organizational life. Rather obvious to my outsider's eyes was a disconnect between what happened at the "girl level" and what happened among the professionals. At the girl level, there were circles, agreements, and rituals for learning and remembering what Parker Palmer calls "the thing in the middle," the reason for coming together. There was play and creativity, connection to nature, all things that strengthen girls—and adults! In the day-to-day workplace, I saw none of the non-rational, emotional, soul-level content and I began to imagine ways to connect the system to the practices which were the DNA of its birth and growth through many years of life.

Diagnosing, then attempting to heal like a poet, rather than a statistician or technician, for the space of the nine months of my work with them, I was percolating an ever deeper understanding of how women's organizations often "out-Herod Herod," wearing the clothes of the masculine in order to be taken seriously. The organizational culture was symbolically siloed, as opposed to circled, despite its roots in circles of girls.

My understanding of theories and lived experience of feminine development within patriarchy brought in another line of feeling and intuition that pointed to possibilities for transformation of the organization's culture. Women are asked to abandon our girl selves, our physicality, courage, spunk, and independence in order to grow up to a model of adult womanhood that actually marginalizes feminine values. As the organization "grew up" it left behind its girl self, its founding myths, its energizing rituals, and even its connection with nature. Eventually, I met many women across the various business units (even now, writing years later, I can remember their faces and stories). They had entered this organization because, as girls, they had fallen in love with the very things now missing in their lives as women in the workplace. Here again was the old story, the one that brought me into creating a world by, for, and about women in the first place: women not giving ourselves the very things we want to give to the next generation. Somehow, we are deceived into believing that if we empower ourselves, or delight ourselves, we deprive our daughters, as if power and joy were zero sum quantities. Words from the French feminist Luce Irigaray rise up in this context: "And what I wanted from you, Mother, was this: that in giving me life, you remain alive."[7]

And What I Wanted

I wanted to create containers for healing the disconnection that had arisen in this organism, to help it evolve from hierarchy to community through a gradual, respectful, and incremental teaching of practices aligned with its own rituals, symbols, and history. What I got: a one-day retreat for managers from the various business units, held at a retreat center on a beautiful fall day. I wanted Joan to be at the retreat, to "be held" in the container, signifying her commitment to co-creating the new culture. At first, Joan was enthusiastic about participating, but then she decided not to attend; she was very busy and, she said, the others would feel freer to speak their minds in her absence. I strongly disagreed with this, but I could not persuade her of the importance of practicing a both/and leadership I describe in more details in the next chapter.

A Container for the Day

Working like a poet, I spent long, time-out-of-time hours crafting a container for the day, incorporating playfulness and seriousness of purpose, celebration of diversity, and focus on common purpose. I contacted all the participants ahead of time, asking them to read a chapter from *The Girl Within*[8] by Emily Hancock, and naming my intentions for our work together: *Creating the climate for sustainable, mission-driven change based on authentic relationship, truth-telling, renewed joy and commitment in alignment with organizational history, spirit, and values.*

The flow of the day married practices learned in developing the culture of Women Writing for (a) Change with what I had learned in researching the organization's format for working with girls. I planned to alternate overt "teaching" activities with elements of play, getting to know one another, experiences in nature, and shared food.

When the managers arrived, we had a buffet breakfast. To help make connections among people from several different geographical areas as well as our corps of five WWf(a)C facilitator/participants, we played "people bingo," a game in common use in the organization and generously organized by my inside coordinator, Caren. Ahead of time, through e-mail contact, Caren had solicited "lightweight" facts about each participant's life, e.g., I grew up in the scrap metal capital of the United States; I won a prize for lip-synching to Patsy Cline's "Crazy" when I was nine; I am the oldest of nine siblings.

After breakfast and the awarding of prizes for top scores in people bingo, we gathered in a circle of about thirty-five and listened to "The Lost Girls," a poem by Linda Pastan.[9] The first thing I lifted up after reading the poem was the absolute importance of confidentiality. Without preaching, I spent some time focusing on the importance of freeing one another to think outside the usual boxes, to express feelings which were both real and not "the whole truth" of what a person feels. I opened the floor for discussion about confidentiality, and gave several examples in which I distinguished between discussing themes and ideas (good) and carrying personal information outside the day's circle in a way which could put a person at risk professionally or personally (bad).

I also shared a lesson I had learned from reading Parker Palmer, which he calls "second level confidentiality." Outside the community, or circle of trust, we would not engage a member of the circle about something she or he shared inside the circle unless he or she chose to bring it up. I allowed the words to sink into the circle; then we began our first activity. I asked the participants to write a story from their lives as girls. Possible doorways into a story:

♦   Doing something you loved
♦   Dealing with a loss
♦   Being at your favorite place
♦   A friendship
♦   Making a discovery
♦   Experiencing a change in life as you knew it

After writing time, participants were invited to read either whole stories or excerpts. Passing was encouraged as an honorable choice, but only four or five of the thirty passed.

We shared lunch and then moved into a time for reflection and inquiry. I facilitated a discussion of "The Girl Within" reading, weaving in some of the theories and insights I was bringing to the table for their consideration.

Our second activity was a fast-write. I encouraged them to write freely, without concern for punctuation, grammar, etc., to one or a combination of these prompts:

♦   "Who Is" the organization as you now experience it?
♦   What are its strengths and gifts?
♦   What's working/what needs work?
♦   "Who Are" you in the organization?
♦   Who/how do you want to be?
♦   Write at least one story from your life at work, showing elements of the organization and you in it.

Participants divided into small groups that were facilitated by members of our consulting group, trained in our leadership academy. Facilitators taught and modeled small group practices and reiterated confidentiality.

We then returned to the large group for another time of reflection and inquiry. This included read-backs, discussion of themes, and questions and answers. I discussed the creation of circles, communities of practice, and containers to sustain change.

After another period for play—the hokey-pokey—we collaborated on a letter to the CEO. I asked them to include:

♦   what we see from where we stand about the organization;
♦   what is needed;
♦   what we want;

- what we will contribute;
- what we learned today;
- how we are feeling about today's retreat;
- what we are taking away from today's retreat; and
- what we need to keep the momentum of change.

We then engaged in a ritual to close the circle.

As we were cleaning up the space, taking down chairs, and packing up, Joan came into the building for what I gathered was another meeting. I was surprised to see her, but delighted when she said something to the effect that "from the buzz I got on the way in, it looks like good things happened here today." I felt that way too; I was exhausted and incredibly happy for the depth, the laughter, and the hope generated by the experience all of us had created.

Retreat Aftermath

Stopping by a local tavern to celebrate, our consulting team members were thrilled when we read soul cards from the day. We had asked participants to write to questions such as: What were the gifts, what were the challenges of the experience? What did you learn? What did you contribute? What seems important to do next?

Every, and I mean *every* card was thoughtful and—as much as I hate to use a generic word—*positive* about the experience. The only shadow, expressed mostly in the closing conversation of the day, was the concern that the feeling of community and the promise of the day might be not be sustained by a commitment from the organization's leaders. Given the long-term relationship I had with Joan, who by then had been selected as the CEO of the new entity, I had been reassuring that the intent was to integrate both the spirit and the practices of the day into the ongoing creation of the new culture.

A Sampling of Soul Cards from the Retreat

We have arrived at the "people" portion of our journey. Let's continue throughout our teams to bring people into the fold. Let's make them part of the "bottom line," investing time, money, and resources. As Mary said we must focus on a healthy group of women to raise healthy girls. Thanks for today!!!

Gifts: the opportunity to have assistance and guidance in this transforming time. I would have loved more time, a two-day program that allowed for social evening time. It appears as though our cultural differences will be respected and nurtured at the same time. It was a good day, a very good day. Thanks for making us part of the process.

I was totally out of my comfort today. I don't write anything or have a good personal container but I leave here today starting anew. I truly believe this re-organization will be hard, challenging work that will change as we grow. I look forward to helping every way possible. This workshop will help me develop into a strong leader. Thank you!

(1) Sharing my feelings with others, and being respected for my ideas and feelings, no put-downs. (2) Getting to know my sisters. (3) I hope other staff members will have the same opportunity to participate in this event.

Gifts: Meeting new people with same ideals for girls. Being able to find my inner container and be a part of a larger container. Challenges: getting all, other staff, volunteers, and girls—on the same wavelength or circle; learning all we need to know.

Gifts of the day: the power of women together works for the girls and doesn't stop when we become women.

Gifts: wow, what a warm feeling I am walking away with, brought us together as one and we got to used to the word *we* instead of *you* and *us*. Challenges: everyone wants to be heard, but can we *really* listen to everyone? In the busyness of everyday work, can we really implement it?

Gifts of the day: coming together with our future coworkers, sharing our fears and our dreams, realizing *we all* have fears, even Metro starting to build relationships, knowing we're all in it for the girls and volunteers. Challenges: making it a smooth transition, including as many as possible in the decision-making, improving communication "casting a bigger net," alleviating fears of staff!

Gifts: meeting counterparts from sister groups and hearing their stories. Seeing similarities among women—regardless of background, age, etc. in respect to their valuable, memorable life experiences. Challenges: To create the containers as an ongoing/ available resource. Being able to integrate concepts into daily work.

I am inspired by the collective passion in this group, a deep desire and also a feeling of being uprooted, left out—who are we? I sense a confusion about the "what next," expressing that there have been experiences of making changes one month and then having a month's worth of work erased or undone by another change. The women here want *connection and transparency.* [from a facilitator card]

Today gave me the following: rediscovered writing, connections to other staff members, really enjoyed small group work, great facilitators. I leave conflicted about creating work containers. In the past, I have gotten mixed messages about this practice. Will the culture accept this practice?

Oops!

It turns out I was wrong to be reassuring about leadership's intent to sustain and learn to integrate the remarkable insights and movements of the day. I prepared carefully for the debriefing, crafting a container to help Joan and her director of organizational development, neither of whom had attended, to have an experience of the retreat. Members of the facilitator team helped me transcribe soul cards, and we forwarded them along with a summary report in time for Joan to prepare for the meeting. Caren, a leader who had been instrumental in helping to create the retreat, Andrea Nichols, and I attended the meeting.

After months of living with this project, I offered the highlights of my diagnosis, research, and plan:

1. Capitalize on the investment in this retreat by acting now to communicate that you have heard their needs and concerns and are moving forward to create "communities of practice," circles in which leaders learn to *create containers* to seed the cultural transformation, to communicate what is going on, to hold the confusion and tension of change, and to participate in creating new ways of being and working together.

2. Establish a circle of Transformation Teachers or Change Conductors who are learning and teaching the new culture as part of their jobs—not as something "extracurricular."

3. Narrate at all times what you see from where you stand in leadership and ask for their stories of what they see from where they stand. The Change Conductors will help you create methods to do this.

4. Continue to name the challenge: "We are allowing the culture to take a shape more aligned with its mission, moving from silos to circles," from hierarchies in which women cannot see one another to circles (or "flocks") in which leaders can see one another and assist one another when staying airborne is a challenge.

5. Honor the necessity of "landing." When the flock is exhausted, and has lost its direction, don't be afraid to call for days or partial days of reflection. (Part of the "Toyota Miracle," as I understand it, was that they were not afraid to stop the assembly line. Their cultural transformation and changes in processes began with line workers' stories of what worked in manufacturing and what did not, putting the stories into experiments, then stopping to reflect on what was working and not working.)

6. Name the practice of holding both/and: honoring the new culture *and* letting people grieve the old; staying connected to tradition *and* allowing new shape to grow out of that tradition; both collective discernment *and* clarity about who the decision-makers are and why in a given situation.

Methods

1. I recommend a one-year prototype in which a circle of eight, two from each group, meet regularly to learn to create containers on two levels:

    a.) individuals as containers, learning tools of personal reflection, intuition, inquiry, delegation, self-care and development;

b.) the organization as a container where an environment for healthy systems might evolve.

2. The Circle members would meet one day a month with alternating geographical areas hosting.

3. We would plan the curriculum to teach new concepts and give them new tools. They would then have practice assignments within their organizations.

4. At the end of six months, these leaders would be ready to create their own circles of culture conductors who would teach concepts and tools, spreading the processes across all levels including volunteers and girls.

5. CEO and manager participation and buy-in are critical— though I don't know what this will look like as yet. We will work on this to help leaders be both co-creators and decision-makers in areas where "the buck stops with them."

Things Fall Apart

At the debriefing, my first clue that our forward movement was in jeopardy was the fact that Joan had not read any of the preparatory materials. She was distracted and upset, and waved away the container I had created to reconnect to our shared purpose. She began to talk in a disconnected way about how much the work had cost and how she had heard "certain things" that upset her and made her worry this wasn't the right direction for the organization. She suggested maybe it was too early for this kind of effort, and it might not be a good idea to connect managers with their girl-selves because, after all, "girls are different today."

Writing this, I look at the notes taken by Caren during the meeting, and I am still unclear as to what happened, even after years of studying the story and many hours trying to write about it in a way that will contribute to my own understanding. For readers of this book, I want to tell all the truth about my own "not-knowing," and I want to encourage you as you attempt to translate conscious feminine work into a world created on such a different template.

It became apparent that Joan was afraid of something, possibly related to her feared loss of ability to hold employees accountable. Andrea and I listened to the fragments of her story: a phone call from someone, and an apparent breakage of confidentiality that included the content of another participant's writing or speaking. All this made Joan frightened and angry, and clearly, she was going to pull the plug on the experiment that we had created with so much hope. I felt I could rely on the considerable relationship capital Joan and I shared, given our one-on-one sessions leading up to the retreat, but I was unable to engage her on a level that would allow us to focus on what the organization could achieve with the continued exercise of courage and trust.

Andrea and I left the meeting stunned and confused—confused about everything except that without exactly hearing the words, we knew *we would not be continuing the work.* When we got into the car I asked Andrea, "What just happened?" She replied, "I think we got fired."

What I'm Beginning to Understand

A colleague asked me why I chose to focus on a failure story. It is because I want to manifest the values I say I hold: saying what happened (as I experienced it), and telling full stories as opposed to partial. I believe the only healing stories are true stories, and true stories have both the light of success and shadow of failure. The retreat itself was a rousing success! But I failed to sustain the relationship with Joan that had made the work possible. I also failed the larger organization and its members and clients served by not knowing how to teach or convey that the work of cultural transformation is not an overnight cure. Transformation is a healing process engaged through time and in a conscious field of energy, what I call the container.

Here are a few truths I take from this writing of the story: (1) The work *is* daunting; (2) I do not know how to make it any easier than it is right now, nearing the end of this cataclysmic first decade of the twenty-first century; (3) it is worth the effort; and (4) it is incredibly satisfying, joyful work for me—the direct delivery and the work itself, but not the convincing leaders to take a chance on healing.

Understanding More and More Deeply

Telling this particular story also has shown me how fragile are our footholds on the climb out of industrial-age systems. The values of command and control and the fear of losing authority when we choose transparency are deeply internalized in all of us. I am certainly familiar with my own retreat into the warrior's daughter who emerges, fierce and imperious, when things feel "out of control." Certainly the schools in which most of us learned the ways of the world were created in the partial story Isaac Newton knew to tell: the universe runs like a clock. We are most comfortable in the familiar workings of mechanistic systems in which people are creatures rather than creators. Even more fragile are our footholds in the Herculean effort of climbing out of the wasteland created by the older, more disastrous banishment of all that is *the feminine*—right-brained, holistic, nurturing, collaborative, feeling, intuitive—from public, i.e., organizational, life.

All of this is to also say the work we did with this organization was an honor, an opportunity for great learning, and I am grateful Joan had the courage and the vision to infect the old with the germ of the new.

The Universal Wound

I want to emphasize that our consulting work comes from working in the margins, the rich and fertile places where the feminine thrives: among women and girls, artists, and healers. At the same time, the work is thoroughly applicable to men, and to organizations of all kinds. And here is why: we entered the wound of the excised feminine on the stories and in the voices of women, only to encounter the universal wound of *the way things are*, the out-in-the-open secret of a culture crippled by the incapacity to hold critical wholeness, the necessary-to-life both/ands. Diagnosing illness in systems is as simple, many times, as reconnecting:

♦   health to healing professions (in our work in health care);

♦   teaching to learning (in our work in schools);

♦   spiritual capital to material capital (with religious orders and congregations);

♦   collaboration to competition (in work with entrepreneurs and businesses);

♦   wisdom to knowledge (in working with academics); and

♦   creating a tourist destination to creating quality of life for locals (in working with a tourism bureau).

Confirmation by Night

Finally, I feel confirmed in having chosen this daunting, complex story about bright beginnings and disappointing endings by a dream given me the night following a marathon day at my desk trying to tell it:

> I am given an antique stringed instrument by its maker, a dark-haired craftsman of indeterminate age. The instrument, a smallish guitar, is beautiful in an almost unearthly way; it is made of dark wood, polished to a soft sheen. I am awed and grateful, but when I pick up the instrument to play it I cannot seem to do so. I realize that is has been strung for right-handed playing and, of course, I am left.
>
> Afraid of appearing ungrateful, and determined to master right-handed playing, I try and try, but cannot. I return to the maker (the setting seems like an Italian shop street) and ask if he can re-string the instrument for left-handed playing. He demurs. I describe my hard work to master the instrument as it is; I plead my case in what I feel is a reasonable, and a respectful way. The maker takes the instrument from my hands and, rather than change the stringing, he breaks the beautiful instrument into pieces, fragile neck first.

Exercise 16-2: Taking It Further

1. If possible, invite your colleagues to share their stories from exercise 16-1 in a confidential circle that you, or one of the others, volunteer to create and facilitate. After listening to the stories, offer one another read-backs, but not critique of either style or content. Then do a ten-minute fast-write together to this prompt: "Having heard the multiple versions of our shared story, I set my intentions to change my participation in our next attempt by . . ." Share the fast-writes. Close the circle.

   If you are doing these exercises alone, read your own story aloud, and then write to the prompt above.

2. Another way to continue working with this material of bright beginnings/disappointed endings, especially if it was a significant, feeling-laden event in your working life, is to write the story several times. A good tool for surfacing

new details and remembering things you might have for-
gotten is to start each version of the story in a different
place. Begin with the ending, start in the middle, write a
version which is a "prequel," write another which is an
imagined "sequel," capturing how things "ought to have
happened" from your point of view. Obviously, you can use
these tools in a colleague circle as well. This set of tools is
an excellent way to do after-action-reviews of performances or projects.

17.

Teachers Writing:
A Model for Authentic Leadership

No one who ever signed a check for a re-engineering
had his job re-engineered.

Peter Block[1]

As I survey the landscape of late 2008 I see more than ample evidence of organizations in systems failure, and traditional leaders impotent to do more than slow, or (at times with short-sighted interventions) hasten the disintegration. At the same time, conscious feminine strategies for healing and reinvigorating are viewed and resisted as too slow, too simple, too expensive. I also suspect that even well-intentioned leaders fear the surrender of traditional notions of authority and status, and the reexamination of their own identities with regard to work and life.

A common theme in stories about failed organizational transformation is often leaders' failures to see themselves as participants. A leader who wants to restore life and love to her organization will need to transform her relationship to the system. She does not "get reengineered" nor does she "reengineer"; she shifts her job description from doing disconnected, high-level tasks to doing the work of building the community. The leader moves into the circle while remaining clear-eyed and communicative about how she is *both* a member of the circle *and* a steward with unique responsibilities, and therefore authority, for seeing the larger system and caring for it. This chapter describes a prototype of what is needed now: a transparent, authentic leadership creating ways to discern with others "what really matters," as a basis for action in the world.

Participative Facilitator

A breakfast table conversation at a writing retreat originally turned me to contemplation of a universal element of the Women Writing for (a) Change process that remains nonetheless remarkable in the culture at large: that is, the participative role of the facilitator/teacher.

"What I notice that's unusual to my experience is that you both, as you call it, *hold the center*, and you participate in the circle as a writer," observed Maureen Martin, a Chicago hospice chaplain, physician, and then newcomer to WWf(a)C.

Carol Walkner, transplanted to Cincinnati from New York jumped in, "I think that's part of what causes the change, the shifts in our lives when we participate in this work."

When I asked her to say more about this, Carol noted that the teacher's writing offered as part of the mix of voices and themes deepens the safety of the container. It communicates that, while a writer is being witnessed and held by someone whose commitment is to service, the leader is not studying the writer from afar, evaluating at the safe remove of the nonrisking observer. "So, we can go deeper and deeper—to where the shifts happen and become transformation," finished Carol.

"That's radical, and so simple—so much a given here—you might overlook it," mentioned Layla, an occasional participant in WWf(a)C workshops.

I trace this element of WWf(a)C back to the early 1980s when, as a participant in the Ohio Writing Project at Miami University of Ohio, I eagerly embraced the writing project tenet that *teachers of writing should write*. The habitual stance was the writing teacher as above and uninvolved in the struggle of finding language for thoughts and feelings. *Writing with students* was groundbreaking and was hailed as either a heretical or a common sense practice, depending on who was speaking.

The orthodoxy of the removed teacher, the nonwriter or secret writer, is at least twofold in its origins. One layer of the subject-object relationship lines up with the tradition of the scientist-observer recording "objective" data. Despite the Heisenberg principle, which taught us that all observations are affected by the presence of the observer no matter how subtle her presence, *the myth of the disconnected* has persisted, and has deeply scarred educational—and leadership—models.

The truth is that learning is a transaction affecting both teacher and student. Put another way: though we are not in the *same* relation to what we are gathering to learn, teacher and students are all learners in the classroom or circle. This is radical because it goes to the root of unexamined power relations, embodying this truth: teachers and students have—and need—different roles in a given set of circumstances, but we are the same in terms of our humanity and need for mutual respect, not to mention our openness to learning.

The way this truth is revealed in our WWf(a)C circles is that teachers write, and we share our writing in both large group and small group settings. We are transparent about our delights and our struggles in shaping language, and this alone is a source of learning for the students who join us. They see us at work with words. They may well see, and be comforted by the fact, that we are not necessarily "better" writers than they are. We may not even be—though we often are—more practiced and more experienced. What WWf(a)C faculty communicate to the students is that we are all practicing writers, and we have devoted ourselves to learning how to "teach writing." We are devoted creators of relationships which allow words to emerge, to be heard, polished, made truer to their intent—and more beautiful.

When I work with public and parochial school teachers of writing I say that this is the element I would choose, if forced to choose *one element*, of how we do what we do. We are practicing writers, and we drop the screen on our own writing practice, our own crafting with words.

Are there boundaries, cautions about this? Yes, of course. All dances, to be dances, must have steps—rules, if you will. However, participating in the dance is more art, less science, than *watching* the dancers and *correcting* their steps. The guiding principle I lift up in mentoring others is: Always remember, we are there for them; they are not there for us.

This principle can be unfolded in a number of ways, but one important application of this principle is that I do not take up too much space with my own writing. I recognize that most students would too easily defer to the teacher who wanted to push the boundaries of time and space, and center her words and her needs.

In the early days of WWf(a)C while I was still beginning to articulate what I knew to be true, two or three women created knock-offs of our program. I allowed them to "pick my brain" so they could start their own schools. In one of the latter attempts, a woman, who had been in a WWf(a)C class only six weeks and had never been a teacher, decided she was going to launch her own school in a small college town a moderate distance away. At the time, I felt that she had every right to do so, as long as she didn't call it Women Writing for (a) Change. (Her attempt prompted me to trademark the name of the school.) She called her school Writing Women. She bought a building, and built a lovely program of complementary arts around the core of writing classes. One of my mentors, who lived nearby, described a Writing Women read-around as "the big writer-teacher in the center with her little writer-students arranged on either side of her as if in Ziegfeld tableau." More time and attention was devoted to the work of the writer-teacher. Hers were deemed the "better" pieces; her students read complementary, shorter, and "not as good" pieces.

My friend was horrified, but we were both consoled by the knowledge that such a practice of teaching-learning would not likely persist. We predicted one of several possibilities would unfold, or maybe a combination. For the school to succeed, the teacher might mature in her practice and be affected by the power and maturity of her students' voices. Or, the students would not put up with this for long. Rather than diminish their growth as writers, they would either abandon the teacher or help reform the process. Without teacher maturity or student-writers' growth, the school would fail.

Writing Women closed and I speculate that the unconscious "taking up of space" by the founder-teacher was a factor. I have found the need to maintain a delicate balance: the teacher/ leader must be "big" enough, strong and authoritative enough to be an initiator. She must provide a model of grounded energy that the writers trust. Alongside this cultivation of "bigness," she must cultivate a watchfulness about her own power; it is very easy to get addicted to "being the center," when our real job is "holding the center." I advocate that leaders/teachers have professional spiritual companions who will help them be self-reflective and honest. At WWf(a)C, we have practices which support teachers' development as strong, "big," confident leaders who do not develop a cult of personality around themselves.

One of my proudest moments was hearing a WWf(a)C writer, a skillful poet and corporate attorney, say of her long-time participation in the Tuesday night class, "I started my time at WWf(a)C with Mary as my teacher for several semesters. Over the years, I've had every faculty member as a teacher each for at least a semester, usually two at a stretch. The process and the community still work, despite the teachers' obvious differences. What this tells me is that we're not dealing here with a cult of personality."

Let me give some specifics about my own practice of being a teacher-writer. I read short pieces. If there is a shortage of time in small group, I don't read at all, reminding students that, though I am proud to be a writer among them, I am there to put their writing first. I prefer not to read first or last at a read-around, reluctant to be in a position that might indicate "better" or "more important" in any way. If I am the first or last reader it is because no one in the community claimed that position or wanted it, and I will remark on this as the preface to my reading. (These guidelines apply to in-class reading of work; performances sometimes require me to read first to set the context.)

Teachers at WWf(a)C do not keep traditional therapeutic boundaries. We do reveal ourselves in our writing, and I believe this is a powerful communication of woman-in-progress, writer-in-progress that is echoed around the circle by the other writers and women-in-progress. Students have often remarked upon this role modeling by teachers—for example, on soul cards: "When I hear the struggles and challenges, the secret fears and flaws of women who are so wonderful, so amazingly together, I think it's possible *I* am wonderful and amazing too. I'm not so alone with my doubts, or my fears of inadequacy."

One important caveat is that I do not think teachers should read or share inordinately dark personal material with students. What do I mean by this? I cannot give any rules here either—only indications. I would not read anything that conveyed such self-doubt, fear, or struggle with personal darkness, that women either feared trusting me or, a more likely scenario, tried to take care of me. I learned to walk this careful but not rigid line while teaching high school students. With teenagers I shared my poetry, my journal entries, and my essays about teaching. I did *not* share sexual material, criticisms of faculty or administration, or the deep pain of the divorce I went through during my tenure as a high school teacher.

This work of conscious feminine leadership is not suitable for exhibitionists, narcissists, or divas of any stripe. Needy people make horrible teachers and leaders because they are far too apt to twist the relationship to serve their own needs. At the other end of the spectrum, the way of working I'm describing is not amenable to writer-teachers who cannot be vulnerable, or who need to be right and *the* authority on writing or life. No dogmatists need apply, only nimble-footed dancers, who love continuing to create the dance.

Undivided Woman-Teacher

The "other fold" of the participatory leadership model that I'm aware of resonates with culture more than with science. I am haunted by the words of Margaret Starbird in *Goddess in the Gospels*:

> I was gradually becoming aware of my own bondage to the "sun god" and the burnout and utter exhaustion it was causing, the desert I was becoming. Until that point I had willingly, and even enthusiastically embraced the path of service to others, but now I was in pain, my health deteriorating, with no time for anything but meeting the demands of my composite roles.[2]

A daughter of generations of West Point commanders, wife of the same, and mother of five children, Margaret became a near-casualty of the war between service as constructed within patriarchy and service to her own spirit, her own gifts of intellect and scholarship. She suffered a nervous breakdown in her middle years, entering a mental hospital from which she both feared never returning to the needs of her family—and surely *feared* returning to what she herself called a cage of "command performances" and duties.

Service professions, among them teaching, are laid down on the same pattern and cut from the same cloth as mothering: having awesome responsibilities alongside little—and only conditional— authority and resources with which to fulfill them. The "good" mother—and teacher—must be all service to others and have no regard for self. Or, as I used to observe within the institution of public school teaching, we are taught that whatever contributes to our well-being is, by its very nature, inimical to the well-being of our students! Implausible as it might seem, I was not surprised to read a woman's passionate argument that teachers *should not* write, in the pages of *English Journal*! She claimed that our own writing steals time we should be devoting to helping students become better writers, *steals* from them literally. Teachers are apparently under contract to serve the needs of students, for all hours of the days, weeks, months, and years. We should be reading their papers, grading their papers that—if we are assigning enough writing—will rise to mountains of unread manuscripts needing our careful correction.

It is radical down to our very roots to fashion a life that balances, or even *allows*, for the needs of those who serve to be considered alongside the culture's needs and demands for our service.

Margaret Starbird speaks further, poignantly:

> My husband's job as a battalion commander in the elite 101st "Screaming Eagles" Division at Fort Campbell required me to participate in an endless stream of social events, command performances, and activities related to his troops, in addition to caring for our five children, who ranged in age from five months to eleven years old when we arrived.
>
> The whole three-year assignment has melted into mush in my memory, except for a few highlights. . . . My whole life was one of trying to juggle commitments and meet deadlines without being late to anything (a cardinal sin in the army!). I felt like a trained lioness, jumping through the fiery hoops, and experienced true compassion for the caged beasts in the circus when it came to town. I was not in the desert during this time; I was the desert.[3]

I have seen far too many women, my own mother included, used up and discarded unnecessarily. Surely the unlived lives of our mothers are of no benefit to daughters or sons; to the contrary, many of us are haunted by a debt we owe, in a bargain neither we, nor they, ever consciously made. Similarly, I have seen far too many fine teachers, mostly—but not only—women, become deserts, dried up and embittered, distanced from the ideals which led them to the profession in the first place.

To write while teaching, to keep one's own gifts alive while mothering, is to water into health and beauty the all-too-familiar wasteland of family and institutional life.

Anna / Dancer[4]

She began taking ballet at age three and performed professionally in Paris as a teen, but Anna left her dreams of dancing behind when she married and had children. Now she teaches her daughter, working with her three or four hours a day in their home. Anna hopes that one day her daughter will fulfill her dreams and dance as a member of a world-class Corps de Ballet.[5]

I.
I try to imagine what you teach her,
Anna, pictured in the morning paper,
how you teach your daughter, Anna,
to dance what you renounced.

I try to imagine why you teach her
this dance: formal, brutal
in its demands upon a woman's life,
in its demands upon a woman's body—

always the torturous shoes,
enforced delicacy of bone and line,
bodies shaped to suggest breaking.

II.
Mother myself, and teacher,
I am dreaming, I am teaching
toward a world in which our daughters
shed the silly tutus and toe-shoes,
and dance, full-footed and fleshy
in all the bodies of their lives:
taut or soft,
elegant or arthritic
pregnant, or ripe with age,

in which they leave behind
only those dreams
only those dances which reduce them
to porcelain figurines,
mincing and preening,
gathering dust
on the whatnot shelves of their lives.

III.
Won't you join me, Anna,
in renouncing renunciation,
in teaching our daughters by refusing
to give up our dreams,
by continuing to dance,

by contributing to a new repertoire,
abandoning the classic roles:
princesses and sylphs,
ingénues and swans,
Dying Swans,
Anna, there is too much dying
in this dancing they would have us
train our daughters to!

I'll have no part in teaching
the traditional positions,
the requisite steps in a dance
that divides a woman against herself,
stipulates she be mother or
dancer, teacher or performer.

Join me, Anna,
in refusing to teach our daughters
to bend to the bar
in refusing to turn them over
to the dance-masters
who will finish the work
of making them loyal members
of the company,

pretty ballerinas
who have nothing to say,
are graceful and useful
in the service
of the Corpse de Ballet.

18.

Conscious Feminine and Linguistic Leadership in a Time of Planetary Crisis

Language does our thinking for us.
Kathleen Hall Jamieson[1]

Leadership's task: to help everyone find their voices.
Peter Block[2]

The paradoxical nature of both/and facilitation described in the previous chapter is one of many lessons I learned about leadership over the years of making up Women Writing for (a) Change as I went along. As someone who learns best by creating, I founded the Feminist Leadership Academy of Cincinnati (FLA) as a community to enact conscious feminine leadership. FLA and what we learn by doing there is a book of its own, but I do not want to end this book without pointing to what leadership from the conscious feminine can look like on the ground. I want *to say, to save,* a little of what we have learned in the FLA incubator of leadership, so that our learning will be woven into the DNA of re-imagined leadership, which is desperately needed if we are to stop the madness.

Linguistic Leadership

A critical aspect of leadership as practiced in FLA is that we are a language-generating, meaning-making, meaning-evoking community. Listening to women's stories, poems, and journal entries in the earliest days of Women Writing for (a) Change, I heard that leadership was emerging powerfully in writers' lives because they were listening to themselves on the page, being listened to and listening to one another in the classes. I recalled Shelley's proclamation that "poets are the unacknowledged legislators of the world."[3]

Leaders speak things into existence. Conscious feminine leaders create containers for *themselves and other members of their field* to speak things into existence. Conscious feminine leadership provides the healing complement to traditional leadership models. Traditionally, leaders fixate on their own speaking, with no regard for what happens *after* the words, and no sense of responsibility for connecting words in real time to others' words, beyond the imperial question-and-answer session. The conscious feminine leader is aware of the impact of her words She invites others into speech, and points to ways words can become action in the world.

The Current Field

There is much talk in organizational and leadership theory about "the field," a term fostering the understanding that everything is energy. I will borrow the image here to amplify the necessity of including conscious feminine patterns into leadership.

A typical scenario: a leader speaks to groups with whom he or she has little relationship, beyond the frame of his or her theories, ideas, or adventures. In settings which are so much the norm that to even suggest disrupting them is to create scandal, the leader speaks at length, either off the cuff or from a set of prepared remarks which have become boilerplate. He or she is busy, flying all over the world doing important work, spreading important ideas. His time is precious; fees are high. She becomes a profit center for groups who hire her to give lectures. The groups can be sure she will draw a large crowd and help them secure both dollars and recognition. If this setup is not "the only game in town," it is the only game that seems to matter to people who attend conferences and lectures with important leaders. The attendees seem to be collecting charms on a bracelet, or lines on a resume: "studied with so-and-so in South Africa"; "heard famous thinker such-and-such in Toronto and Santa Fe." If the ideas are powerful and the speaker can communicate well, the energy is inspirational, thrilling, and often motivating. In my experience, however, the energy rarely extends beyond the conference hall, and maybe into discussions afterward in hotel bars and at receptions. Rarely is the energy channeled into the creation of leadership for a planet in crisis. The crisis stems precisely from the rarefied masculine-way-alone style of leadership that bears stunted fruit.

A Small Digression on Shame

Let me first clear the space by saying what I do not want. I do not want to end the practice of keynote speeches, ideas for the sake of ideas, or art for art's sake. Nor do I want to disparage those who deliver great speeches, engage in cutting-edge science, and delve more deeply into the sky or the workings of the brain. Above all, I do not want to shame anyone, not even the great men at whose feet I have been unwilling to sit hour after hour. By happy coincidence, I discovered the words of Gregory Bateson in the introduction to a book on healing shame. His words have become my mantra: "The pattern that corrects is the pattern that connects."[4] Shamed early and often for carrying the feminine gifts of feeling and nurture into public life, I never want to be an instrument of knee-jerk anti-intellectualism, or anti-masculine-ism, or any other simplistic solution. I do not want my remarks to be taken as an argument for destroying the masculine self, as if that would be a final solution. I do not believe in final solutions.

Make Space for the Unexpressed

I want those who have power because their lives and ways of leading have been sanctioned by the dominant culture to use that power to make space for the unexpressed, the underprivileged values of life and leadership. Since they are insiders by virtue of their abilities in areas valued in traditional culture, I want them to have the courage to open the door to what has been forced outside. I invite them to create containers for the feminine: to sit in the circle, be vulnerable, let go of their certainties, and actively engage new practices in their own persons and within the organizations in which they hold power. If it is too late for them to learn the feminine within or demonstrate it without, then I want them to get out of the way so those who are willing to learn can be seen and heard. By getting out of the way, I do not mean a shamed warrior's suicide. Rather, I suggest surrendering: sitting down and shutting up for a long enough time to balance all the years of standing up and taking up too much space. More nicely put, I want them to enjoy being *in* the container, listening, nodding, and taking notes, as women have since we have been allowed in public containers at all—schools and businesses and a little crust of visibility in some churches. I want them to bring some homemade food, make coffee, welcome people at the door and sit for a time at the feet of the feminine; I believe all this is necessary to be part of the project *of connecting by correcting.*

Put in poetry, I want to cultivate leadership to correct:

1. History
litany
of
bloody dates
shouted

by
fat coaches

at
good girls
in
white blouses.

We take
careful notes
of
pogrom, witch hunt,
holocaust

enshrine
beefy heroes
in our
museum minds

telling
their stories
instead
of our own

to
pass tests
win grants
get jobs

surviving
by memorizing
our own
exclusion.

2. Herstory
rising
in the smoke
of
washtub
cookpot
witch burning
holocaust

Heartstory

of childbed
marriagebed
sickbed
deathbed

so many
sheets
stained
by pleasure
and
pain

then
bleached pale
and hung
in the sun
to
fade

Mystory

of women's lives
written
stitched
plaited
quilted, patched
and painted,
and all too often,
packed away
in a
chest
without hope.[5]

Leadership That Corrects

Failures of leadership are so thoroughgoing that many people
argue for abandoning the word *leader*. I consider myself a survivor
of the war waged against women by the systematic desecration of
all the words we claim for naming ourselves whole and honorable,
so I'm not in favor of ceding linguistic territory. Daunting though
it may be, I'd rather participate in the task of speaking into existence a leadership of wisdom and delight, inviting others to play
my "what if" game.

What If I Said "Leader"
and It Evoked an Image of Someone Who . . .

Always kept sight of what is in the middle?
What are we gathered here to give life to?
Told her own stories and made space for yours?
Asked, "What can we make of this?"
Rather than "Whose fault is it?"
Didn't privilege some stories over others for the sake of political
correctness
Or the need to appear cool, or in the know?

Had the courage to ask, "What's going on in the room right now?
What is not being said?
What am I feeling?
What are others feeling?"

Spent time and energy creating spaces for people to generate
meaning,
To take risks,
To tell the truth,
To make commitments?
Was courageous enough to integrate life-giving and soulful tools
into practice:
Circles, silence, flowers, poetry, stories,
Knowing that it might expose him to ridicule
Knowing that it *would* expose *her* to ridicule?

Knowing, all the while, that the culture reveres and rewards discon-
nection,
Calling it "pure genius,"
"scholarship."
What if the Leader had enough integrity and imagination to con-
nect:
Theory with practice
Research with action
Ideas with implementation
Activism with compassion?

In short, what if we said "leader" and that word connected with
someone who was conscious that publicly enacting feminine values made her (or him) more vulnerable, less valued, and did it anyway, intentionally and respectfully? Conscious feminine leaders act
in spite of all the pitfalls, because we are running out of time. We
recognize the futility of doing things the way we always have: the
maimed, half-brained, closed-heart way, the hero's way, the warrior way, the purist's way, the way of masculine = public, feminine
= private.

Digression and Paradox

As I have said elsewhere in this book, I align with Carl Jung's idea
that the feminine and the masculine are innate and universal patterns
in the human psyche. Archetypes of feminine and masculine are not
restricted to gender but are present in both women and men; they are
more about structures of consciousness than about sex organs. That
said, my own belief, based on experience and observation, is that
women are more likely to be practitioners of conscious feminine

leadership because we live in bodies which make cycles more apparent, and which can incarnate the great both/and in a way that men's
bodies cannot. I do not agree with Freud that biology is destiny but I
do recognize that, with our ability to birth another life, only women
have the bodily knowledge of being both *self* and *self with other*. Given
how little is actually left after men's leading for millennia, and with
women's bodily knowledge of the great both/and, I am passionate
that women become the teachers of conscious feminine leadership. I
believe we have nothing to lose and much to gain by embracing
women leading for (a) change.

Imagine my frustration when I see men having more authority
and credibility espousing the feminine than women do. Men, in far
greater numbers than women, author books about living systems
and feminine, holistic leadership models, while rarely enacting
those theories in the organizations and conferences where they are
the celebrated centers. This paradox awakens a deep knowing: I
see without full realization that I have taken on something that
appears to be impossible in my lifetime: genuine and wholeheart-
ed embrace of the feminine as well as the actual persons and practices of the feminine, by all of us still bathed in patriarchy.

A Primer of Conscious Feminine Leadership

"We" are "they" and "the system is us."
Don't talk about what "they" or "the system" won't let you do.
  Don't feed the beast by warring with "them" or "the system."
  Lead from where you are; do not wait to ascend the ladder.
By the time you get there, you have paid such a high price,
you dare not notice the ladder is against the wrong wall.
  For each piece of work which is yours to steward:
  Invite a potential, community
  Create the space for all voices to be heard
  Gather all the stories.
Remember: "conversation" privileges the masculine.
  Plan intentional beginnings and endings
  Hold the creative tension between process and product,
openness and boundaries,
risk and safety.
  Care for the container on a regular basis
  Set your intentions publicly;

Avoid hidden agendas.

    Ask others to do the same.

Create context and define terms for maximum inclusion.

    Serve the work.

Open the space

Set boundaries around it.

    Clarify the process of decision-making: who, how, why and by when?

    Clarify how long decisions will remain in place before revisiting them.

    Give up the need to be seen as a player, smart, cool, or in the know.

    Find your joy by serving the greater whole.

This list-in-progress is more useful within a community of practice than within a book about leadership. However, the list points out some of the themes you can begin to explore as you translate conscious feminine and linguistic leadership into your setting.

A Fable, a Place to Begin, a Poem

A Native American Fable: A grandfather was talking to his grandson about how he felt. He said, "I feel as if I have two wolves fighting in my heart. One wolf is the vengeful, angry one. The other wolf is the loving, compassionate one." The grandson asked, "Which wolf will win the fight in your heart?" The grandfather answered: "The one I feed."

Exercise18-1: A Place to Begin

Create a lineage of leadership for yourself. Place yourself within a line of real people from your life who fed the loving, compassionate part of you. (I am not an advocate of throwing out the baby of tradition along with the sometimes foul bathwater of hierarchy. In fact, hierarchy has been and still is useful in emergency, and other contexts.) Write the names of your leadership forbears, and remember stories about them. Write the stories and study them for clues to as yet unexpressed or underexpressed elements in your leadership self.

I choose to place myself in the leadership tradition of the conscious feminine, to place my self in service to the conviction that we will never restore the messes we have made or the natural and organizational places (and words) we have desecrated, until we admit to the very early, if not original, sin of banishing the feminine from our public lives, from our notions of authority, value, and power. I intend my words and work to be part of a conversation and a movement to redefine the meaning of leadership in an era of crisis brought on by gamesmanship and greed of Leaders-as-We-Have-Known-Them. They posture and pillage on the brightly lit stages of press conferences, trade expos, lecture halls, board rooms, pulpits, even nonprofit dog-and-pony shows, created to show donors that "something is being done with their money."

I choose to act as if leadership is love, put to good use, wherever there is need. And where isn't there a need for love?

Lineage poem

Early Letter in Spring II, 2006

Dear Mother,

This morning the prayer words
"Mary Queen of Heaven"
float into my reverie
on our, yours & mine
stalk of motherline,
grandmothers pruned long
before we could know them.

Today I am naming you
Isabel Queen of the Kitchen,
Chairwoman—though we said "man" then—
of the annual Crestline High School
Marching Band Uniform Fund
Spaghetti Dinner.
In the new, state-of-the-art
South Elementary School
kitchen, you reigned.

With my girlfriends in our frilly
servers' aprons setting tables in the cafeteria
I watched you above bubbling pots

of homemade sauce, your non-recipe/recipe,
stout Italian woman weaving
among the other mothers
prepping salad, cutting homemade pies
setting kettles to boil for pasta,
your never-manicured, clean hands
speaking your language of encouragement,
direction-without-condescension.
It strikes me now how this was
the only place I could watch you perform.
Women then were so far behind
scenes, the cleaning, ironing, arranging flowers
stage-hands for priests and principals,
petty town politicians, policemen
all the princes
of our lives.

But through the kitchen pass-through
a proscenium of sorts, I saw how
you inspired—

my friends all loved you
brothers' friends too
crowded our tiny concrete porch summer nights where you
reigned from a porch rocker set between geranium pots
dispensing no-nonsense advice.
You joked and laughed
but *always* appropriately.
You were steadfast that mothers should be mothers
not faux girlfriends flirting and preening.

You courted no one, did not engage
in village intrigue
what could be intense competition
for small town prestige.

Mother, your reigning was
the raining-love-and-common sense
kind of Queenship

If you had
a status-conscious,
bone in your body I never felt it
press in on me
and we hugged often.

(Dad said his mother was cold;
stoic Scotch-Welsh
the Pierces
were a more imperious lot
with their books and well-spoken
aloofness
in coal-mining towns)

Despite the jealous rumor of one
of my friends' mothers that
"you pushed me" into achievement:
band, choir, honor society,
musical theater—

Oh, not a bit of it
you made space for me to express
what your life suppressed but did not
extinguish

just love, put to good use.

Epilogue:
Growth, Change, Letting Go

I have moved as much from kitchen to kitchen
as from house to house, seeking to meet
my mother among the bowls and spoons,
even more in the movement
from table to stove,
stove to table, and
back again.

I have moved from kitchen to kitchen, as if
the shape of this room would shape me,
make my life larger or smaller,
    better or worse,
    richer or poorer.

In early old age, I have moved to the first eat-in
kitchen of my life since quitting my mother's
table-cramped kitchen,
universe I still explore.

Telling my life in kitchens
instead of rivers and mountains,
marlins and grails, I must either
bow to the knowledge of my own smallness
    or ask:

What am I to learn in each galley,
closet, L-shaped, homely room?
    And what will I teach?

What is mine to make here?
    Whom shall I feed?

I have traveled so far from my mother's life
how dare I go farther?
makes each move treacherous.

I have traveled so far from my mother's life
how dare I go farther?

leaving her behind.

As someone who grew up with powerful messages about the dangers of "getting too big for your britches," I have found it excruciating to have been called to work that requires me to put my deepest self on the line so publicly. Following intuition, dreams, and "inner knowing" without support of statistics, measurement of outcomes, and other forms of sanctioned knowing amplifies the "Who-do-you-think-you-are?" voice in my head to sometimes unbearable volume. On the other hand, I am aware than I have not so much invented the school and its processes as I have quilted it, re-membered it from cherished pieces put into my eager hands by a lineage of women. First and most potent among them is Isabel Rose Caliendo Pierce, whose kitchen I have re-created over again and again, sometimes repeating the unhealthy patterns she helped make and were her unmaking, and sometimes weaving more life-giving patterns from the depth of her capacity to love.

Writing this book, I see more clearly that the work of my life and hers, the work of Women Writing for (a) Change, is Mother Love in all its faces: gentle, fierce, nurturing, rigorous, life-giving, and life-surrendering. It is no easy thing for a "below average" woman to become conscious of being a portal, a voice for the distorted and diminished feminine. This is work for finer vessels, more eloquent voices, and larger personages, for braver, and less insecure women. Only yesterday, a cherished friend and colleague admonished me, "Stop being the mother!" She is only the latest in a long line of people warning me of the psychosocial entanglements and near impossibility of being mother in a healthy way. Mother in our culture signifies something to be used and thrown away, a sentimentalized relationship, or a relationship to be shucked off like old clothes on the way to autonomy. I sighed, "I know, I know, I'll try . . ."

But even as I spoke, I heard the inner voice saying, "How can I stop? It's not what I do, it's who I am." I suspect that I am laboring to give birth, at times against my will (given the pain), to the honored, co-equal, co-creative Mother.

To Relate, Not Identify

A good friend and mentor reading drafts of this book told me, "In your prose, but not in your poetry, I hear an under-voice, tentative, and frightened, saying 'Please, don't think I'm making too much of myself. Please don't hurt me or mortify me. Hear what I'm trying to say.' It weighs down your sentences and muddies your writing style to have all that equivocation, and well, fear." My wise friend is right. Fear weighs down my life too, has weighed me down into depression, anxiety, and a desire to run away, to get me to a hermitage, or maybe a country where I don't speak the language, so "my mouth," as my mother always warned me, "won't get me in trouble."

In *Dancing in the Flames: The Dark Goddess in the Transformation of Consciousness*, by Elinor Dickson and Marion Woodman,[1] I discovered a distinction which has been a touchstone for me as I ponder the role of an individual in receiving and passing on something beyond herself, and her understanding.

> To "identify" is to become the God or Goddess without the feminine ground to reestablish the boundaries that return us to our humanity. To "relate" is to know that the ego is the instrument through which the divine energy flows. Pavarotti relates when he honors the divine for his gift, and when he steps off the stage and becomes just plain Luciano enjoying his pasta.[2]

My task, then has been to have an ego large and whole enough to receive and to transmit the energy that has chosen me and for which I have made various containers, while never allowing myself to *identify*, to believe that *I* am the container. A danger for any leader is that he or she would let others' need for certainty and "bigness," what I sometimes call a need for "guru-ness," force her to wear the false face of the all-knowing divinity. A far greater danger for me, given my particular history and temperament, is that I allow others' fear of female power to shame me into suppressing my energy behind Emily Dickinson's coy question, "I'm nobody, who are you?" I am both a firm believer in horizontal sharing of power *and* a believer that we must learn to create female lineages, i.e., herstory, as well as history.

Nothing whole and healthy, no organization, no school or church, can be built on the lie that women's stories and contributions do not matter, are minor, or less. I have seen many women compromised at the soul level when they try to fashion female power and leadership, while they remain unconscious or in denial that they do so within a culture allergic to feminine whole and holiness. I suspect that I could write a book tracing the erasure of the feminine in organizations founded by and for women. My own alma mater, for example, Ohio Dominican University, formerly College of St. Mary of the Springs, began its adaptation to the financial realities of the times in 1968, when I was a sophomore. It began with a name change and the enrollment of a few men. By 2008, the disconnect from the feminine source is so complete that I open my alumnae magazine to see news of the second lay president in the school's history, and second man. That the de-feminization is, if not complete, pretty close to it, was made clear to my eyes when the school fielded a football team.

A Film Example

A powerful image of identifying rather than relating was brought home to me in the ending of the 1999 film *Elizabeth*, that chronicled the life of Elizabeth I of England from childhood to the beginning of her reign. Elizabeth had been installed on the throne by the violent overthrow of forces loyal to Roman Catholicism and to Mary, Queen of Scots, Elizabeth's half-sister and rival. As only one—but a far-reaching—consequence of this sea of change, Catholic devotion to the Blessed Mother, the last vestige of goddess worship in England, was all but suppressed.

In the denouement of the film, a youthful and heretofore spontaneous Elizabeth circles a white stone statue of Mary, the Blessed Mother. Elizabeth ponders the face of the statue, as if trying to understand Mary's power to inspire. In the next scene, Elizabeth cuts off her long hair, and very deliberately, ritually, covers her face with white, plaster-like make-up. Having masked her humanity and femininity she goes out to greet the riotous throngs. I read this scene as Elizabeth *identifying* with the goddess, putting on the false face of divine power in order to be "big" enough to rule as the first female monarch of England.

In identifying with the goddess, even as she suppressed connection with the Divine Feminine, Elizabeth lost touch with what

Woodman and Dickson call the grounded feminine. I see this as a danger for contemporary women leaders and for celebrities, as well. In order to convince others of our power, we lose touch with our human limits and identify with the projections of those in our communities. Some want to worship or give away their own power—and responsibility—and invest power and responsibility in "larger-than-life" leaders or "divas." Others will unconsciously work to diminish the leader's power, thereby making it impossible for her to carry out her responsibilities. They are recreating the mother-child dynamic within patriarchy: mothers bear the most responsibility for the well-being of children, while having the least access to resources and authority to provide for those children.

A New Season

Fall has always been my favorite season, as it was my father's, who said his church was sitting under an old hickory tree on a Sunday morning listening to a squirrel cutting on a nut, while the rest of the family attended Mass.

It is late fall, October 2008, as I end the story for now. In chapter 6, I described the WWf(a)C ritual of creating the container for our work by passing fire in bowl around the circle. This morning, I sit in the still-dark, watching a candle stutter in the very cut glass bowl we used throughout most of the formative years of the Cincinnati school. This container for protecting the fire of the feminine made its way around thousands of circles as we moved from space to space, from the first rented room, to the writing house, to the writing hall above the Ironworkers union hall. In 2006 we moved to what many of the writers now call "the center," a fully wheelchair accessible building, to hold a more diverse circle of writers, a building to hold the center of our expanding-into-the-wider-world vision of the conscious feminine, of women and girls getting a fair hearing. The center, sometimes called the "mother school," was imagined and purchased by the almost superhuman efforts of a small group of committed women as a permanent home for the hearts and words of women and girls. A student of history, I have been driven by the knowledge that whatever benefits women and girls for ourselves alone rarely survives a generation, as it is the first casualty of larger cultural chaos and wars in particular. Women's movements are not only abandoned, they are erased or demonized, then reinvented, at great cost, over and over again.

Fire

Some of the deepest learning in our Feminist Leadership Academy and among the WWf(a)C practitioners and site owners has been in the area of self-care. How not to burn out or burn up in the effort to conduct the repressed energy of the conscious feminine into an unconscious, and even hostile, world? Beth Lodge-Rigal, our Bloomington, Indiana, sister and owner of WWf(a)C Bloomington, introduced us to the teachings of Karla McLaren. In her CD set, *Energetic Boundaries,* I caught this phrase: "Female fire elements have a hard time in the world."[3] I am a fire element, an astrological Leo, moreover someone prone to fury at the unaccountable and unconscionable insistence on splitting wisdom from knowledge, heart from head, feminine from masculine. I have been fiery in my dedication to the vision of the divine marriage, the crucible of the grounded feminine, but I have tried not to burn others, nor burn myself to ashes of bitterness and resentment. My private efforts to both protect the fire of my vision and passion and to not let the fire become an egotistical, out-of-control conflagration have been aligned with my work in the outer world—creating containers for the fire of inspiration and transformation. I have sought out others to create containers for me to lay down my fire, to fall down, to surrender to not knowing, grief, and my own fragility and exhaustion. Colleagues have created containers in which I have been the fortunate participant, able to write, think, and learn, able to be myself, not a persona, a more or less than human person/woman.

This Book as a Container

In making this book I have not *talked about* my containers, but have shown them to you: poems, dreams, communities, symbols, rituals, and suggestions for you to create containers of meaning in your places, both private and public. Nearing the end of the writing, I see that I have written myself into an awareness that a new pattern is emerging, or, to adapt a phrase, that I/we may have come to the end of this particular rope or thread.

After all, in the WWf(a)C candle ritual, the candle is blown out and held with as much intention and attention as it is lit. In its own bittersweet way, autumn is as rich and fecund as summer.

Why Not Just Say What Is Happening?

In my favorite season, I have spent this week doing just that. Sitting in each of the Cincinnati writing circles this glorious week of October 2008, I have sketched out the history of the movement, summarizing the most recent chapter. On June 20, 2008, we celebrated the successful completion of our capital campaign, the arduous eighteen-month effort to purchase free and clear a home for our expanding movement. It was the last step in a path of stewardship I discerned in 1998: (a) to establish a school (FLA) that will bring and evoke conscious feminine leadership for the movement and from the movement into the larger world; (b) to secure a home to be owned by the community, a place of our own for cherishing and protecting the fire of the feminine; (c) to write the story.

2008 yielded a bumper crop of activity and joy. Leaders from all three classes of FLA—The Pioneers, Builders, and Weavers—met for a week of writing, and self and community care. We wove a container for staying connected to and from the movement. Happily, we bridged with our young leaders, teens in the Young Women's FLA. We wrote and read together, eating, talking, and laughing in "girls café," the social container created during leadership retreats. Girls filled the Cincinnati center with stories, poetry, a mosaic project, and singing. Women from Bloomington, Indiana, Burlington, Vermont, and Indianapolis participated in Cincinnati Girls' Programs, in preparation for bringing work to their schools. I signed a contract with Sorin to publish the story of WWf(a)C in the larger world. My colleagues here and throughout the country responded to news of our story's publication with "You go, girl" enthusiasm. FLA sisters formed a community of practice to read my new chapters and "test-drive" the exercises.

What's Happening Now?

It is fall 2008. Enrollment in our programs has fallen off by almost half. While teachers from across the country report that consciousness of the greater purpose of the work has never been higher, resources have never been more scarce. The stock market has crashed, though we don't like to use the word "crash" in public. Many women have lost their jobs or have seen their retirement accounts eviscerated. Money is scarce; fear is abundant; political intensity, distraction, and health and family needs have pulled women away from their writing and from participation in WWf(a)C.

We bringers-of-the-feminine are trying to re-member money back to its proper connection with purpose and value. In the meantime, we do not know how to do that any more clearly than anyone else who is caught between paradigms and in the blowback of a systemic conflagration caused by the very thing our presence in the world is trying to remedy.

How to say it? Too much Father, too little Mother is the simplest, but perhaps simplistic way; or maybe overvaluing of the masculine energy, undervaluing of the feminine. I went to our WWf(a)C classes to say, "This set of containers is threatened. I came to say what's happening now and I don't know what will happen next." Afterward, I understood at a deeper level, yet again, why it is so difficult to say what is happening: when people do not have adequate inner space to hear, some turn to fixing, blaming, guilt, shame, or anger. I said to our circles, "I did not come to this place to either transmit or receive the old reactions."

Clarity

I came as a carrier of Mother. I carried the fire from my mother whose own mother, Filomena Lucia Franceze Caliendo, died of childbirth when my mother was two. From this primal breaking of the container that haunted my mother throughout her life, I learned that the essence continues, even when the forms are broken. I see that, as usual, I knew this truth first in poetry, said it to myself in a poem I wrote in 1998, late, late autumn of the millennium.

Letter in Spring, or How You Did It

Dear Mother,

1. Last night I was startled by the sight
of a full moon spilling from a cloudbank,
a moon like none I remember seeing,
not the pale, disinterested disk of winter,
it was a pouring-light, lover's-touch,
kitchen-lamp moon,

a white yolk, thick and glistening.

2. This morning I spilled from clouded sleep
into the memory that today you would have been eighty,

into new light on my old question:

how out of your un-mothered life
did you pour such love on me,
I swim in it still—
years after your death?

3. I think now you rose in the night, mother,
and stood over me, pouring kitchen-lamp
lover's-touch light.

Deep in my girl's sleep,
I did not see you there,
thick and glistening.

4. By morning you had slipped under the world again.

5. It was the zenith of the century, the golden fifties
backlit by bomb-burst, the blaze of heroes' glory,
the sky was filled with father: My father, the holy
father, our father was in heaven, Our mothers
were everywhere exiled.

6. The sun is going down now, the millennium ending.
Daughters are awakening to see Our Mother who
is in heaven, full and glistening, Our Mother pouring
her lover's-touch, kitchen-lamp love into a burned world.

Finally, I came to say that no school of my making, if I have breath in my body to prevent it, will be grafted onto masculinized patterns, the very unconscious, unexamined ways of being in the world that have burned us to a wasteland in the first place. Rather than destroy the essence of something to save the container, which would ever after be a place alive with death, I am happily able to follow the wisdom of my favorite Mary Oliver poem, "In Blackwater Woods":

and, when the time comes to let it go,

to let it go.[4]

Mary Pierce Brosmer
October 2008

Writers' Comments

Have you ever felt appreciated, listened to . . . really special? Telling and hearing and honoring words and stories in a community is the founding philosophy of Women Writing for (a) Change. WWf(a)C offers a safe, inviting space where women's voices are heard and affirmed. I don't know what I expected when I signed up for my first WWf(a)C semester. I guess the writing, sure—and the sharing. What I wasn't prepared for was the unconditional acceptance, the encouragement. The writing allowed me a tangible way to empty a cup that was often overflowing with others' pain. And at the same time it allowed me to leave filled and topped off.

Amy Malcom

[When] I stepped through the front door of the Ironworkers union hall . . . to begin a semester writing class I didn't understand the name of the school. Women Writing for (a) Change . . . what kind of change? Three and a half years later, I leave . . . a new person. I stand taller. I walk with a surer stride. I extend a firmer handshake, beam a broader smile, evince a brighter glow.

At WWf(a)C [I experienced] a profound change. I received both the motivation to write my truth and the encouragement to speak it.

Sally Schneider

I carried the burden of being German from the time I was thirteen years old. I took it on and made it mine, when I saw *The Diary of Anne Frank* as part of a theatre subscription. At first I thought, Anne Frank seemed just like me. But she had to hide in a tiny apartment . . . because she was Jewish and the Germans were killing the Jews. I had never had to fear for my life because of my beliefs, my nationality, my religion or the color of my skin. Through the years, I started to believe that the chasm between Germans and Jews was too big to ever be overcome. Although I had Jewish friends and colleagues . . . I never dared talk about the Holocaust, never tried to share my own feelings of guilt, never understood how my Jewish friends could even start to love me. In my Women Writing for (a) Change circle I have a writing sister whose father and grandmother were Holocaust survivors. Each time I heard her read about their cruel memories, a sharp sting went through my heart and tightened it. And yet, hearing her write about her pain encouraged me to write about mine. So I did. And through my writing, I uncovered the depth of the sorrow and distress that come with "being born guilty." I started to deal with it. But the real breakthrough came when I read about my anguish in one of our read-arounds. The Jewish writers in the circle told me that they never realized how much pain there is on both sides. We hugged at the end of the class and I felt for the first time that I was coming to terms with my past.

I think we were helping to heal the wounds of history by showing each other the scars it had left for all of us.

Rita Bosel

[My writing] gives my soul a voice.
It has helped me to learn to be with myself and with the silent spaces in my life and I am learning to use them well.

A Day in the Life of the Newbie Volunteer Neelu

I always knew writing made me happy, that it made me feel like a free bird soaring in the skies. But what I did not know was that, there was an organization solely dedicated to this purpose—to make people happy through writing. That is what Women Writing for (a) Change does on a daily basis—help people achieve that elusive happiness by providing a safe and comfortable setting where one can explore the world both within and outside of them through the power of writing. This post is about how I got here and what I did on my first day at WWf(a)C

I had registered with an organization called Business Volunteers for Arts hoping to share my knowledge and contribute my skills in a meaningful way to the community. That is where I was matched with WWf(a)C and I officially started volunteering duties from last week. I loved it from the moment I visited here. Everybody was so warm and friendly and the ambience of the place made me feel like I always belonged here.

Most people are quite curious to know what I do here—so yeah, I work the databases and am into some kind of database arm twisting to make it behave and produce the kind of reports the staff here wants it to. Or should I say my job is to "fulfill dreams" which is how Mary first requested me for a report. OK for now I will go with, "My job is to fulfill dreams." Sounds fancier doesn't it?

I also had the privilege of attending my first writing class on the very same day in the evening. And I must say this—it was *amazing*. It was a wonderful experience. To be honest, that was the first time I was reading out something I had written to other "real" people. All I could think of at that moment was: Huh! So this how what I have written sounds. And to see people looking at you compassionately and taking in every word that you read out and then to provide their special feedback. It really makes you feel important. Trust me, it's a very special kind of high!

The first thing I said to Bron after I met her the next day was, "Bron, you should rename the organization as Women Meeting for Happiness instead of Women Writing for a Change." Because to me writing seemed like only a part of the overall experience. You could clearly see the change in the happiness levels and the smiles on the faces of all the women before and after the class. If only I could do some before and after pictures to show it to you all.

So that was my 1st day at WWf(a)C—database in the morning, happiness (writing class) in the evening. Watch out for my other posts as I share my experience on this WWf(a)C journey.

Neelima Kodomuri
http://blog.womenwriting.org

I am a writer. A real writer. Of this, I have no doubt, because of Women Writing for (a) Change.

Anni Gibson

I wish I had learned these things earlier in life. I wish I had experienced at a younger age the deep acceptance of my inner experience that I have been given at WWF(a)C.

Carol Stewart

I could hear my own thoughts. I loved that when I read what I wrote, I could finally give what I felt a voice. It awakened my soul to new horizons. . . . I don't know how I lived my life without this tool. It has helped me to grow in leaps and bounds.

Kaya Kotzen

To Whom It May Concern:

I am writing to support the dream of Women Writing for (a) Change to raise enough capital to find a permanent home. The Wellness Community of Greater Cincinnati—Northern Kentucky has been one of the many beneficiaries of Women Writing for (a) Change's efforts over the years, as Mary Pierce Brosmer donated her time to facilitate a series of writing groups for the women of the Wellness Community. These women, all of whom were coping with a diagnosis of cancer, were given a powerful opportunity to learn to use creative writing skills they barely knew they had to express thoughts and feelings churning within them. One participant said, "Sometimes I don't know what I'm thinking until I start to write."

The impact of the WWf(a)C group was impressive and has been sustained. While the WWf(a)C program at the Wellness Community ended nearly two years ago, its legacy lives on in the form of a weekly professionally facilitated journaling group, Writing into Wellness, that meets at the Wellness Community every Friday afternoon. Several of the writers from the original group remain actively involved, inspiring new writers who enter the group to lay aside their fears of not being a "good enough writer" and to simply write what flows from the heart. The words which follow are not only beautiful, but powerful, insightful, and inspiring. One of our weekly writers told the facilitator, "There are things that come out on paper that I feel like my body needs me to get out."

Bonnie B. Crawford, MSW, LISW, Program Director

We are like a mother's anniversary ring, sparkling with the colors, sharing brilliance. There is strength in the setting that holds these jewels in this circle, a strength that can't be broken by societal pressure.

Tina Neyer

In the three years since becoming involved with Women Writing for (a) Change, I've heard Brosmer repeat the phrase "telling the truth of women's lives" umpteen times without really understanding what it meant to me.

I've seen what it means to the grandmother speaking for the first time about childhood abuse, the divorcee learning to define and express herself outside the role of wife and mother, the emotionally drained teacher reclaiming her calling, the business professional letting down her guard, or the shy teenager testing out her voice.

Stephanie Dunlap

Standing at the store counter, I filled out a credit card application: age, income, credit history, marital status—as if a checklist of boxes could contain me! How quick we are to profile one another, I thought, to assign an impersonal label and then a pigeon-hole marked "poor" or "straight" or "married" or "professional." Neighborhoods, schools, and workplaces reinforce this segregation, and we are all diminished—cut off from one another and even from ourselves.

Yet there are chances to break out. . . . At my first session, I was impressed by the spirit of reverence, the respect for silence as well as self-disclosure, the homelike setting, the warm laughter. We began in a circle and were led through a carefully orchestrated set of activities—silence at first, passing a candle, a quotation from an admired author, a "fast-writing" exercise, then time to break into smaller groups and share our own writing. . . . By the end of the evening, two and a half hours later, I felt as if I'd found a safe harbor, a chance to be known and appreciated.

"It's like what church ought to be. I always come away feeling like a better person," says one person who described herself as a lifetime member.

Indeed, my course was marked by a spirit of reverence. Care was taken to encourage people to speak freely. The physical space was carefully prepared. Ground rules were laid. The facilitator knew how to promote a spirit of respect for every person. I was not surprised to learn that many women return, enrolling over and over.

We all listened with respect, often finding common ground. My group of twenty included an amazing variety of individuals. I got to hear the inner musings of a minister and a car mechanic, a punk bisexual and an elderly nun, a young black woman voted "most likely to succeed" in high school and an older white woman who'd set aside a stellar career to care for her elderly mother. Old and young, Christian and Jew, black and white, conservative and progressive—all these polarities were represented in one circle.

At times my own stereotypes were revealed. There were no formal intro-
ductions, so we got to know each other slowly through what each writer
chose to disclose. I'd pegged one older woman as a sheltered grandmother,
only to discover weeks later that she was a nun who'd lived many years in
Africa, teaching villagers how to deliver babies!

"Another Woman's Story," by Trudelle Thomas, Professor at Xavier
University and author of *Spirituality in the Mother Zone,*
(Mahwah: Paulist Press, 2005)

If she had a place like this . . .

(Dedicated to the Women Writing for a Change Community)

If she had a place like this
where people listen with respect
would her constant hand wringing
have lessened occasionally to a relaxed pose
of confidence in her lap

If she had a place like this . . .
where people listen with tenderness
would the anxiety and despair
that fed her mind and
turned her life
into a dance w/ land mines
Disappear

If she had a place like this . . .
Where wounds of an imperfect life can be shared
would she have experienced being known?
understood she was not alone, but welcomed
in a community that stands for the soul of each and every?

If she had a place like this . . .
Where feelings are important, dreams have value
Would she have spoken the dark secrets of her abuse
Asked for help
Escaped
Another bruise
Another humiliation
Being a statistic

I often wonder, I will never know
This place didn't exist in her time
Thank god, it exists in mine

SH, May 2007

Appendices

List of Exercises for Part Three

Women Writing for (a) Change
Small Group Questionnaire (Held in Confidence)

Name _____

Phone#(H) _____ (W) _____

It is not necessary to answer each question.

1.   My ideal listener is someone who could offer me

2.   When I listen to a writer, I can offer her

3.   This semester I probably will miss _____ classes. (if you know them, put them here)

4.   On average my guess is that this semester I will spend about _____ hours a week writing.

5.   I will probably be writing about

6. and it will be in the form of

These next two questions are important and also not important. I trust instincts, attractions, and I want them to be factors in placing you. And I also believe that "discomfort is informative." *Please state what you want, and know that I may not be able to work out all requests. I would never high-handedly ignore your requests!*

7. I would like to have the following women in small group with me:

8. I would not like to have the following women in small group with me: *Please limit to one or two at most.*

Other Comments:

Women Writing for (a) Change
Creating the Container to Hold Our Words

"To teach is to create a space in which the community of truth is practiced."
"Boundaries create the space for reverence."

Parker J. Palmer,
To Know as We Are Known: A Spirituality of Education

Since the beginning of Women Writing for (a) Change (in September, 1991), certain simple practices, and the structure of the school itself, have grown out of deeply-held values.

Women Writing for (a) Change is a container which both evokes and holds the words of women. All the women and girls who attend classes, workshops, book discussions; all faculty and staff; all who support Women Writing for (a) Change Foundation; and all women who are part of the wider "Circle around the Circle," make the container as deep and safe as possible for the work we do here. At the beginning of each semester, and occasionally in between, it is necessary to name some of the elements which are crucial to the learning.

1. **Community.** Each individual woman and the class as an entity shape the space, are the space, into which the words fall. Each of us gives words and receives words. We are both writers and members of the audience who hear the words of the other writers. Our regular presence to one another, our taking ourselves and one another seriously, showing up, paying attention, being prepared for each class, really listening—these are a few of the gifts of being in community. Writing does not exist in a vacuum—it exists in a reciprocal relationship with audience—those who hear and respond to the words sent out. We attempt to remain conscious of this relationship in WWf(a)C. It is an important part of how we learn to write, how we learn what images, patterns, and rhythms affect our listeners.

2. **The Physical Space.** As we are on the second floor of a building which needs to be locked during evening classes, we ask each woman to take a turn being greeter. The greeter arrives thirty minutes before the start of class. The teacher will let her in, and the greeter will welcome class members downstairs until fifteen minutes after the start of class, unless all members have arrived, at which time the greeter will join the circle upstairs and be responsible for listening for a knock

253

and/or watching the door-light (the doorbell on the outside of the building does not ring; a light upstairs on the teacher's table will light when the doorbell has been pressed) in case there is a late arrival.

Our space consists of four classrooms: Earth (the largest room, running the full length of the west side of the building), Air (small room off Earth), Water (the large room on the east side of the building), and Fire (off Water.) At times the Office may also be used for small groups. There are restrooms on both sides of the building at the end of the hall. There is a phone in the Office and another in the Water room if you need to make a call. The phone ringer is turned off during class, so any phone calls during that time will go into our voice-mail system. The copier and computers in the Office are for faculty and staff use only.

3. **Gathering the Community**. As women arrive, there will be hot water for tea in the Water room. Some women choose to socialize before class in this space; *the other rooms are kept quiet for those who want to write or gather themselves before class begins.* Please be in the circle at the start of class. The teacher will light the candle and the flame will be passed from woman to woman. The movement of the candle begins the making of the circle, and women are encouraged to use the time to become quiet and attentive. When you receive the candle, you can *set your intention* for the night, and when you watch each woman with the candle, you can support her intentions for herself. The making of the circle happens yet again when the stone is passed and each woman says her name.

4. **Leaving the Community**. At the close of class, women in the circle will receive index cards. Here they are asked to write words to the community about their learning experience for that evening. (*What did you feel, notice, learn? Any gifts? Any struggles? Any suggestions? Any questions for the group?*) As women are finishing their cards, the teacher blows out the candle and passes it (darkened) around the community, unmaking the circle and closing it for the evening. Leaving the circle, writers will put their index cards in their class's basket. Women are encouraged to read the cards before or after class.

The greeter will help the teacher restore the space. Greeter and teacher will leave together.

5. **Teacher Boundaries**. Since the teacher may be engaged in preparation or reflection prior to class, she may not be available, except in a casual, social way, before or after classes. *If you have questions during the week, you can leave a voicemail message—272-1171,*

mailbox 3, or e-mail me at mpierce@one.net, and I will do my best to respond promptly.

6. **Confidentiality**. What a woman reads here, or speaks from her heart here, *must stay here* unless she gives her permission otherwise. This includes writing which may be in preparation for publication.

What sometimes feels uncomfortable and challenging about what we do here is that we are attempting to be conscious, while unconsciousness in its many manifestations (carelessness, projecting, blaming, reacting, etc.) is more common in our culture. As a result, women are sometimes *self-conscious about being conscious* (going slow, being ok with silence, using symbols and rituals.). What at first might feel clumsy, eventually becomes graceful and grounding. And perhaps we lose our anxiety when we come to see how the conscious creation of the container for our words keeps us writing, and when we see that no one is ever shamed for "not doing something right," for *hospitality* is another deeply-held value of WWf(a)C.

Organizational Chart

To bring the feminine more fully into expression by supporting the voices and stories of girls and women of all races, classes, and nations.

I. School, LLC
Founded 1991

The mission of Women Writing for (a) Change (the school) is to help individuals and organizations craft more conscious lives through the art of writing and the practices of community.

A. Leadership
- 1. Founder
- 2. Executive Director
- 3. Associate Director
- 4. Faculty

B. Programs
- 1. Writing Classes
  - a. All Women
  - b. Co-ed Classes
  - c. All Men
  - d. Virtual program

C. Feminist Leadership Academy

D. Affiliate Schools
- 1. Bloomington IN
- 2. Burlington, VT
- 3. Grand Junction, CO
- 4. Birmingham, AL
- 5. Louisville, KY
- 6. Indianapolis, IN
- 7. Portland, OR
- 8. Traverse City, MI

E. Consulting for (a) Change

F. Sources of Support
- 1. Tuition
- 2. Consulting contracts

II. FOUNDATION 501(c)(3)

Founded 2000

The mission of Women Writing for (a) Change Foundation is to foster healthy writing communities where the words of women and girls from all classes, races and ethnic backgrounds, and life circumstances are nurtured, developed and celebrated.

A. Leadership
    1. Board of Trustees
    2. Executive Director
    3. Young Women Program Director
    4. Community Partnership Director
    5. YW and Partnership Faculty
    6. Volunteers

B. Programs
    1. Young Women Writing for (a) Change
    2. Young Women's Feminist Leadership Academy

C. Scholarships
    1. for girls; high school and college
    2. for women

D. Ownership of fully accessible building at 6906 Plainfield Rd. Cincinnati, OH 45236

E. The New Media Circle

F. Community Partnerships, such as:
    1. YWCA Battered Women's Shelter
    2. Lighthouse Youth Services
    3. Talbert House
    4. Kennedy Heights Community Center
    5. High Schools
    6. Contemporary Arts Center

G. Sources of Support
    1. Individual and Corporate Gifts
    2. Foundation Grants
    3. Rent from School and Others
    4. Tuition

Women Writing for (a) Change Foundation
Statement of Philosophy

The Mission

The Women Writing for (a) Change Foundation is a not-for-profit organization in the Cincinnati area. The Foundation fosters a healthy writing community where the words of women and girls from all walks of life are nurtured, developed, and celebrated.

The Philosophy

The WWf(a)C Foundation believes it is essential that women and girls have a safe space in which to speak and write their truths, to share their words and to open their imaginations without limits. The truth of our lives can be a fragile thing, and no one should be silenced, belittled, or misunderstood.

The WWf(a)C Foundation supports the existence of a community that we consciously and intentionally create together. This community is a living entity that continuously needs the loving attention of its members so that its values will be maintained. In this community, we offer safe environments where feminism is practiced, where there is respect for the words and experiences of all women and girls, and where we can take ourselves seriously as writers. In this community, there is reverence for our time together. We listen and respond to one another in a noncompetitive way with the intent to raise up what is powerful and strong in each of us.

The WWf(a)C Foundation embraces the concept of hospitality—we intend to welcome all women and girls who come to the WWf(a)C programs and to extend to them kindness and respect. We believe that diversity enriches our lives, and we welcome differences in race, class, culture, sexual orientation, life experience, writing style and skill, opinion, personality, and belief system.

The WWf(a)C Foundation acknowledges that both openness and the setting of healthy boundaries are required for art to be made and communities to grow and deepen. We believe that we can care for others without forgetting to care for ourselves. Respect for one another is a primary concept in our community.

The WWf(a)C Foundation believes that there is joy in the act of creating, that there is pleasure in the beauty of words, and intimacy even in silence. When women and girls are free to express themselves, they are a powerful force for change and healing.

The WWf(a)C Foundation is committed to learning how women can mentor and be mentored, can bring together the wisdom and authority of elders with the wisdom and authority of novices.

The WWf(a)C Foundation is devoted to a feminist process of making art and building community. This process is life-giving, life-affirming, non-coercive, and mutually respectful. When this process is practiced by women and girls, it benefits all of society, men as well as women.

The WWf(a)C Foundation recognizes connections between: art and politics, art and spirituality, art and life, writer and audience, history and the present, the present and the future. We honor the women who went before us: family members, personal mentors, feminist writers, activists, and teachers. They have brought us to where we are today, and we hope to lead and nurture the women who will take our places in the future.

History

The WWf(a)C Foundation was established in 2000 as a sister organization to the WWf(a)C school. The School, founded in 1991, has experienced rapid growth. In 1998, participants in WWf(a)C created a committee structure, which raised and administrated funds for women and girls to attend programs at the school's Writing Hall at reduced or no cost. The committees also focused on outreach, development, and marketing circles.

In September 1999, the group began the process of incorporating this committee structure as a not-for-profit organization, in order to provide adequate human and financial resources for these outgrowth activities. In September 2000, this Task Force incorporated as WWf(a)C Foundation's founding Board of Trustees. WWf(a)C Foundation was recognized as a non-profit by the State of Ohio in 2000 and by the Internal Revenue Service in 2001. Its primary roles are to reach the diverse population of girls and women in the Greater Cincinnati area and to raise and administer scholarship funds for girls and women who would not otherwise have access to the mentoring, creative support, and safe, empowering environment offered in WWf(a)C.

The Foundation also sponsors outreach programs which deliver creative writing programs and performances to women and girls in greater Cincinnati's diverse communities, through collaborations including YWCA, Peaslee Neighborhood Center, Urban Appalachian Council, and Enjoy the Arts.

Women Writing for (a) Change Code of Ethics

Leaders certified by the Women Writing for (a) Change movement agree to abide by this code of ethics as a sign of their commitment to core values as manifested in:

- helping others find inner truth and authority through the art of writing and the practices of community;
- holding the lives of others in sacred trust;
- modeling healthy boundaries in all connections and relationships pertaining to WWf(a)C; and
- maintaining honest relationships with students with regard to money.

The following rules are based on the above values:

1. Leaders will recognize their responsibilities with regard to clients'/students' writing: to hold students' writing in confidence by not sharing it outside of faculty and supervisory relationships without permission; to keep ownership /authorship of writing in the writer's hands (i.e., not exert undue influence over writers to change their words or publish them); and, to never co-opt or plagiarize the writing of students.

2. Recognizing that leaders/teachers are seen as having more power and influence in a relationship, leaders will:

   Not engage in romantic or sexual relationships with students.

   Always maintain clarity that their role is "to hold," not to "be held" by their students, those whom they are mentoring.

   Set up the classroom/community based on valuing the individual, rather than motivating by fear, competition, or favoritism.

   Remember that power is defined within the principles of WWf(a)C as "empowering" rather than "coercive."

3. Leaders/teachers may have other kinds of relationships with students (e.g., friendships, professional or business associations), but careful and ongoing attention must be given to

teachers acknowledging and clarifying the boundaries of the relationship, and to whom has what role in a given setting (e.g., massage therapist as student).

4. Leaders will honor the lineage of WWf(a)C in the spirit of naming the honorable connection.

In the event of possible unethical conduct, a certified leader is in jeopardy of having her certification revoked. She will be invited to tell her story to a listening and decision-making board consisting of the Founder of WWf(a)C or her appointee, and two other members: one chosen by the founder or her appointee, the other by the woman telling her story.

I, _____, agree to abide by the Code of Ethics as delineated above.

Sample Class Agendas

Sample 1

Living and Leading Like a Poet, Class 11

The past, present and future are all properties of consciousness. The past is recollection, memory; the future is anticipation; the present awareness. Therefore time is the movement of thought. Both past and future are born in the imagination; only the present, which is awareness, is real and eternal. It is.

Deepak Chopra, The Seven Spiritual Laws of Success

The inner artist is always torn between two worlds; on one side family, friends, leisure, laziness, and on the other the fulfillment of the inner urge to create, to write. How can we honor the inner Artist? In part, by creating a schedule, a system that is true to the way we write, and true to our physical self.

John Lee, Writing From the Body

7:00   Opening the Circle (Read "Assateague Island, October" by Marjorie Saiser)

7:10   Check-In: We'll read soul cards from our Read-Around then have some debriefing discussion about the event.

7:30   Writing Time: 20 minutes: First, re-read today's poem.
   ♦   If you were to ask for "healing," for forgiveness, what specifically would you ask for?
   ♦   Imagine yourself on a shoreline. What would you ask of the waves?
   ♦   That time I . . . When I . . . Take this . . .
   ♦   Write from the shoreline.

8:00   Small group meetings

9:00   Large Group Reflection

9:15   Acknowledging our connection to community/soul cards

9:30   Closing the Circle

Writing Suggestions for the Coming Week

1. a. Take time to read through all the material you've begun this semester. What lines surprise you? What do you find that you have no memory of having written, but you feel to be intriguing? Consider picking up the thread of some passing thought you expressed, but moved on from before. Fresh writing can begin here with what you've already generated.

    b. Write a list of unanswered questions you have about your childhood. Start with your conception and ask away. The list itself might make an interesting piece. You may want to take one of these questions and answer it.

    c. What do you know about your astrological sign? Read your horoscope in the paper every day and write it down. Write some kind of response to it and have fun with it. What does your sign say about you? What do you have to say about your sign?

2. Keep working with your fast-write from today . . . the shoreline . . . the waves and what healing they offer.

3. Follow your muse.

I believe that movements start when individuals who feel very isolated and very alone in the midst of an alien culture, come in touch with something life-giving in the midst of a death-dealing situation. They make one of the most basic decisions a human being can make, which I have come to call the decision to live "divided no more," the decision to no longer act differently on the outside than one knows one's truth to be on the inside.

Parker Palmer
The Grace of Great Things

Sample 2

Mistakenly, "Tradition" is often thought of as words, rules, or doctrines handed on or handed over. But in a strange paradox this is not actually its meaning. For no such "thing" as "tradition" exists to be handed over. Rather, it is the action of handing on and handing over that is the tradition.

Maria Harris, Dance of the Spirit

10:00	Say your name/soul card/anything you need to say to bring yourself into the circle. (Opening poem "Pre-Holiday PMS" by Ginger Andrews)
10:20	Fast-write: 1. I don't want to . . . I hate . . . You could start . . . 2. What are pointers you discovered for a successful holiday? 3. My experience at the read-around . . .
10:30	Read-around/read-backs
11:20	Small Groups
12:15	A little conversation, announcements, soul cards, Closing

Writing Suggestions and Practices for the Coming Week

1. Explore your feelings re: the upcoming holidays.
2. What is one thing you hope happens during the holidays; one thing of the merry mess you would like to skip? How might you bring about your hopes?
3. Imagine your perfect holiday.
4. Spend some time remembering holidays of the past. Describe in as much detail, using as many senses as possible, what you remember.
5. Explore what happens to you when you cook. What is your favorite recipe?
6. Describe any catastrophes of previous Thanksgiving dinners (turkeys not thawing, turkeys falling on the floor, wine spilling on your father-in-law . . . an argument . . .) Or what is the worst holiday you survived, the worst item on the menu?

7. What is your relationship with a charge card? With shopping? (Got a story?)

8. Answer the following questions with lists. Lists are great jump starters. Then explore the lists.

- What are five ways of being you have "inherited" from your family. How have you been nourished or not by your family, by a certain person?

- What does your family "know" from tradition, according to the definition in the quote above?

- What do you as a person pass on to society? What does society know of life from your life?

- Make a list of Hanukah or Christmas presents. Your list: item, person, why?

Listen to your muse.

Sample Meeting Agendas

Sample 1

The Courage to Write: Fostering Creativity and Community
(Presented to Chatfield College Faculty and Staff, September to April, 2004, Gathering 1)

> As we dream of a safer, saner world,
> we must dare to stand beside our few well chosen words.
>
> *Sam Hamill, open letter on 9/11/2004*
>
> Autumn Equinox;
> day equals night and light balances darkness,
> as the season of completion and contentment begins.
>
> *Edward Hays, Prayers for a Planetary Pilgrim*

4:00   Gathering the Community (Opening Poem, "Ritual to Read to One Another" by William Stafford)

4:20   Writing in Community

4:40   Reading in Community (confidentiality, double confidentiality)

5:20   Conversation in Community

 ♦   How do we understand the possibilities of our work?

 ♦   Thoughts about how to shape our two campus and virtual communities?

 ♦   How to invite more colleagues?

 ♦   Reading, writing, posting between gatherings

6:00 Conclusion

1. Writing to bring to next gathering: "Stories of Emergence." Write the story of your relationship to Chatfield from "In the beginning . . ." through the story of your presence in this Courage to Write project. Touch on events, themes, relationships that have been woven into your history here.

2. Writing suggestions for posting: Read the intro and first chapter of *The Courage to Teach* by Parker Palmer. Choose three

short passages from this section. Begin by quoting Palmer, then write how his words line up or don't line up with your teaching life.

Sample 2

Strategic Planning Meeting on Social Media

I love you, gentlest of Ways,
who ripened us as we wrestled with you.

Rainer Maria Rilke

11:00   Opening with writing for five minutes to: what do we want social media to do to feed our organism?

11:05   List of goals

11:10   Reduce to three and prioritize

11:25   What do we have now and how could we make it more strategic for meeting our goals?

12:00   Lunch break

12:15   Workshopping / Revision of our social media presence

12:45   Next steps

1:00   Close

Notes

Preface

1. Archibald MacLeish, *Collected Poems 1917–1982* (Boston, MA: Houghton Mifflin, 1985), 106.

2. Frank Partnoy, interviewed by Steve Croft, *60 Minutes*, October 5, 2008, www.cbsnews.com/stories/2008/10/05/60minutes/main4502454.shtml (accessed 10/30/2008).

3. Quote attributed to Oliver Wendell Holmes, Jr. *Wikipedia*, http://en.wikiquote.org/wiki/Oliver_Wendell_Holmes,_Jr. (accessed June 5, 2009).

4. May Sarton, "An Observation," *A Private Mythology* (New York: W.W. Norton, 1966).

5. Sherwood Anderson, *Winesburg, Ohio* (New York: Random House, 1999).

Introduction

1. Auden's words were: "Speaking for myself, the questions which interest me most when reading a poem are two. The first is technical: 'Here is a verbal contraption. How does it work?' The second is, in the broadest sense, moral: 'What kind of a guy inhabits this poem? What is his notion of the good life or the good place? His notion of the Evil One? What does he conceal from the reader? What does he conceal even from himself?'" John Berryman, "Auden's Prose," *New York Review of Books* Vol. 1, No. 1 (February 1, 1963), www.nybooks.com/articles/13750 (accessed on June 5, 2009).

2. Mary Pierce Brosmer, definition of feminine developed in 2004.

3. Doug Pibel, "Pete Seeger: The Power of Song," *Yes Magazine*, Issue 44 (Winter 2008), www.yesmagazine.org/article.asp?id=2123 (accessed on October 11, 2008).

4. Robert Sardello, *Facing the World with Soul: The Reimagination of Modern Life* (Great Barrington, MA: Lindisfarne Books, 2004), 58.

1. Surveying the Landscape

1. Robert Bly, *Iron John: A Book about Men* (Reading, MA: Addison Wesley, 1990).

2. Terrence Real, *How Can I Get Through to You?: Reconnecting Men and Women* (New York: Fireside, 2002), 90.

3. Peter Senge, C. Otto Scharmer, Joseph Jaworski, and Betty Sue Flowers, *Presence: Human Purpose and the Field of the Future* (New York: Doubleday, 2004).

2. Beginnings: In the Names of My Mother and My Father

1. See Janet Kalven's history of this important experiment in feminist utopian community: *Women Breaking Boundaries: A Grail Journey, 1940–1995* (State University of New York Press, 1999).

2. Published in Marge Piercy, ed., *Early Ripening: Contemporary American Women's Poetry Now* (Boston: Pandora Press, 1988).

3. In the One, Holy Catholic (and Apostolic) Church

1. This quote has been attributed to James Baldwin and others, but, at the time of this printing, the specific reference has not been identified.

Part II. Groundwork

1. Kay Leigh Hagan, "Orchids in the Arctic: The Predicament of Women Who Love Men," *Fugitive Information* www.terry.uga.edu/~dawndba/4500orchids.htm (accessed October 5, 2008).

2. Lisel Mueller, "Why We Tell Stories" www.poemhunter.com/poem/why-we-tell-stories/ (accessed October 12, 2008).

5. The Circle as Conscious Container

1. Carolyn G. Heilbrun, *The Last Gift of Time: Life Beyond Sixty* (New York: Ballantine Books, 1998), 138.

2. Annie Rogers, "Voice, Play, and a Practice of Ordinary Courage in Girls' and Women's Lives," *Harvard Educational Review* 63:3 (Fall 1993): n. pag.

6. Rituals to Create Containers

1. Adrienne Rich discussed the principle of reverse in a talk which I attended.

2. Margaret Wheatley, "Leadership in Turbulent Times Is Spiritual," www.leader-values.com/Content/detail.asp?ContentDetailID=168 (accessed October 12, 2008).

3. Parker Palmer, *To Know as We Are Known: A Spirituality of Education* (San Francisco: Harper & Row, 1983).

4. Jenn Reid, "Ritual as a Post-Modern Device," 250; citing Hélène Cixous, "The Laugh of the Medusa," trans. Keith Cohen and Paula Cohen, *Signs* 1: 4 (1976): 875–93.

5. A business aside here: my conviction that the growth of something should be organic and natural, emerging with the particular gifts of person and place, made it easy for me to embrace a "licensing" model, in legal terms, for sharing the work. Licensing encourages difference; franchising dictates uniformity, which would be deadly in more ways than one, to the creative and entrepreneurial essence of WWf(a)C.

6. These altars have continued to be a valuable prompt, used frequently in Young Women Writing for (a) Change. What a thrill it is to move through the rooms of the hall seeing what the girls hold sacred, lovingly and artfully arranged!

7. Maria Harris, *Women and Teaching: Themes for a Spirituality of Pedagogy,* Madeleva Lecture in Spirituality (Mahwah, NJ: Paulist Press, 1988).

8. Megan Miller, Young Women Writing for (a) Change, Full-Day Teen Program 2003.

7. Creating Writing Prompts

1. Guy Gugliotta, "Monkeys, Dolphin Say 'I Don't Know': Research Suggests Higher Mammals Able to Think About Thinking," *Washington Post*, November 28, 2003, www.washingtonpost.com/ac2/wpdyn?pagename =article&contentId=A17485-2003Nov27&notFound=true (accessed October 22, 1008).
2. See www.poets.org/viewmedia.php/prmMID/5792 (accessed October 22, 2008).
3. Ilene Beckerman, *Love, Loss and What I Wore* (Chapel Hill, NC: Algonquin Books, 1995).
4. Sue Bender, *Everyday Sacred: A Woman's Journey Home* (New York: HarperCollins, 1995).

8. Sharing Writing in Small Groups

1. Attributed to Rita Dove.
2. June Singer, *Boundaries of the Soul: the Practice of Jungian Psychology* (New York: Anchor Books, 1994). Chapter 10 is called "Dreaming the Dream Onward: Active Imagination."
3. www.etymonline.com/index.php?search=criticism&searchmode=none (accessed October 22, 2008).
4. See Catherine Keller, "Nelle Morton: Hearing to Speech" in *The Christian Century* (February 7–14, 1990).
5. Audre Lorde, *Sister Outsider: Essays and Speeches* (Berkeley, CA: Crossing Press, 1984).

9. Read-Around

1. Audre Lorde, *Sister Outsider* (1984).
2. Jean Baker Miller, *Toward a New Psychology of Women* (Boston: Beacon Press, 1976).
3. Brenda Ueland, *If You Want to Write: A Book about Independence and Spirit* (St. Paul: Graywolf Press, 1988).
4. Carolyn Heilbrun, (NCTE convention, Baltimore, November, 1989).

10. Listening Within, Moving Out

1. Krista Tippet with John O'Donohue, "The Inner Landscape of Beauty," *Speaking of Faith*, NPR, February 25, 2008, http://speakingoffaith.publicra-dio.org/programs/john_odonahue/index.shtml (accessed October 22, 2008).
2. Eckhart Tolle, *The Power of Now: A Guide to Spiritual Enlightenment* (Novato, CA: New World Library, 1999), 1.
3. Ibid., 1–3.
4. Peter Senge, Otto Scharmer, Joseph Jaworksi, and Betty Sue Flowers, *Presence: An Exploration of Profound Change in People, Organizations and Society* (New York: Doubleday Business, 2005), 79–81.

5. C. Otto Scharmer, *Theory U: Leading from the Future as It Emerges* (Cambridge, MA: The Society for Organizational Leadership, 2007), 24.
6. Ibid., 24.
7. Ibid., 24.
8. Ibid., 25.
9. Gregory Bateson, *Mind and Nature: A Necessary Unity* (Cresskill, NJ: Hampton Press, 2002).
10. Stanley Kunitz and Genine Lentine, *The Wild Braid: A Poet Reflects on A Century in the Garden* (New York: WW Norton, 2007), 13.

11. Moving Out, Family

1. Pete Hamill, *Forever* (New York: Back Bay Books, 2003).
2. Philippe Sands, interview by Bill Moyers, *Bill Moyers' Journal*, May 9, 2008, www.pbs.org/moyers/journal/05092008/watch2.html (accessed October 22, 2008).
3. Utah Phillips, interview by Amy Goodman, *Democracy Now*, www.democracynow.org/2008/5/27/utah_phillips_1935_2008_legendary_folk (accessed October 22, 2008). Includes January 2004.

12. Weaving the Social Fabric

1. William Stafford, "A Ritual to Read to Each Other," www.poemhunter.com/poem/a-ritual-to-read-to-each-other/ (accessed October 22, 2008).
2. Robert Pack, *Waking to My Name: New and Selected Poems* (Baltimore: Johns Hopkins University Press, 1980).
3. Bernard Lietaer, "Beyond Greed and Scarcity," *Yes! Magazine: A Journal of Positive Futures*, Summer 1997, www.yesmagazine.org/article.asp?ID=886 (accessed October 12, 2008).
4. Ibid.
5. Dee Hock, *The Birth of the Chaordic Age* (San Francisco: Berrett-Koehler, 1999), 30.
6. Muriel Rukeyser, *Houdini* (Ashfield, MA: Paris Press, 2002).
7. William Carlos Williams, *Asphodel, That Greeny Flower and Other Love Poems* (New York: New Direction Books, 1994), 9.

13. Revitalizing the World of Work

1. Williams, *Asphodel* (1994).
2. David Whyte, *The House of Belonging* (Langley, WA: Many Rivers Press, 1996).
3. Quote attributed to Buckminster Fuller, source unknown.
4. Hock, *Chaordic Age* (1999), 116.
5. "Insanity is doing the same thing over and over again and expecting different results." Variations have been attributed to different sources, including

Benjamin Franklin, Albert Einstein, an old Chinese proverb, and Rita Mae Brown. http://en.wikiquote.org/wiki/Insanity (accessed October 22, 2008).

6. Hock, *Chaordic Age* (1999), 103.

7. Helen Luke, "Money as the Feminine Principle of Exchange," *The Way of Woman* (New York: Doubleday, 1995), 54.

8. Coleman Barks, trans., *The Essential Rumi* (Garden City, NY: Quality Paperback Club, 1998).

14. The Planet Passing Through Us

1. Hock, *Chaordic Age* (1999), 5.

2. Attributed to Ralph Waldo Emerson; source unknown.

3. Peter Van Dijk, "Paradise Regained," *Ode Magazine,* July/August 2008, 49.

4. Leonard Shlain, *The Alphabet Versus the Goddess: The Conflict Between Word and Image* (New York: Compass Books, 1998), vii.

5. Steven R. Kellart and Edward O. Wilson, ed., *The Biophilia Hypothesis* (Washington, D.C.: Island Press, 1993).

6. Mary Pierce Brosmer, *Poems to a Coming Grandchild* (2000).

7. Richard Louv, *Last Child in the Woods: Saving Our Children from Nature Deficit Disorder* (Chapel Hill, NC: Algonquin Books of Chapel Hill, 2005), 68.

8. Ibid., 13.

9. Ibid., 14.

10. Philip Appleman, *New and Selected Poems, 1956–1996* (Fayetteville, AR: University of Arkansas Press, 1996).

11. Hock, *Chaordic Age* (1999), 1.

15. Care of the Container

1. Brunonia Barry, *The Lace Reader: A Novel* (New York, NY: William Morrow, 2008), 162.

2. John Burnett, "Dr. John: 'We're Gonna Be Back' in New Orleans," NPR, March 2, 2006, www.npr.org/templates/story/story.php?storyId=5240124 (accessed October 22, 2008).

3. Marion Woodman, "Symptoms and Addictions as Guides," audiotapes of lectures given at *The Heart of Healing: Exploring the Theory and Practice of Wholeness,* tape #2 (Berkeley, CA: Conference Recording Services, New Medicine Tapes, 1993).

4. Margaret J. Wheatley and Myron Kellner-Rogers, *A Simpler Way* (San Francisco: Berrett-Koehler Publishers, 1998).

16. Writing the World of Work: A Story From the Field

1. Hock, *Chaordic Age* (1999), 274.

2. Ibid., 276.

3. Marge Piercy, "The Seven of Pentacles," from *Circles on the Water* (New York: Alfred A. Knopf, 1982).

4. Hock, *Chaordic Age* (1999), 274.

5. www.etymonline.com/index.php?search=poem&searchmode=none (accessed October 27, 2008).

6. Parker J. Palmer, *A Hidden Wholeness: The Journey Toward an Undivided Life* (San Francisco: Jossey-Bass, 2004).

7. Luce Irigaray, "And The One Doesn't Stir Without the Other," in *Feminist Social Thought: A Reader*, ed. Diana T. Meyers, (Florence, KY: Routledge, 1997).

8. Emily Hancock, *The Girl Within* (New York: Ballantine, 1990).

9. Linda Pastan, "The Lost Girls."

17. Teachers Writing: A Model for Authentic Leadership

1. Peter Block, "Spirit at Work Teleconference," aired May 29, 2008, available from www.designedlearning.com.

2. Margaret Starbird, *The Goddess in the Gospels: Reclaiming the Sacred Feminine* (Melbourne, Australia: Bear Publishing, 1998), 62.

3. Starbird, *Goddess in the Gospels*, 58.

4. Mary Pierce Brosmer, *Voices from the Middle*, NCTE 3:1, 1996, 41.

5. Quote from an article in the *Cincinnati Enquirer*, early 1990s.

18. Conscious Feminine and Linguistic Leadership in a Time of Planetary Crisis

1. Kathleen Hall Jamieson, interview by Bill Moyers, *Bill Moyer's Journal*, October 10, 2008, www.pbs.org/moyers/journal/10102008/profile2.html (accessed October 27, 2008).

2. Peter Block, notes from lecture at Chatfield College, St. Leo Campus, St. Martin, Ohio, 2004.

3. Percy Bysshe Shelley, "A Defense of Poetry," www.bartleby.com/27/23.html (accessed October 27, 2008).

4. Bateson, *Mind and Nature: A Necessary Unity* (Kresskill, NJ: Hampton Press 2000).

5. Mary Pierce Brosmer, 1985.

Epilogue

1. Elinor Dickson and Marion Woodman *Dancing in the Flames: The Dark Goddess in the Transformation of Consciousness* (Boston, MA: Shambhala, 1996).

2. Ibid.

3. Karla McLaren, *Energetic Boundaries: Practical Protection and Renewal Skills for Healers, Therapists, and Sensitive People,* audio (Boulder, CO: Sounds True, 2003).

4. Mary Oliver, "In Blackwater Woods," *American Primitive* (New York: Little Brown, 1983).

Glossary

The "inside language" of a community only becomes jargon if the insiders use it unconsciously and without hospitality.

Mary Pierce Brosmer, 1995

Crosstalk: Large-group conversation open to all, facilitated by the teacher, without using the talking stone.

Fast-write: Writing fast enough to stay a step ahead of the inner critic or editor.

Greenbook: A Greenbook reading is an opportunity for a writer to share a longer piece of writing with the large group, and to be held by the larger circle. It is an opportunity for the writer to receive support in the way of read-backs, but it is not a setting for feedback. A total of thirty minutes is available, although it is recommended that the reading be a little less, to allow for read-backs from the class. There are spaces for three Greenbook readers per semester.

Read-around: Sharing a piece of writing in the large circle. Each woman has a portion of time in which to read. Passing is an honorable option. Confidentiality is expected.

Read-backs: During read-arounds listeners write words and phrases which move them in some way. Space in the Circle is opened at the end of read-around, and these words are read aloud in no special order (like polyphonic music, an interweaving of words).

Soul cards: At the end of each class, 3" x 5" cards will be passed to each woman. Take a few minutes quietly to write some words to the community about how the evening felt to you, e.g., *What did you feel, notice, learn, appreciate? Any gifts? Any challenges, suggestions, questions for the group?* The cards will go in a designated basket (each class has its own basket) and are available to be read as a way of keeping in touch with the tone and feel of the class. The soul cards are a way to handle both *light and shadow* in a nonthreatening way, and to make sure that negative feelings are not buried or shamed.

Bibliography

Anderson, Sherwood. *Winesburg, Ohio.* New York: Random House, 1999.

Appleman, Philip. *New and Selected Poems, 1956–1996.* Fayetteville: University of Arkansas Press, 1996.

Baker Miller, Jean. *Toward a New Psychology of Women.* Boston: Beacon Press, 1976.

Barks Coleman, trans. *The Essential Rumi.* Garden City, NY: Quality Paperback Club, 1998.

Barry, Brunonia. *The Lace Reader: A Novel.* New York, NY: William Morrow, July 2008.

Bateson, Gregory. *Mind and Nature: A Necessary Unity.* Kresskill, NJ: Hampton Press, 2002.

Beckerman, Ilene. *Love, Loss and What I Wore.* Chapel Hill, NC: Algonquin Books, 1995.

Bender, Sue. *Everyday Sacred: A Woman's Journey Home.* New York: HarperCollins, 1995.

Block, Peter. Lecture given at Chatfield College, St. Leo Campus, St. Martin, OH, 2004.

Bly, Robert. *Iron John: A Book about Men.* Reading, MA: Addison Wesley, 1990.

Bornstein, David. *How to Change the World: Social Entrepreneurs and the Power of New Ideas.* New York: Oxford University Press, 2007.

Dickson, Elinor, and Marion Woodman. *Dancing in the Flames: The Dark Goddess in the Transformation of Consciousness.* Boston, MA: Shambhala, 1996.

Hamill, Pete. *Forever: A Novel.* New York: Little, Brown & Co., 2003.

Hancock, Emily. *The Girl Within.* New York: Ballantine, 1990.

Harris, Maria. *Women and Teaching: Themes for a Spirituality of Pedagogy,* Madeleva Lecture in Spirituality. Mahwah, NJ: Paulist Press, 1988.

Heilbrun, Carolyn G. *The Last Gift of Time: Life Beyond Sixty.* New York: Ballantine Books, 1998.

Hock, Dee. *Birth of the Chaordic Age.* San Francisco: Berrett-Koehler Publishers, Inc., 1999.

Jamison, Kathleen Hall. From an interview on *Bill Moyers' Journal.* Air date: October 8, 2008.

Kellart, Stephen, and Edward O. Wilson. *The Biophilia Hypothesis.* Washington, D.C.: IslandPress, 1993.

Kalven, Janet. *Women Breaking Boundaries: A Grail Journey, 1940–1995.* State University of New York Press, 1999.

Kunitz, Stanley, and Genine Lentine. *The Wild Braid: A Poet Reflects on A Century in the Garden.* New York: WW Norton, 2007.

Lorde, Audre. *Sister Outsider: Essays and Speeches.* Berkeley, CA: Crossing Press, 1984.

Louv, Richard. *Last Child in the Woods: Saving Our Children from Nature Deficit Disorder.* Chapel Hill, NC: Algonquin Books, 2005.

Luke, Helen. "Money as the Feminine Principle of Exchange," *The Way of Woman.* New York: Doubleday, 1995.

MacLeish, Archibald. *Collected Poems 1917–1982.* Boston, MA: Houghton Mifflin, 1985.

McLaren, Karla. CD set. *Energetic Boundaries: Practical Protection and Renewal Skills for Healers, Therapists, and Sensitive People.* Boulder, CO: Sounds True, 2003.

Oliver, Mary. "In Blackwater Woods," *American Primitive*. Boston, MA: Little, Brown, 1983.

Pack, Robert. *Waking to My Name: New and Selected Poems*. Baltimore: Johns Hopkins University Press, 1980.

Palmer, Parker. *To Know as We Are Known*. New York: HarperOne, 1993.

———. *A Hidden Wholeness: The Journey Toward an Undivided Life*. San Francisco: Jossey-Bass, 2004.

Piercy, Marge. "The Seven of Pentacles," from *Circles on the Water*. New York: Alfred A. Knopf, 1982.

Piercy, Marge, ed., *Early Ripening: Contemporary American Women's Poetry Now*. Pandora Press, 1988.

Real, Terrence. *How Can I Get Through to You?: Reconnecting Men and Women*. New York: Fireside, 2002.

Rogers, Annie. "Voice, Play, and a Practice of Ordinary Courage in Girls' and Women's Lives." *Harvard Educational Review*, 63:3 (Fall 1993).

Rukeyser, Muriel. *Houdini*. Boston, MA: Paris Press, 2002.

Sardello, Robert. *Facing the World with Soul: The Reimagination of Modern Life* New York: Lindisfarne Books, 2004.

Sarton, May. *A Private Mythology* New York: WW Norton, 1966.

Shlain, Leonard. *The Alphabet Versus The Goddess: The Conflict Between Word & Image*. New York: Penguin/Compass, 1999.

Senge, Peter, Bryan Smith, Nina Kruschwitz, Joe Laur, and Sara Schley. *The Necessary Revolution: How Individuals and Organizations Are Working Together to Create a Sustainable World*. New York: Doubleday, 2008.

Senge, Peter, Otto Scharmer, Joseph Jaworksi, and Betty Sue Flowers. *Presence: An Exploration of Profound Change in People, Organizations and Society*. New York: Doubleday Business, 2005.

Starbird, Margaret. *The Goddess in the Gospels: Reclaiming the Sacred Feminine*. Melbourne, Australia: Bear Publishing, 1998.

Tolle, Eckhart. *The Power of Now: A Guide to Spiritual Enlightenment*. Novato, CA: New World Library, 1999.

Ueland, Brenda. *If You Want to Write: A Book about Independence and Spirit*. St. Paul: Graywolf Press, 1988.

Van Dijk, Peter. "Paradise Regained," *Ode Magazine*, July/August 2008.

Van Gelder, Sarah Ruth. "Money: Print your Own!," *Yes! Magazine*, Summer 1997. Bainbridge Island WA: Positive Futures Network, 1997.

Wheatley, Margaret J., and Myron Kellner-Rogers. *A Simpler Way*. San Francisco, CA: Berrett-Koehler Publishers, 1998.

Whyte, David. *The House of Belonging*. Langley, Washington: Many Rivers Press, 1996.

Williams, William Carlos. *Asphodel, That Greeny Flower and Other Love Poems*. New York: New Direction Books, 1994.

MARY PIERCE BROSMER is a teacher, poet, feminist visionary, and the founder of Women Writing for (a) Change. She also founded the Feminist Leadership Academy of Cincinnati, where she works to build a sustainable community of women leaders in order to incorporate conscious feminine values and principles into many different types of organizations. In 2007 Pierce Brosmer won the Athena Award from Cincy Business for her leadership as a social entrepreneur and was recognized by Leading Women, Inc. as an Outstanding Leader of 2005. Her poetry has been featured in such places as *English Journal*, *Sojourner*, *The Women's Forum*, and *Early Ripening*.